T0314266

Law and Macroeconomics

LEGAL REMEDIES TO RECESSIONS

Yair Listokin

 Harvard University Press

Cambridge, Massachusetts
London, England
2019

Second printing

Library of Congress Cataloging-in-Publication Data

Names: Listokin, Yair, 1975– author.
Title: Law and macroeconomics : legal remedies to recessions / Yair Listokin.
Description: Cambridge, Massachusetts : Harvard University Press, 2019. |
    Includes bibliographical references and index.
Identifiers: LCCN 2018034037 | ISBN 9780674976054 (hardcover : alk. paper)
Subjects: LCSH: Law—Economic aspects—United States. | United States—Economic
    policy. | Recessions—Law and legislation—United States.
Classification: LCC KF5900.L57 2019 | DDC 339—dc23
LC record available at https://lccn.loc.gov/2018034037

For Steph

Contents

LAW AND MACROECONOMICS

Introduction

The Great Recession of the late 2000s, cost untold trillions in lost output. It roiled long-settled political orders in the United States and Europe and put tens of millions of people out of work. In many countries, anemic growth rates and high unemployment continue. And even in those countries where growth is more robust, macroeconomic policymakers worry about what will happen when the next recession strikes, because, although there is much agreement over the causes of the Great Recession, officials still lack the tools to reverse such a downturn when it next occurs.

The cause of the Great Recession, as macroeconomic policy institutions from the International Monetary Fund (IMF) to the Federal Reserve have concluded, was inadequate "aggregate demand." Private-sector spending collapsed in the wake of the financial crisis of 2008 and took nearly a decade to recover. With too much saving and too little spending, firms were unable to sell all the goods and services that they could produce, grinding the economy to a halt.

To stimulate aggregate demand, policymakers had at their disposal conventional macroeconomic instruments: monetary and fiscal policy. Despite good reasons to think that monetary policy would be ineffective, it became the primary response to the Great Recession. Central banks implemented aggressively expansionary monetary policy during the Great Recession, growing the money supply by previously unthinkable amounts in order to lower interest rates (Figure I.1). These policies likely prevented the Great Recession, triggered by the "the worst financial crisis in global history, including the Great Depression,"[1] from causing even more pain than it did.

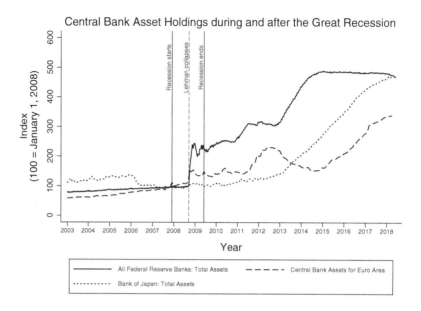

Figure I.1 After an extended period of remarkable stability before 2008, central bank assets exploded in response to the Great Recession.

Data Source: Board of Governors of the Federal Reserve System, "All Federal Reserve Banks: Total Assets" [WALCL], retrieved from FRED, Federal Reserve Bank of St. Louis, https://fred.stlouisfed.org/series/WALCL; European Central Bank, "Central Bank Assets for Euro Area (11–19 Countries)" [ECBASSETS], retrieved from FRED, Federal Reserve Bank of St. Louis, https://fred.stlouisfed.org/series/ECBASSETS; Bank of Japan, "Bank of Japan: Total Assets for Japan" [JPNASSETS], retrieved from FRED, Federal Reserve Bank of St. Louis, https://fred.stlouisfed.org/series/JPNASSETS; Bank of England, "Bank of England Balance Sheet—Total Assets in the United Kingdom" [BOEBSTAUKA], retrieved from FRED, Federal Reserve Bank of St. Louis, https://fred.stlouisfed.org/series/BOEBSTAUKA.

But the unprecedented monetary expansion raised continuing fears of financial market bubbles. And even this monetary "shock and awe" campaign failed to provide the needed stimulus to prevent the incalculable harms of the Great Recession. For many, this failure was no surprise. The "zero lower bound" on interest rates constrained the effectiveness of even the most aggressive monetary policy. Because interest rates can't go much below zero, only so much stimulus was available. As the *Economist* observed in late 2016, "Central banks have been doing their best to pep up demand. Now they need help."[2]

While monetary policy was vigorous, discretionary fiscal stimulus—passing new laws to increase government spending and decreasing taxes to stimulate aggregate demand—was, after an initial burst, left largely untested. Political gridlock at the federal level in the United States, constitutional debt restrictions in U.S. states and the European Union, and concerns about excessive government debt in many countries meant that discretionary fiscal stimulus never came close to compensating for the decreased demand prompted by the 2008 financial crisis. Indeed, many governments reduced public spending during the Great Recession, as unexpectedly low tax revenues led to belt tightening.

With monetary policy impotent and fiscal policy dormant, many of the world's economies face a pressing question: "Are we ready for the next recession?"[3] Grave uncertainty about the answer to this question is demonstrated by the previously implausible policy measures that are now under serious discussion. Policymakers such as Ben Bernanke, former chair of the U.S. Federal Reserve, and Mario Draghi, chair of the European Central Bank, have considered distributing "helicopter money," in which the central bank prints money and sends it directly to citizens, if economic conditions deteriorate in the future.[4] And in the Eurozone, the IMF has pushed for the creation of a "centralized" fiscal institution to "cushion economic shocks," advocating a fundamental expansion of the European Union's mandate for the sake of better macroeconomic policy.[5]

Law and the Great Recession

In this book, I propose a different macroeconomic policy tool: law. True, law is already part of fiscal and monetary policy. But too little attention is paid to the effects of law on macroeconomic policy's success and failure when short-term interest rates are constrained by the zero lower bound. I also will argue for the benefits of novel legal instruments—and novel uses of existing legal instruments—for stimulating aggregate demand when monetary policy is ineffective. I group these under the umbrella of "expansionary legal policy." And I bring law's focus on designing institutions, known as "institutional design," to bear on the preexisting macroeconomic tools of monetary and fiscal policy.

The Great Recession made law's effects on fiscal policy vivid. Recall, for instance, the tens of billions of dollars the U.S. Congress earmarked in 2009 for "shovel-ready" infrastructure projects. The goal was to quickly replace faltering private demand with government spending by enacting a new law. But laws, regulations, and bureaucracies stymied these efforts to spend quickly. Commenting on the U.S. government's failure to rapidly spend infrastructure appropriations, President Obama concluded, "There is no such thing as a shovel-ready project." Law—which, from now on, I will use as a shorthand for law, regulation, and administration—spurred investment directly via the passage of a fiscal stimulus package and then got in its way.

In addition to facilitating better fiscal or monetary policy, law also shifts demand without calling upon fiscal or monetary policy. For example, when a construction project is approved, construction spending increases, at least in the short term. A legal decision thus changes spending without any change in fiscal or monetary policy. On a much larger scale (almost $400 billion in 2015 in the United States), electric-utility regulation also affects aggregate demand.[6] If utility regulators approve a utility's rate increase, then utility consumers have fewer dollars to spend and utility investors have more. If utility consumers spend more of their money than investors do (almost certainly the case), then the utility regulator's decisions affect aggregate demand. Approving higher rates lowers spending, while keeping rates low raises spending. And just as utility regulation affects aggregate demand, so too will many other legal decisions.

I argue that, in limited circumstances, law should promote spending. If expansionary monetary policy is constrained by the zero lower bound on short-term interest rates and expansionary fiscal policy is constrained by constitutional limitations, political gridlock or fear of excessive government debt, then expansionary legal policy, such as utility regulation that keeps rates low in recessions and private debt forgiveness (via bankruptcy law), offers a third way for stimulating aggregate demand. I will discuss both of these options, and others, in detail.

Although law is not currently part of the U.S. macro toolkit, there is no reason it couldn't be. During the Great Depression of the 1930s, policymakers relied on legal instruments such as the National Recovery Administration, which regulated industry, and the Federal Housing Administration, which regulated the housing finance market, to stabilize the economy. Likewise, the post–World War II Bretton Woods regime of international macroeconomics was premised on legal controls restricting the movement of capital across borders. And during the inflation of the 1970s, the U.S. government responded with price controls. Although these legal interventions were not always successful, it is striking that we now assume they can never work and so never even consider legal policy options. We have abandoned what used to be integral tools of macro policy.[7]

In other policy areas, law and regulation often substitute for government spending and taxation; they aren't just tools to prevent malfeasance. Like fiscal policy, law mitigates harmful "externalities." For instance, carbon emissions can be abated using a carbon tax (fiscal policy) or by environmental regulation (law). When the Obama administration failed to pass a comprehensive statutory plan to limit emissions of carbon dioxide, it turned to aggressive regulatory action under the Clean Power Plan. And (again like fiscal policy) law provides public goods. The government can inspire economic growth by funding scientific research (fiscal policy) or by fostering profit potential through patent and copyright (law). If the goals of taxing and spending include stimulus at the zero lower bound, then so too should the goals of law, which is often a substitute for fiscal policy.

Just because law can promote or hinder spending and affect the business cycle does not mean it should always be used to do so. To evaluate expansionary or contractionary legal policy, we need to compare the pros and cons of using law for macroeconomic ends with those of alternative macro instruments, primarily monetary and fiscal policy. I find that law offers an unwieldy instrument of macroeconomic policy. As a result, we should consider expansionary legal policy only when monetary and fiscal stimuli are unavailable. Even then, regulators, judges, and administrators should stimulate aggregate demand only when they have the discretionary power to do so. They can't change the law to promote spending—they can only use the discretion the law already gives them to do so. Legislatures, by contrast, enjoy greater scope to pursue expansionary legal policy.

Unfortunately, limitations on effective monetary and fiscal policy may become all too common in the future. With interest rates languishing near historically low rates even after a prolonged period of expansion, recent papers estimate that the zero lower bound may constrain future attempts at monetary stimulus as often as 40 percent of the time.[8] In addition, constitutional debt restrictions, political gridlock, and fears about growing government debt burdens make expectations of decisive discretionary fiscal stimulus ever more unrealistic.

In comparing expansionary legal policy with monetary and fiscal policy, I bring together law and macroeconomics, augmenting the microeconomic perspective that has dominated my academic field of "law and economics" over the past half century. Law and economics has argued that law should be used to maximize the size of the microeconomic pie. But law and economics has ignored the effects of law on aggregate demand, leaving the prevention of recessions to monetary and fiscal policy. The desperate search for new macroeconomic policy tools indicates that this division of labor is not a reasonable one.

Law and Macroeconomics is intended for economic policymakers, economists, lawyers, and anyone interested in public policy. Economists and policymakers seeking new tools for stimulating slumping economies will hopefully find in law a promising macroeconomic policy instrument. Economists should also find new ways of examining the virtues and drawbacks of monetary and fiscal policy from an institutional design perspective. Lawyers may discover here a new baseline for evaluating laws and regulations: in addition to asking whether a law is just, fair, administrable, or microeconomically efficient, we should consider that law's effects on the macroeconomic environment. A legal decision that is right when the economy is healthy may well be wrong at the zero lower bound on interest rates. I will argue that the decision should come out differently because the macroeconomic context is different. Law and macroeconomics thus extends law to a pressing social problem that has recently been outside its scope—namely, the constraint imposed on stagnant economies by inadequate aggregate demand.

My discussion does not exhaust every link between law and macroeconomics. I do not discuss "law and finance" or "property rights and economic growth," which consider the effects of legal traditions and institutions on long-run macroeconomic outcomes such as gross domestic product (GDP) and stock-market valuations. These literatures are of fundamental importance. Like most of law and economics, however, these literatures focus on law's role in expanding an economy's productive capacity (its supply side) rather than spending (the demand side). In this book, by contrast, I focus on the demand side—specifically, how law can stimulate demand to mitigate recessions when monetary policy does not suffice.

I also do not emphasize financial regulation. No doubt, better regulations reduce the probability of financial crises, with long-lasting macroeconomic effects. But such regulation has been explored amply by lawyers and economists. In addition, even the best financial regulation is doomed to periodic failure. Carmen Reinhart and Kenneth Rogoff identified eight separate episodes of global banking crises between 1900 and 2008, suggesting that there may be no way to regulate our way out of such events.[9] In light of this history, law must offer responses once crises have struck in addition to trying to prevent crises through prophylactic regulation.

Indeed, there is no better time to ask more of law. The Great Recession's shadow falls over the global economy still, in the form of slower growth even in countries that have ostensibly recovered and exceptionally low interest rates across the industrialized world. With rates so low, there will be little space for monetary policy when the next downturn inevitably strikes. And the lack of a decisive fiscal response to the Great Recession demonstrated that fiscal policy is unreliable as a substitute for monetary policy. It is therefore crucial that we understand how law can be a more effective tool for easing downturns.

Plan of the Book

Part I examines monetary and fiscal policy from a legal perspective.

In Chapter 1, I provide an overview of Keynesian and new Keynesian macroeconomics for readers unfamiliar with this literature. In brief, I explain that temporary increases or decreases in spending alter output briefly but also induce changes in interest rates and, ultimately, prices. These changes in interest rates and prices gradually return the economy to its "natural" output level, determined by supply factors. (Readers interested in a simple formal economic treatment—the "IS-LM" model—of the topics discussed in this chapter and all future chapters should consult the Appendix.)

Chapter 2 examines fiscal policy when interest rates are well above zero. I explain why fiscal stimulus, obtained through lower taxes and higher spending, raises aggregate demand while fiscal contraction lowers it. "Discretionary" fiscal policy is enacted by legislatures and is generally viewed as an ineffective stabilization tool. In particular, the requirement for legislative action means that the government will move too slowly to offset most fluctuations in aggregate demand. I discuss the desirability of using "automatic" fiscal policy, in contrast with discretionary fiscal policy, to stabilize an economy in recession. With automatic fiscal policy, deficits increase quickly when incomes fall and shrink quickly when incomes rise, without need for legislative action and the political challenges that poses.

To conventional macroeconomic accounts of automatic fiscal policy, which focus only on government spending and income taxation, I add a third instrument of fiscal policy—"tax expenditures." These are government subsidies delivered through the tax code. An example of a tax expenditure is the charitable deduction in the U.S. income tax code, which reduces taxable income for each dollar a taxpayer gives to charity. The government has decided to subsidize charitable giving, so the giver faces a lower tax payment after giving to charity, even though the giver's income hasn't decreased. In 2016, U.S. tax expenditures were worth approximately $1.5 trillion, or 7.9 percent of GDP (more than nondefense discretionary spending).

Unlike the conventional tax and spending programs emphasized by macroeconomists, tax expenditures tend to be automatically destabilizing. A good example of the automatic destabilizing effects of tax expenditures is the (now limited) deductibility of U.S. state income taxes from federal taxable income for the purposes of calculating federal income tax liability. This tax expenditure provides an effective federal government subsidy to taxpayers for paying state income taxes and (indirectly) to the government spending funded by state income taxes. An extra dollar of state spending financed by state income tax requires state residents to give up less than one dollar of after-tax income because the dollar paid in state taxes is deductible from federal income.

State income tax liabilities go up when income rises in booms (lowering deficits) and go down in recessions (increasing deficits). The state income tax therefore automatically stabilizes the economy, as observed by macroeconomists. But the tax expenditure for state income taxes—the federal subsidy for making tax payments to states—destabilizes the economy. If state income tax payments rise in booms and falls in recessions, then the effective federal subsidy through the tax expenditure also rises in booms and falls in recessions. This destabilizes the economy by reducing a government subsidy in a recession and increasing the subsidy when incomes are high.

The destabilizing effect of the deductibility of state income tax payments from federal taxes and other similar tax expenditures is quantitatively important. Recent empirical estimates suggest that tax expenditures reduce the stabilizing properties of the U.S. income tax code dramatically.[10] But these destabilizing effects of tax expenditures have gone unexamined by macroeconomists, who do not study alternative forms of fiscal policy like tax expenditures. Given the destabilizing properties of tax expenditures, we need to either reduce our reliance on them or pass laws limiting their destabilizing properties. I conclude Chapter 2 by describing the destabilizing properties of other important but neglected instruments of fiscal policy, such as matching grants and some government insurance programs.

Chapter 3 examines monetary policy when interest rates are well above zero. Expansionary monetary policy stimulates spending by making money abundant and lowering interest rates, while contractionary policy inhibits spending by raising interest rates. All Western democracies delegate authority over monetary policy to independent and expert central banks.

Monetary policy offers a powerful tool for mitigating the economic effects of shifts in aggregate demand. But Chapter 3 observes that many jurisdictions do not retain control over monetary policy. Individual U.S. states and member nations of the Eurozone forgo the benefits of monetary policy to facilitate trade and political integration. In Chapter 3, I ask why any jurisdiction would give up such a powerful macroeconomic tool, described as the "only [macroeconomic] game in town" in the title of one recent book on macroeconomics.[11] I explain that the "impossible trinity" of international macroeconomics offers governments a stark choice. They can either promote trade through shared or fixed currencies, or they can promote macroeconomic stability by retaining control over monetary policy, but not both.

This remains true unless the jurisdiction chooses to enact capital controls—the third prong of the impossible trinity. With capital controls, jurisdictions pass laws to impede the movement of capital across borders, going so far as to deny the enforcement of an otherwise valid contract when enforcement would enable a violation of another country's capital control regime. Capital controls complicate law but allow jurisdictions to get the trade-promoting benefits of fixed exchange rates without relinquishing control over monetary policy. Using capital controls to enable stable exchange rates and monetary flexibility is a perfect example of the possibilities opened by law and macroeconomics—by asking more of law, regimes with capital controls, such as the Bretton Woods regime of 1944–1971, enable better macroeconomic outcomes.

In Chapter 3, I also compare monetary and fiscal policy as tools for macroeconomic policy. I explain why economists favor monetary policy over discretionary fiscal policy for stimulating and inhibiting economies when interest rates are well above zero. According to this conventional wisdom, monetary policy is effective because it is implemented by an expert and nimble central bank that is able to respond effectively to fluctuations in demand. Fiscal policy, by contrast, requires a slow-making legislative body populated by politicians to respond to rapid aggregate demand fluctuations. When monetary policy is not an option, however, fiscal policy remains the primary macroeconomic policy tool.

Chapter 4 emphasizes the onerous costs of liquidity traps, in which short-term interest rates are constrained by the zero lower bound. In a liquidity trap, spending falls short of the economy's capacity to produce. But a fall in interest rates cannot quickly return the economy to its natural level of output because interest rates cannot go (much) below zero. Without a fall in interest rates to induce borrowers to spend excess savings, output falls below capacity and unemployment rises.

Because output is not constrained by capacity at the zero lower bound, economic policies that increase capacity do not raise output. Instead, a lack of demand constrains output. Policies that increase aggregate demand therefore increase output in a liquidity trap.

The Great Recession was itself a liquidity trap, with short-term interest rates stuck at zero for more than five years. The costs of the Great Recession exceeded almost all predictions. Not only was there a pronounced plunge in short-run output, but long-term growth rates, too, appear to be down. This problem is known as *hysteresis*, whereby a short-term slump leads to a long-term decline in the economy's growth rate. The simplest example of hysteresis comes from the labor market. Long-term unemployment causes skills to deteriorate; after people have been unemployed for a year or longer, the chance they will ever work again drops dramatically. Thus, a short-term deterioration in the economy can have long-term negative effects.

What is more, the effects of liquidity traps are not confined to the labor market. Because the costs are shared unevenly—the unemployed suffer grievously, but most workers lose relatively little—liquidity traps can foster political upheaval. Sluggish economies offer fertile ground for politicians seeking to overturn established political and economic orders, even if these are more productive than their proposed replacements.[12] In the United Kingdom, angry voters chose Brexit, rejecting Britain's long-standing (and mutually beneficial) economic integration with the European Union. In the United States, angry voters elected Donald Trump to the presidency, even though Trump promoted economic and social policies, such as trade protectionism, that rejected both bipartisan orthodoxies and conventional economic wisdom. Although the Great Recession is not the only cause of these political upheavals, it almost certainly made them more likely. Given the possible losses from such popular surges of anger, the politically driven costs of liquidity traps can dwarf even their direct multitrillion-dollar effects.

The liquidity trap is not the only plausible account of the Great Recession and other prolonged recessions and depressions. Chapter 5 also presents two other accounts. Like the liquidity trap, the "secular stagnation" view emphasizes the problem of the zero lower bound on interest rates. But the secular stagnation view emphasizes the possibility of inadequate aggregate demand persisting for a generation—longer than most macroeconomists think liquidity traps should last. The "debt supercycle" account of the Great Recession emphasizes the role of insolvent borrowers and an insolvent financial sector in perpetuating, as well as triggering, a slump in aggregate demand. I argue that the correct account of the Great Recession has relatively small implications for expansionary legal policy because, under each account, the problem is inadequate aggregate demand that can be addressed by legal intervention, among other policies. As a result, I use the terms "zero lower bound" and "liquidity trap" as synonyms for prolonged recessions even though some macroeconomists prefer to emphasize other causes of the worst recessions.

Because liquidity traps are so dangerous, macroeconomic policymakers try hard to avoid them—and to exit them quickly once they begin. In Chapter 5, I examine how well monetary and fiscal policy mitigate liquidity traps. I find both deeply flawed.

Monetary policy's primary stimulus instrument—lowering interest rates to stimulate borrowing for investment and consumption—becomes impotent in a liquidity trap. Interest rates cannot go (much) below zero because negative interest rates would cause people to dump financial assets for cash, which yields a zero interest rate. As a result, macroeconomic policy options at the zero lower bound are limited to "unconventional monetary policy" and expansionary fiscal policy. Unconventional monetary policies were widely and aggressively deployed during the Great Recession, but they proved insufficient in stimulating aggregate demand. Such policies also give unprecedented power to central banks, as emphasized by Paul Tucker in an important 2018 work.[13] Indeed, the unconventional monetary policies of the European Central Bank violated the simplest interpretation of the Maastricht Treaty that created the Eurozone. (The European Court of Justice ultimately permitted the policies, using a strained interpretation of the law that I critique but ultimately support.) If unconventional monetary policy backfires—and the risks will always be great—then the closely guarded and invaluable independence and power of central banks will be at risk. To avoid turning to such controversial policies in the future, policymakers should look for alternatives.

As for expansionary fiscal stimulus—both automatic and discretionary— many empirical and theoretical papers have demonstrated its effectiveness in response to the Great Recession. But the mere fact that expansionary fiscal policy can be effective in a liquidity trap does not remedy fiscal policy's inherent institutional flaws. Automatic fiscal policy boosts demand—government deficits reached unprecedented heights in many nations from 2009 to 2015—but not enough to counter a slump the size of the Great Recession. Discretionary fiscal expansion can be more aggressive and tailored to the size of the slump, but discretionary fiscal policy is subject to constitutional restrictions, the whims of legislators, and fears that government debt will undermine economic growth and social stability. Indeed, after an initial round of discretionary fiscal stimulus in the immediate aftermath of the financial crisis, most industrialized nations turned toward austerity to reduce deficits and debt burdens, in spite of considerable evidence that fiscal stimulus was effective at stimulating the economy.

Macroeconomic policy failed to end the Great Recession. In this context, it is not surprising that some advocate the use of radical policies such as helicopter money in future liquidity traps. With this policy vacuum in the background, Chapter 6 considers institutional reforms to improve fiscal policymaking. I argue that simply teaching lawyers—the professional class from which politicians typically emerge—some macroeconomics will help to ensure that states enact appropriate fiscal policy. We cannot be surprised if, having never learned about the urgency of fiscal stimulus at the zero lower bound, legislators do not spring into action when interest rates are zero.

I also support the abolition of constitutional deficit restrictions. Instead of requiring that budgets be balanced each year, I argue that jurisdictions should consider cyclically adjusted deficit restrictions. These require zero deficits when economies are operating at capacity. But when unemployment and output plunge, deficit spending should be allowed. These deficits should be balanced by surpluses run in boom years. I also advocate rule-based instruments of fiscal stabilization. Governments should pass laws mandating that if interest rates are zero and unemployment rates high, tax rates should be lower and government spending higher. Finally, I consider the creation of an independent agency for fiscal stabilization policy—the fiscal equivalent of a central bank. Although I am open to the idea in principle, I am skeptical that such an agency will ever attain democratic legitimacy because fiscal policy is viewed as more integral to government than monetary policy. More plausibly, I propose a fiscal policy–coordinating office within government. This office would ensure that consistent and sensible attention gets paid to macroeconomics at times when the macroeconomic implications of decisions loom large. In many countries, analogous offices like the Office of Information and Regulatory Affairs (OIRA) in the United States ensure that diverse government actors apply consistent standards to questions of microeconomic policy. A similar office for macroeconomic affairs would facilitate fiscal stimulus without threatening democratic legitimacy.

Concluding Part I, Chapter 7 identifies overlooked opportunities for regulatory fiscal stimulus. Tax collection agencies, such as the Internal Revenue Service (IRS) in the United States, implicitly make fiscal policy. When the IRS interprets the income tax code in a way that lowers tax revenues, it stimulates aggregate demand. At the zero lower bound, the IRS should exercise its policy discretion in favor of rulings that stimulate the economy by lowering tax collections. Other government agencies also play an important role in public spending. If an agency implements a spending program with unconstrained funding (such as Medicaid or Medicare) more aggressively, then demand will be stimulated. Because fiscal stimulus is extraordinarily valuable at the zero lower bound, agencies should favor more aggressive spending than they do in ordinary times.

Chapter 7 also discusses limiting principles for stimulus attempts by regulatory agencies. First, agencies should stimulate the economy only within the bounds of their preexisting discretion. They cannot violate laws in pursuing stimulus, only use their preexisting discretion. Second, regulatory fiscal stimulus needs coordination. By establishing an office of fiscal policy oversight, government ensures that agencies use sensible and consistent standards as they attempt to stimulate the economy.

Fiscal stimulus at the zero lower bound enjoys broad support from economists, even though using fiscal policy for macroeconomic purposes complicates fiscal policy's other ends—provision of "public goods" like education and redistribution from rich to poor in pursuit of a more just society. The consensus in favor of expansionary fiscal policy at the zero lower bound indicates that we should tolerate policies that may not be ideal from a microeconomic public finance perspective in order to mitigate macroeconomic inefficiencies.

If this consensus applies to fiscal policy, then we should consider something similar with respect to law. Like fiscal policy, law concerns the allocation and redistribution of goods and services in pursuit of a more just society. If we are willing to sacrifice some fiscal policy goals in order to improve macroeconomic policy, then we should at least consider sacrificing some traditional legal goals to achieve the same end.

Whereas Part I offers a legal and institutional analysis of the traditional tools of macroeconomic policy, Part II examines the macroeconomic effects of law. I focus on several examples, including the debate over the approval of the Keystone oil pipeline, the regulatory agencies of the early New Deal, and the price controls imposed by Congress and President Nixon in 1971.

Chapter 8 concerns the long-running regulatory debate over Keystone. I show how different the debate would have been had politicians and regulators accounted for macroeconomic conditions. Proposed in 2009, construction on the Keystone pipeline was prohibited by the Obama State Department on the grounds that it was not in the "national interest." Republican politicians claimed that approval for Keystone would create jobs—one element of the national-interest standard—but President Obama responded, "There is no evidence that that's true."[14] Neither party was correct. Both claims depended on the state of the business cycle, yet they were stated as immutable truths.

The construction process would have directly employed over 42,000 workers. In an economy producing at its capacity (as it was when Keystone received approval from the Trump administration in 2017), these jobs would have mattered little for unemployment, because Keystone's construction workers would probably be working in other jobs. However, when the State Department delayed the project in 2010–2011 and rejected it in 2013, the economy was producing below capacity. Demand constrained output, and monetary policy could not stimulate aggregate demand because of the zero lower bound. Increased aggregate demand would have increased employment. If Keystone had been approved in 2011, then its construction would have put underemployed labor and capital to work without requiring government spending. Law—in the form of regulatory approval for Keystone—would not merely have shuffled spending from one source to another: it would have expanded output. U.S. unemployment would have decreased in the short run and, if hysteresis effects were avoided, in the long run as well. Keystone may not have been in the national interest for other reasons, even in 2011, but the State Department was remiss in not considering macroeconomic effects in its evaluation.

While a macroeconomic perspective of law may have been economically beneficial had it been applied to Keystone, there also may have been drawbacks. I explore costs and complications in Chapter 9. Keystone is a case where prioritizing the macroeconomic goals of law entails sacrificing other such goals, specifically environmental protection. Adding factors to legal decisions also makes law more complicated: it is hard to know how the State Department should balance the promise of more aggregate demand at the zero lower bound with other considerations of national interest.

However, these costs and complications, though considerable, should not be exaggerated. In the case of Keystone, expansionary legal policy should not be equated with lower environmental standards. Approval for the pipeline could have been conditioned on attaining a more stringent pipeline safety level, the additional costs of which would also have boosted spending. Furthermore, the incremental costs of more complicated decision-making look marginal when the regulator is already applying an open-ended standard such as the "national interest." It is not as though adding macro to the policy mix complicates what would otherwise be straightforward regulatory analysis.

Still, other institutional weaknesses make law a clunky instrument of macro policy. As noted, regulators, administrators, and politicians lack macroeconomic expertise. They may therefore misjudge the state of the business cycle, favoring job creation even when stimulus is not indicated, as when Keystone was approved by the Trump administration in 2017. In addition, many projects requiring legal approval are implemented after long time lags, complicating law's utility for macro policy. Finally, if law is to vary with the business cycle, opportunistic judges and litigants may be able to justify wrongheaded policies on macroeconomic grounds.

These are valid concerns, but they counsel restraint in the use of law for macro ends—not maintenance of the monetary- and fiscal-policy status quo. We should turn to law only when other options are constrained.

The case for legal stimulus is strongest when short-term interest rates are at or very near zero, for four reasons. First, monetary policy is ineffective at the zero lower bound. Second, historically, zero interest rates provide a strong signal of inadequate aggregate demand. Third, periods of inadequate demand associated with zero interest rates tend to be long-lasting, reducing concern about the slow implementation of many legal policies. Finally, zero short-term interest rates are easily observed even by nonexperts. Legislatures, regulators, and judges should therefore strongly consider expansionary legal policy at the zero lower bound.

It is essential that we plan for the zero lower bound. The latest research predicts that U.S. monetary policy will be constrained by the zero lower bound as often as 40 percent of the time in the future.[15] Interest rates in the United States are also higher than they are in most other industrialized countries, suggesting that the zero lower bound will frequently constrain monetary policy in most developed countries, as it has in Japan for most of the last thirty years.

The zero lower bound is not the only appropriate context for expansionary legal policy. Under the "debt supercycle" theory of deep recessions, expansionary legal policy can substitute for a broken credit system in bringing economies with broken financial sectors back to health. Expansionary legal policy offers a remedy for the deep recessions that follow financial crises and the bursting of asset bubbles—even if short-term interest rates exceed zero. In addition, expansionary legal policy offers options to depressed jurisdictions that lack control over monetary policy in a currency union. If, reflecting healthy economies in other parts of the currency union, monetary policy in a depressed jurisdiction is inappropriately tight, then expansionary legal policy offers an alternative stimulus instrument.

In any of these three contexts, expansionary legal policy should be considered. But macroeconomic considerations should dictate legal decisions only when the decision will clearly increase spending and when the macroeconomically desirable legal ruling requires little sacrifice of other legal goals, such as equity. Expansionary legal policy is thus best suited to legal decisions where the merits would be in equipoise, excluding macroeconomic factors and when one outcome clearly raises spending relative to the other outcome.

Even judicious use of expansionary legal policy will incur significant costs, but they are worth paying because the damage of sustained downturns is so great. It is worth making a sacrifice in order to mitigate liquidity traps and the deep recessions that follow financial crises. Indeed, policymakers make much the same choice when they apply fiscal stimulus in these contexts—overspending, by typical standards, in hopes of jump-starting a moribund economy. We need to think of law as another flawed macro policy tool with different institutional strengths and weaknesses than monetary and fiscal policy. At times, law may be the best tool we have for stimulating the economy, even if we wish there were better alternatives.

In Chapter 10, I turn to prominent historical examples of the use of law for macroeconomic ends. The early New Deal response to the Great Depression in the United States relied heavily on law, rather than fiscal policy, to stimulate a depressed economy. (Monetary policy, in the form of ending the gold standard, was also a factor.) Indeed, Keynes himself criticized the laws passed during President Franklin Delano Roosevelt's first hundred days for their emphasis on regulation over fiscal stimulus. The signature policy of FDR's famed "hundred days" was the National Industrial Recovery Act (NIRA)—and not the end of the gold standard. The NIRA created a regulatory agency charged with increasing spending by eliminating expectations of deflation by allowing business and workers to collude to increase prices. (With deflation, a zero nominal interest rate associated with holding cash translates into positive "real" returns, as cash buys more goods in a year from now than it does now. Ending deflation thus lowers the real return—measured in goods—from holding cash, encouraging spending.) Although NIRA was ultimately ruled unconstitutional by the U.S. Supreme Court, an end to deflation followed NIRA's passage and initial implementation.

Although it was not guided by sophisticated macroeconomic theory, the early New Deal experiment in using law for macro ends was a qualified success. The U.S. economy performed very well from 1933 to 1937. The recession of 1937–1938, which brought an end to this period of growth and prolonged the Great Depression, was caused by fiscal contraction and tight monetary policy, not a failure of expansionary legal policy. If expansionary legal policy focused more explicitly on stimulating private spending directly rather than working through the price channel, then we should expect it to be even more effective in the future.

The United States again turned to law during its next bout of macroeconomic instability—the Great Inflation of the 1970s. To curb inflation, Congress authorized and President Nixon imposed price controls implemented by an administrative agency. The plan worked in the short run but ultimately failed, leading to queues at gas stations and grocery stores without controlling inflation. I argue that, in this case, the unique institutional costs of legal policy loomed large. Price controls imposed extreme, rather than marginal, harms on the economy. Mitigating these costs demanded impossible levels of economic expertise and information. It is also important to keep in mind that price controls were imposed for political as much as economic reasons, at a time when other macro policy options, such as contractionary monetary policy, were available.

Like other macro tools, though, even price controls have their place. Here my example is Greece. I argue that, in the course of a disastrous recession ongoing since 2010, Greece should have imposed a uniform mandatory deflation of 10 percent on all prices and most debt contracts.[16] The best option for mitigating Greece's depression would have been to devalue its currency. Doing so would have made Greek labor more internationally competitive by making Greek goods and services cheaper relative to the costs of similar products produced in nearby countries. As a member of the Eurozone, however, Greece was unable to devalue its currency, so, instead, Greek wages and other prices needed to fall in absolute terms. As Milton Friedman predicted, this internal price adjustment imposes much higher costs in terms of unemployment and lost output than a currency devaluation. I argue that to mitigate these costs, Greece should have designed a package of price controls and other legal measures to mimic a currency devaluation.

In Chapter 11, I offer specific examples of expansionary legal policy. Each example meaningfully stimulates spending, lies within the domains of regulators or judges, and can be implemented without unreasonable time lags.

I first explore public-utility regulation as an instrument of expansionary legal policy. Many utilities are natural monopolies, and government administrators regulate their prices. At present, public-utility rate regulation ignores the business cycle. Instead, regulators are directed to keep prices as low as possible, consistent with ensuring utilities a market rate of return on capital. But the guaranteed-return standard has a perverse effect, leading to higher prices in downturns and lower prices in booms. This is because many of a utility's costs—such as those of building and maintaining power plants and distribution networks—are fixed. When demand drops in a downturn, the utility sells less output to offset its high fixed costs and therefore needs to raise prices to earn its required return on capital. In a boom, by contrast, the utility offsets fixed costs over more output, allowing it to charge lower prices and still earn a market rate of return.

Not only does this sort of regulation end up straining consumers in hard times, but it also has deleterious effects on aggregate demand. At the zero lower bound, consumers struggle with shrunken incomes. Meanwhile, utilities hold onto capital rather than spend it on investments in production for which there is less demand. Thus, when regulators approve higher prices to offset lost demand in downturns, aggregate demand goes down because consumers reduce their spending by more than the utility company and its shareholders increase their spending.

I argue that utility regulators therefore should reject rate increases at the zero lower bound and instead push for lower utility rates. Utility regulators should also evaluate the utility's capital investment plans. The more the utility plans to invest, the more receptive regulators should be to rate increases. Either declining utility rates or increases in utility investment will raise aggregate demand—just what is needed to raise output and employment at the zero lower bound.

Utility regulators cannot simply insist on lower rates in downturns. To provide an adequate return on capital and ensure continued investment in regulated utilities, regulators need to allow higher prices and returns when interest and unemployment rates are normal. Indeed, the average return on utility stocks would need to increase because it will be more correlated with the rest of the market. In effect, countercyclical utility regulation moves business-cycle risks from utility consumers to utility investors.

Next, I turn to a legal policy tool that goes back at least to the time of Hammurabi: the use of debt modification during economic contractions. Debt forgiveness or modification stimulates aggregate demand because debtors and creditors have different propensities to spend. Debtors spend—that's why they are debtors—and creditors save. If the economy is suffering from a spending shortage, then a transfer from debtors to creditors raises spending and stimulates the economy. Some, such as Atif Mian and Amir Sufi, have argued that, in the wake of the Great Recession, the United States and other countries needed a range of new debt forgiveness statutes.[17] I focus on debt forgiveness policies that do not require additional legislative action, arguing that existing bankruptcy laws provide considerable scope for the type of debt restructuring that is needed.

Bankruptcy attempts to balance debtors' needs for a fresh start with creditors' claims to repayment. The balance is difficult to define and therefore involves a fair amount of discretion. For example, federal student loans are not typically eligible for discharge but may be if the borrower can demonstrate that repayment will cause "undue hardship." I argue that, at the zero lower bound, judges should exercise the discretion granted them to offer more debt forgiveness than they would in ordinary times. A time-varying standard of undue hardship is realistic—it is harder for debtors to repay when unemployment is high and incomes are low. Macroeconomic conditions also tell us when the social goals of a fresh start are especially important. At the zero lower bound, the spending triggered by relief of student debt would benefit the debtor and the surrounding community. Debt forgiveness can harm private credit markets, but this is of less concern when the government is the lender or the guarantor. In such cases, a bankruptcy discharge operates as fiscal policy channeled through the legal system.

But judges need not limit themselves to discharging government-owned debt. Bankruptcy procedures for discharging private debts offer further opportunities for expansionary legal policy. Judges exercise considerable discretion in all aspects of bankruptcy. Indeed, research shows that the amount of debt relief granted in any given case varies considerably depending on the identity of the judge hearing the case.[18] If bankruptcy judges exercised their discretion by discharging more debt at the zero lower bound than at other points of the business cycle, then they could stimulate aggregate demand without dramatically disrupting the market for credit.

Finally, I emphasize the importance of judicial remedies for stimulating aggregate demand. Judges don't simply vindicate legal rights—deciding who wins and who loses a case. They also fashion remedies—how the winner's interest is protected. These remedial choices have important implications for aggregate demand. Consider a case in which residents challenge a proposed construction project in their neighborhood, arguing under tort law that the development interferes with their right to "quiet enjoyment" of their property. Let us assume that the neighbors are right under the law. What remedy should the court apply? Should the court issue an injunction, preventing the developer from building until the neighbors agree to a revised proposal, or should the court allow the development to go forward and then require the developer to compensate the neighbors with damages for the harm caused?

I argue that, at the zero lower bound, courts should favor the damages remedy. In that case, the builder still builds, spending on workers and capital, some of which would otherwise lie idle. Under the injunction, by contrast, the builder needs to secure permission from all of the neighbors to go ahead. At the very least, securing permission delays the project at a time when alternative opportunities for labor and capital are scarce. And unless the builder is a skilled negotiator, there is a good chance the injunction will prevent construction indefinitely.

The damages remedy thus increases aggregate demand relative to the injunction. At any given time, many proposed spending projects are subject to litigation. In these cases, favoring damage remedies over injunctions at the zero lower bound would promote aggregate demand, while ensuring that plaintiffs' rights remain protected.

Utility regulation, bankruptcy law, and the law of remedies are hardly the only examples of expansionary legal policy. Other areas of law have important implications for macroeconomics. Unfortunately, I am unable to cover all of them in one book. By providing a few salient examples of expansionary legal policy, I hope to trigger the development of other legal tools to mitigate downturns.

Even if the reader doesn't think expansionary legal policy is worth the candle, then I at least hope that law and macroeconomics offers a different and fruitful perspective on law, monetary policy, and fiscal policy. In short, I hope that when the next Great Recession strikes, law will be ready.

Law, Fiscal Policy, and Monetary Policy

ONE

Macroeconomics outside of a Liquidity Trap

In this chapter, I sketch the Keynesian explanation for how economic output is determined and why output fluctuates over time. This explanation sets the baseline for the critical review of the institutions that make macroeconomic policy that follows.

Imagine that the economy is a single business, such as a restaurant. There is no investment in the economy; the restaurant uses labor and a fixed amount of capital to produce and serve meals. Because the restaurant is the only employer in the economy, its workers are also its customers, purchasing meals when they are off the clock by using the money the restaurant pays them. Workers can save their money in cash or lend it at interest to other workers who want to buy more meals than they can currently afford. The restaurant earns money by selling meals. It pays this money to its workers. The restaurant uses its excess money to lend or hold cash reserves.

The restaurant has limited capacity. If all its tables are filled all of the time, then it cannot produce any more—the restaurant economy has reached its "potential output." In addition, the restaurant's prices are fixed in the short run. Prices cannot change quickly in response to sudden upswings or downswings in the demand for meals. The restaurant's daily output is therefore determined by the lesser of potential output or demand for meals. If the demand for meals falls short of capacity, then the restaurant serves only as many meals as ordered, even though it could serve more.

With the assumption of fixed price and variable output, macroeconomics departs from classical microeconomics, and by implication law and economics, which assumes that prices adjust constantly so that the restaurant produces at capacity at all times. In the classical economy, fluctuations in the restaurant's output arise only from fluctuations in the restaurant's ability to produce meals. The assumption of flexible prices means that the restaurant can never be involuntarily empty in the classical economy.

At times, I will add a government and a central bank to this simplified "economy." The government raises money by taxing workers and the restaurant, borrowing from workers who earn more than they spend on meals and taxes, or printing money. The government also spends on meals, the economy's only output. While the government controls tax rates and borrowing, the money supply is controlled by a central bank independent of the government. Both the central bank and government seek to maximize the output of meals while avoiding restaurant queues caused by excess meal demand.

When demand for meals shrinks and the restaurant produces less, it lays off workers. Unemployment rises, and output falls below capacity. Labor and capital sit idle instead of being used to produce meals. At this point, the restaurant economy is in recession, with inadequate demand leading to wasted resources. The economy suffers from an "output gap" equal to the difference between the number of meals actually produced and potential output.

When demand rises, the restaurant employs more people for more hours. Unemployment declines. Once output hits capacity, lines may develop outside the restaurant. Booms caused by excess aggregate demand impose costs because lines are wasteful. And in the long run, booms cause costly inflation as the restaurant raises its prices to raise its profits and prevent lines. In turn, the workers, faced with higher costs for meals, demand higher wages. In the short run, however, prices are fixed.

As a result, both excess and inadequate aggregate demand for meals impose heavy economic costs. Good macroeconomic policy mitigates these costs. If macro policy attempts to do more than offset fluctuations, however, then it will fail. In general, I assume that macroeconomic policy does not change capacity.

Happily, booms and busts will be temporary in the restaurant economy because interest rates equilibrate slumping or booming economies. If demand for meals shrinks, then savings increases. This reduces interest rates. With interest rates down, borrowers increase their borrowing and savers put away less. Both borrowers and savers buy more meals in response to the decrease in interest rates. If interest rates fall by enough, then demand again equals capacity. Likewise, the increases in interest rates that accompany excess demand bring demand back into balance with capacity. As a result, shifts in interest rates temper the sensitivity of the economy to changes in aggregate demand.

Fluctuations in the Restaurant Economy

What causes changes in demand? Myriad factors, often called "shocks," may be responsible. Good weather can raise demand for meals. So might optimism about future economic prospects. According to Keynesian macroeconomics, the total change in meals produced may exceed the initial change in demand for meals caused by the shock because of "multiplier" effects. For example, if workers get paid less because they serve fewer meals as a result of a run of bad weather, then the workers, in turn, buy fewer meals at the restaurant. The initial shock caused by bad weather can be multiplied into a greater decline in output.

The size of the fluctuation depends on the size of the initial shock to aggregate demand (for example, how bad the weather is and how sensitive meal purchases are to the weather) as well as the size of the multiplier effect (for example, whether the restaurant lays off workers in response to an initial decrease in meal purchases) or whether other sources of spending substitute for the decline. Even with the multiplier effect, however, temporary shortfalls in demand should not cause sustained downturns. When the bad weather ends, the demand for meals should return to normal and the recession should draw to a close.

Adding Financial Frictions to the Model

Traditionally, Keynesians attributed prolonged falls in aggregate demand to psychological causes: "animal spirits,"[1] say, or panic. Animal spirits—the instincts and emotions guiding decision-making—could turn a small and temporary decrease in aggregate demand into a large and sustained decline. Minsky, Mian and Sufi, Geneakopolous, and others have put forward more precise explanations of how downturns come about.[2] Instead of simple shocks to demand, prolonged downturns involve leverage effects and financial frictions working in concert.

To illustrate leverage effects, suppose that the restaurant economy features two types of participants: savers and spenders. Savers consume less than they earn, while spenders consume more. Savers lend money to spenders through financial intermediaries such as banks. The economy also features an asset, such as housing, which can be used as collateral for borrowing. Spenders' ability to borrow depends on the value of their collateral; financial intermediaries are reluctant to lend money to spenders who have no collateral to ensure repayment. If a spender owns a valuable house, the spender can borrow more by using the house as collateral.

Now suppose that the economy is hit by a bad event, such as inclement weather. Fewer people buy meals, and some restaurant employees get laid off. The multiplier effect means that the output of meals drops by more than the initial drop in demand suggests it should. The drop in demand does not stop there, however. Some newly unemployed workers are spenders who have accumulated debts, such as mortgage loans. Unemployed spenders default on their debts, and financial intermediaries respond by foreclosing on the collateral securing those debts, such as spenders' homes. The intermediaries then sell the collateral, often at fire-sale prices. The value of assets used as collateral therefore goes down. With collateral less valuable, spenders who are still employed become less able to borrow and so tighten their belts. They reduce their spending on meals. The leverage effect is a vicious cycle, or negative feedback loop.[3]

"Financial frictions"—impediments to the borrowing and savings market caused by asymmetric information between borrowers and lenders—also propagate initial negative shocks to demand. An example is reduced asset prices. When a financial firm's assets lose value, as when hit by leverage effects, this reduces the firm's ability to underwrite financial transactions. In underwriting fewer transactions, the firm channels fewer resources from savers to spenders. Something like this can happen at the scale of an entire financial system, leading savers to sit on their money and leaving spenders unable to borrow. With less borrowing, there is less spending; consumption of meals falls, reducing output and raising unemployment and loan-default rates still more. This increase in default rates exacerbates the leverage effect already described. With asset values down as a result of foreclosure sales, even more financial firms become unsteady, further exacerbating financial frictions and compounding the leverage effect. The negative feedback loop runs again.

Potential Output, Inflation, and the Long-Run Effects of Demand Shocks

After the initial output fluctuations just described, interest rate adjustments bring aggregate demand for meals back into balance with potential output when interest rates exceed zero. If every worker wants to consume fewer meals because the weather is bad, then the interest rate decreases. This makes consumption of meals today more attractive and saving to buy meals tomorrow less attractive than they used to be, increasing the demand for meals today. Output below potential should therefore be a temporary phenomenon when interest rates exceed zero. When interest rates can adjust, the economy's "equilibrium" occurs when output equals capacity.

Although we have assumed that prices remain fixed in the short run, over longer periods prices will ultimately adjust. Price adjustments enable output to return to capacity even if nominal interest rates cannot adjust. If demand for meals is below the restaurant's capacity for a long time, then the restaurant will eventually lower its prices in order to make use of its spare capacity. Knowing that meal prices are lower today than they will be tomorrow, workers consume more meals. The restaurant will keep lowering prices until demand for meals returns output to capacity.[4]

Over the long run, inflation—changes in prices—is determined by two factors: expected inflation and output relative to capacity.[5] If output is below capacity, then inflation falls short of expected inflation. If output is above capacity, then inflation exceeds expectations. This model allows prices to respond slowly to output fluctuations. Inflation cannot adjust quickly enough to prevent output fluctuations, but inflation does respond to output fluctuations as we would expect.

Price flexibility—in which this inflation adjustment process transpires quickly—lowers the stakes of changes in aggregate demand. Indeed, if prices adjust quickly, there is no need to worry about demand shocks, which are quickly offset. But the length of the Great Recession and earlier downturns, such as the Great Depression, indicate that prices don't adjust all that quickly after all.

The behavior of prices in one market familiar to many lawyers indicates just how long price adjustment can take. In 2006, a boom period in the legal market, large law firms increased salaries of first-year associates, who were in high demand, to $160,000. Then, during the Great Recession, the legal market shifted. As demand for legal services fell, clients grew especially reluctant to pay for inexperienced lawyers. Demand for first-year associates from law firms plunged, following client preferences. The supply of prospective first-year associates—typically graduates of top law schools—remained relatively constant, as new graduates could not have foreseen the downturn three years earlier when they matriculated.

If prices were flexible—the implicit assumption of microeconomics and law and economics—then first-year associates would have seen their salaries plummet rapidly, and the imbalance between supply and demand for freshly minted lawyers would have been resolved quickly. In reality, first-year associate salaries at large law firms held steady throughout the recession. Instead of lowering salaries, firms sharply cut the number of associates they hired. Many new graduates took lower-paying legal jobs or were unable to find legal employment at all. As the legal market eventually recovered, first-year associate salaries remained at $160,000, but firms stepped up hiring, with hiring in 2015 finally recovering to 2007 levels.[6]

The case for macroeconomic stabilization policy—monetary, fiscal, or legal—depends upon the length of the "short run." If prices take a long time to adjust, as suggested by the market for law firm associates, then the short run is more relevant and the case for macro stabilization policy stronger. Empirically, prices are asymmetrically flexible. That is, prices—and particularly wages, the price of labor—are much more likely to increase than decrease.[7] This implies a further asymmetry with respect to the speed of adjustment to demand shocks. When demand increases, we can expect prices to increase relatively quickly to bring output down to potential. However, when demand decreases, the price-adjustment process will move more slowly to bring output back to potential. The case for active policy measures—such as monetary policy, fiscal policy, or law—to mitigate decreases in output is therefore stronger than the case for measures to mitigate increases in output.

TWO

Law and Fiscal Policy When Interest Rates Are Well above Zero

Legislatures implement fiscal policy by passing laws. And fiscal policy affects macroeconomic conditions. Unfortunately, that is where the overlap between the law and the macroeconomics of fiscal policy usually ends, rather than where it begins. (This is an optimistic account—the book I use to teach an introductory course on federal income taxation to law students does not even mention macroeconomic stabilization as a goal of tax policy.) In this chapter, I explore fiscal policy stabilization outside liquidity traps from a lawyer's perspective, focusing on the institutions that implement fiscal policy. In addition to laying out the pros and cons of fiscal policy stabilization as a general matter, I focus on a crucial element of fiscal policy—the role of "tax expenditures" (government subsidies delivered through the tax code rather than through direct spending)—whose legal features are ignored by macroeconomists and whose macroeconomic effects are usually overlooked by lawyers. I explain why tax expenditures have unexpectedly pro-cyclical business cycle effects. I also trace similarly destabilizing features in the design of other government programs, such as unemployment insurance fund design.

Economists distinguish between two forms of fiscal policy to stabilize the economy. "Automatic fiscal policy" stabilizers offset fluctuations in aggregate demand without requiring legal changes.[1] Certain parts of the tax code and some government spending programs are notable examples of such stabilizers. During recessions, they serve to raise government spending and lower tax burdens. In booms, they automatically lower spending and raise revenues. An income tax, for example, acts as an automatic stabilizer, raising more revenue in booms (when income rises) and less in busts (when income shrinks). Property taxes, by contrast, do not change directly in response to business cycle fluctuations in output and income and so do not automatically stabilize the economy.[2]

"Discretionary fiscal policy," by contrast, entails legal changes. Faced with lax aggregate demand, legislatures may lower income tax rates or increase the generosity of public benefits in order to spur private spending, or they can directly increase spending by investing in public projects. When aggregate demand recovers, the legislature raises income tax rates and lowers government spending in order to repay the debts incurred in passing the stimulus passage during the recession.

Discretionary Fiscal Policy

Discretionary Fiscal Policy in the Restaurant Economy

Suppose our restaurant economy has fallen into severe recession. An initial, temporary reduction in demand for meals due to bad weather has been exacerbated by leverage effects and financial frictions. Demand for meals falls significantly, and output of meals falls along with demand.

In response, the government can use discretionary fiscal policy to stimulate aggregate demand by purchasing meals directly from the restaurant.[3] The government raises its own purchases of meals in response to the slump in demand. With more meals being purchased by the government, output rises. Expansionary fiscal policy therefore raises output and offsets falls in demand caused by the bad weather and subsequent recession.

Alternatively, the government can lower taxation to stimulate faltering demand for meals during bad weather. When workers, who are also consumers, pay less tax, they have more disposable income. Workers can use some of this additional income to buy more meals, raising output.

If we know (1) the size of the fall in demand for meals caused by bad weather, (2) the follow-on multiplier effects of this shock to overall meal demand, and (3) the multiplier effects on meal demand of a direct increase in government spending or a tax reduction, then well-implemented discretionary fiscal policy can eliminate recessions. Any decrease or increase in aggregate demand gets offset by the appropriate countervailing change in government spending or taxation.

Institutions Making Fiscal Policy

Legislatures and constitutions set fiscal policy. This reflects the central role fiscal policy assumes in democracies.

The U.S. Constitution, for example, orders that "All Bills for raising Revenue shall originate in the House of Representatives." James Madison described the purpose of this provision in the Federalist Papers (58) as follows:

> The house of representatives can not only refuse, but they alone can propose the supplies requisite for the support of government. They in a word hold the purse; . . . This power over the purse, may in fact be regarded as the most compleat and effectual weapon with which any constitution can arm the immediate representatives of the people, for obtaining a redress of every grievance, and for carrying into effect every just and salutary measure.

Although legislatures make fiscal policy, the ability of legislatures to use fiscal policy to stabilize economies in response to macroeconomic fluctuations is often subject to constitutional restrictions.

Many U.S. governmental bodies, including states, municipalities, and single-purpose entities such as water and sewer districts, adhere to "balanced budget" requirements. These requirements oblige the jurisdiction to balance its budget or run a surplus every year. Balanced budget requirements prevent politicians from spending too much in the present, leaving later politicians to plug the gap. Some form of balanced budget restriction applies in forty-nine out of fifty states.[4]

At present, the U.S. federal budget faces no balanced budget restriction. Limitations on debt issuance, however, often constrain deficit spending. And the constitutional flexibility of the federal budget may be about to change. In the United States, twenty-eight states (through 2018) have passed resolutions calling for a constitutional convention to ratify an amendment requiring the federal government to balance its annual budget.[5] If six additional states pass similar resolutions, then a convention for the purpose of imposing limits on budget deficits will ensue.

The European Union imposes slightly less stringent fiscal policy restrictions on its members than the self-imposed restrictions of U.S. states. Article 126 of the Treaty of the European Union ("Maastricht Treaty") stipulates that "Member States shall avoid excessive government deficits."[6] Unlike American states, EU members can run budget deficits—so long as the deficits are lower than 3 percent. Moreover, budget deficits higher than 3 percent can be permitted during "severe economic downturns," allowing member states to retain some macroeconomic flexibility.[7]

The Flaws of Discretionary Fiscal Policy

While discretionary fiscal policy offers the promise of eliminating the business cycle, the real-life institutions of fiscal policy cannot attain this impossible ideal. Legislators suffer from imperfect knowledge as well as an imperfect ability to implement fiscal policy. Once we appreciate these flaws, it will become clearer why it is important to consider, and reconsider, other macroeconomic-stabilization tools, such as those offered by law and macroeconomics.

Balanced Budget Amendments

Balanced budget requirements prevent discretionary fiscal policy stabilization. Indeed, balanced budget requirements are a widely recognized automatic destabilizer.[8] Government revenue from income and sales taxes inevitably goes down during recessions. If government spending must follow government revenue—as balanced budget requirements oblige—then government spending must be cut in recessions. A decrease in government spending reduces aggregate demand and exacerbates the problem of inadequate demand. Balanced budget requirements therefore automatically destabilize the economy.

One theoretical explanation for balanced budget amendments at the U.S. state and municipal level is the problem of spillovers. Stimulus policy diffuses across regions.[9] When a job is created by additional government spending in a small U.S. state like Rhode Island, the new hire purchases additional services produced locally or in a neighboring state but also buys goods, which may be produced in other U.S. regions or other countries. As a result, fiscal stimulus policy in Rhode Island stimulates demand in other jurisdictions near and far. But while demand stimulus spills over out of state, costs remain in the home area. Only Rhode Island taxpayers foot the stimulus bill.

This combination of diffuse benefits and localized costs reduces Rhode Island's incentives to undertake fiscal stimulus. Knowing this, Rhode Island may conclude that the benefits of fiscal stimulus are not worth the costs and adopt a balanced budget amendment. And even if jurisdictions like Rhode Island do not absolutely bar deficit-fueled stimulus, their incentive to pursue stimulus will be reduced as they bear all the costs but get only some of the benefits.

One way to reduce the scope of this problem is to make macroeconomic policy at the broadest possible level. For instance, by undertaking fiscal policy at the federal level, the United States manages largely to internalize costs and benefits of stimulus. When the federal government spends more, most of the increase in aggregate demand remains in the United States rather than spilling over to other countries because trade makes up a relatively small portion of the U.S. economy.

But we also should not exaggerate the demand–diffusion problem as it applies to smaller jurisdictions like U.S. states. During the Great Recession, several studies examined the effects of extra U.S. federal spending in a particular state by comparing the employment response in that state to similar states that did not benefit from as much direct federal spending. While the stimulus programs under study are not identical to state stimulus programs because the debts associated with the federal spending are not localized in the same way as debts associated with state spending, these studies give us a sense of the size of the direct effects of government spending within a state relative to spillover effects in other states. If demand stimulus diffuses widely, then these studies should have found small spending effects of additional spending in the target states. That is, if an additional dollar of spending in Rhode Island significantly raises spending in other states too, we should see little relative increase in Rhode Island's output as a result of an additional dollar spent in Rhode Island. In fact, these studies find large in-state effects.[10] With such a large effect within state, there will be strong incentives for states to pursue fiscal stimulus even though some of the stimulus benefits the residents of other states. As a result, the argument against stimulus policies in smaller jurisdictions in favor of broader-based stimulus programs may be overstated.

Balanced budget requirements provide the simplest explanation for the failure of discretionary policy to stabilize the economy as described at the outset of the chapter. In addition, discretionary fiscal policy suffers from many other flaws that make it an imperfect tool of stabilization, even in jurisdictions that do not foreclose fiscal stabilization with balanced budget requirements.

Lack of Expertise

Getting expansionary fiscal policy right, at any level of government, requires expertise and access to high-quality information. The government needs to know how much private demand has fallen. If it underestimates, then it will not raise spending enough to offset the demand reduction. If it overestimates, the economy will be overstimulated, causing output to outstrip capacity and inflation to rise. In reality, even experts find it extremely difficult to predict the effects of demand shocks. And if experts have trouble assessing macroeconomic conditions, we can expect politicians' understandings to be that much murkier and their legislative fixes far from the mark.

Even if the legislature knows how much aggregate demand has changed, it must also calibrate its fiscal response appropriately. The increase in government spending or decrease in taxes should be just enough to offset the initial decrease to spending, after accounting for the multiplier effects of government spending on output.

The government spending multiplier is the change in output caused by a one-unit increase in government spending. If the government's decision to purchase one meal raised the restaurant's output by one meal, then the government spending multiplier would be one.

Knowledge of the government spending multiplier requires expertise. In theory, there are many reasons why the multiplier may be more or less than one. For example, the extra meal produced may induce the restaurant to pay more in wages. In turn, workers will use their extra wages to buy still more meals. Under this condition, the multiplier is greater than one. Alternatively, if the restaurant is at capacity, then a meal purchased by the government may simply displace a meal purchased by a private citizen. In that case, the government spending multiplier would be zero. And if workers anticipate tax hikes to repay the debt associated with government meal purchases, they may reduce their own purchases accordingly, also reducing the multiplier.

Empirical estimates of the size of the government spending multiplier vary widely (see Chapter 5 for further discussion). The estimates depend on the economic model used for the economy as well as the empirical technique chosen.[11] In addition to varying between studies, multiplier estimates vary across different programs. Because every spending and taxation program is different, the multiplier effects of a particular program will be uncertain even if the legislature knows the multiplier effect of the average government spending program. The right multiplier estimate for one set of economic conditions and types of government interventions will be inapplicable in other contexts.

Using the right estimate of the government spending multiplier is critical for good policy. If a government spending program with an expected multiplier of 2 gets enacted and the true multiplier for that policy under these conditions is 0.6, then the government policy response will be inadequate. If the true multiplier is 2 when the expected multiplier is 0.6, then the response will be excessive. Navigating the literature requires considerable macroeconomic expertise, but legislatures are unlikely to possess such expertise.

Response Lags

Getting fiscal policy right demands not only a great deal of information but also swift action. Alas, fiscal intervention inevitably lags far behind the problems provoking it.[12] First, the legislature must be persuaded that a shock to aggregate demand has occurred, which requires some sort of data-based assessment that itself takes time. Next, crafting a response takes even longer. Legislators must write, debate, amend, and pass a bill that changes fiscal policy to offset the effects of the shock. This process is often tortuous and is made even more difficult under circumstances of divided government. All that adds further delay, which is soon compounded by the time required for implementation. And even after the law is implemented, it can take a while before the multiplier effects of an increase or decrease in spending are felt.

If the response lags are long enough, then discretionary fiscal policy may become ineffective or even counterproductive.[13] For example, the United States passed significant tax cuts in 2001 in response to the bursting of the dot-com bubble and the resulting recession. But the tax cuts did not fully phase in until 2003, when the U.S. economy had returned to its normal rate of growth. Cutting tax rates in 2003 stimulated an economy that already had healthy aggregate demand growth, intensifying inflation pressures.

None of this is to say that discretionary fiscal policy invariably comes too slowly to be useful. Where the legislative process is relatively swift, as in parliamentary systems, the effects of fiscal policy are more likely to arrive on time. In the United States—where the path to legal enactment is full of obstacles such as Senate filibuster and cloture rules and the presidential veto, and where divided government is common—discretionary fiscal policy is harder to do well.[14] The arguments against discretionary fiscal policy therefore apply with greater force in the United States than in parliamentary democracies such as the United Kingdom and Canada, where there is less risk of divided and slow government.

Although economists treat these lags as unavoidable, in fact they stem from institutions, laws, and regulations that could behave differently. Remember those shovel-ready Obama stimulus projects? They weren't delayed by some mysterious and alien force. Rather, according to the U.S. Government Accountability Office, they were delayed by legal and regulatory requirements. For instance, one federal regulation mandated that stimulus projects pay "prevailing wages" determined by the Department of Labor. But in some cases, such as weatherization projects intended to cut down on energy usage, prevailing-wage data were lacking. As a result, spending was delayed while the Department of Labor ran the calculations.[15] Other regulations, such as "Buy American" provisions in the stimulus bill and historic preservation requirements, delayed many construction projects. After the regulatory approval process was finally streamlined in 2011, "some recipients reported that they were weatherizing more homes in 1 month than they had previously weatherized in 1 year."[16]

These laws and regulations are not inherently problematic; indeed, they serve important functions. In ordinary times, we may reasonably decide that lengthy implementation lags are acceptable in light of the benefits of prevailing wages, historical preservation, and other regulations. However, in extraordinary times, stimulus is urgently needed. In Part II, I will argue that ordinary practice needs to change in order to shorten the lags in fiscal policy implementation.

Alternative Priorities for Fiscal Policy

The obstacles already presented would make effective discretionary fiscal policy difficult even if it was the exclusive goal of policy. But fiscal policy traditionally has three goals: funding public goods, redistributing resources from rich to poor, and stabilizing the economy.[17] When we use fiscal policy to stabilize the economy, we sacrifice some of these other goals.

Consider that, in a recession, tax cuts can provide valuable fiscal stimulus, but they also compromise the other goals of fiscal policy. Lower income taxes benefit the rich more than the poor because the rich pay a higher proportion of their income in taxes. The tax cut favored on stabilization grounds therefore undermines aims of redistribution. And if the tax cut lingers after the recession, public goods such as defense or education will go underfunded as the government's revenue has permanently declined. To avoid these undesirable outcomes, legislatures may refrain from stimulating the economy via a tax cut even when it is macroeconomically warranted.

Political Opportunism

The goal of stabilization further complicates the already challenging process of making fiscal policy. This creates opportunities for politicians to take advantage. They can exploit stabilization goals to advance policies that would be unachievable if fellow legislators and the public knew the real reasons behind them.

For example, some politicians seek to lower taxes because they believe the rich already pay too much. Much of the public disagrees. Ordinarily, popular dissent prevents the politician from pushing for lowering taxes. In a recession, however, the politician can promote lower taxes as a stimulus instrument rather than as a shift in distribution that favors the wealthy. Even though the politician's goal isn't really stimulus, he or she advocates for tax-cut stimulus while knowing that, once the cut is enacted, it will be hard to retract. Introducing stabilization into fiscal policy therefore adds a degree of freedom for politicians to undermine other aims of that policy.

Politicians can also use fiscal stimulus to enhance their chances of reelection, a phenomenon known as the political business cycle. Shortly before an election, self-interested politicians support demand stimulus policies they ordinarily would not, such as tax decreases and spending increases. In the short run, fiscal expansion stimulates the economy. This benefits incumbents, whom voters often evaluate according to the state of their own finances. In the long run, however, such policies lead to large deficits and may do nothing to promote stabilization. The economy suffers accordingly.[18]

Fear of political opportunism offers one of the best explanations for the prevalence of constitutional deficit restrictions. If we can't trust politicians to enact the best fiscal policies for long-run growth, then we may decide to constrain their ability to use deficit financing altogether.

Risks of Excessive Debt

Fiscal policy stimulus increases government deficits and debt. At excessively high debt levels, deficit spending may not actually stimulate demand. As the director of the IMF's fiscal affairs department summarized in 2016, "Once markets perceive government debt to be unsustainable, spiraling interest rates and depreciating exchange rates can ensue. In some cases, countries may . . . simply [be] cut off from market access."[19] For countries with high debts, debt-financed fiscal-policy stimulus is simply not an option, as Greece found during the Great Recession. And some countries that could apply fiscal stimulus will be wary of doing so aggressively, lest debt levels increase to the point that they cause a Greek-style market panic.

Weighing the Costs and Benefits of Discretionary Fiscal Policy

Discretionary fiscal policy holds the promise of stabilizing economies when aggregate demand shocks cause output to deviate from potential. When the economy overheats, governments can run surpluses to prevent inflation and other inefficient behavior, such as queueing. When demand is insufficient, governments can raise spending and lower taxes, increasing demand to offset the shock. Fiscal policy stimulus enables the economy to continue producing at capacity rather than lose output and jobs due to a shortage of aggregate demand.

While perfect fiscal policy promises to mitigate the business cycle permanently, the reality falls far short of this ideal. In democracies, legislatures control fiscal policy because of fiscal policy's essential role in governing. And legislatures are ill suited to stabilizing the economy by using fiscal policy, a difficult task for the even the most nimble and expert decision makers. In addition, monetary policy (discussed in Chapter 3) offers an alternative stabilization instrument that suffers from few of fiscal policy's flaws. By the 1990s, most economists therefore "reject[ed] discretionary fiscal policy directed at aggregate demand as a tool of stabilization policy."[20] Not surprisingly, constitutional balanced budget requirements, which foreclose fiscal stabilization policy, grew increasingly widespread during this period.[21]

Ultimately, the consensus against discretionary fiscal policy within economics was not based on any economic theory—a fact that matters to our discussion of law and macroeconomics. Rather, the argument depends upon the institutional framework of fiscal policy: economists reject discretionary fiscal policy when interest rates comfortably exceed zero because monetary policy's institutions work better than fiscal policy's. This argument needs input from institutionalists in law, public policy, and political science, as well as from economists, as I discuss in Chapter 3.

Automatic Fiscal Policy: The Role of Tax Expenditures, the Tax Cuts and Jobs Act of 2017, Matching Grants, and Government Insurance Programs

If discretionary fiscal stabilization is riddled with institutional problems, what about automatic fiscal policy?

Recall that automatic fiscal policy requires no legislative action. Income tax is one example. When demand is weak and income is low, the tax collects less revenue. When demand is strong and income is high, the tax collects more revenue. Thus, high demand is partially offset by higher income tax collections, and lower demand is offset by lower collections. This stabilization occurs automatically; income tax laws need no modification to serve their stabilizing purpose. Some government spending programs also automatically stabilize the economy. For instance, without any change in laws, spending on means-tested programs, such as Medicaid or the Supplemental Nutrition Assistance Program (SNAP), goes up when incomes go down and more people become eligible for benefits. Similarly, unemployment payments go up in downturns because the level of unemployment rises.

The critiques of discretionary fiscal stabilization do not apply to its automatic cousin. Automatic stabilizers demand no expertise to implement. They require no policy choices at all. Automatic stabilizers do not suffer from long implementation lags, because they kick in as a direct function of changing economic conditions. Automatic stabilizers are also tailored to the size of the economic shock. If the income tax is 40 percent, then 40 percent of any positive or negative effect on income due to a demand shock gets offset by the tax, without any need for calibration. Politicians also find automatic stabilizers harder to use opportunistically. Because they apply throughout the business cycle, they do not raise the likelihood of reelection. While a stabilizing income tax helps politicians' reelection chances by mitigating recessions, it will hurt their reelection chances by mitigating booms as well.

But while automatic stabilizers can be useful, and they come without many of the downsides of discretionary stabilizers, they are not easy to fashion. As the IMF's chief economist observed in 2015, "Most countries allow for automatic stabilizers to dampen demand fluctuations, but these so-called stabilizers were never designed with stabilization in mind. Could they be improved—and why has there been so little thinking about it?"[22] In particular, the institutional details of automatic stabilizers have received little attention.

The Income Tax as Automatic Stabilizer: The Role of Tax Expenditures

The argument that income taxes automatically stabilize the economy stems from an incredibly simple model. This model assumes that income is easily defined and taxed. It also assumes that income tax systems have only one goal: to raise revenue. Tax lawyers, unlike macroeconomists, know that real-world income tax systems face insuperable difficulties in defining income and successfully taxing it. Lawyers also know that tax codes have many goals aside from revenue generation. In the United States, the code subsidizes desirable behavior such as charitable giving, providing employees with health insurance, and state-level spending.

But macroeconomists don't study the code as it actually operates, and tax-law scholars largely ignore macroeconomics, leaving us with little sense of how important elements of our tax code and government spending programs, such as tax expenditures, affect economic stability.[23]

Tax expenditures are defined as "revenue losses attributable to provisions of the Federal tax laws which allow a special exclusion, exemption, or deduction from gross income or which provide a special credit, a preferential rate of tax, or a deferral of tax liability."[24] In other words, they reduce revenue that would be collected under the macroeconomists' model code. Prominent tax expenditures include the home mortgage interest and charitable-contribution deductions, which reduce individuals' taxable income, decreasing the amount of income tax they owe.

Tax expenditures substitute for government expenditures. The U.S. Joint Committee on Taxation explains, "Special income tax provisions are referred to as tax expenditures because they may be considered to be analogous to direct outlay programs, and the two can be considered as alternative means of accomplishing similar budget policy objectives."[25] For example, instead of directly providing health insurance, the government subsidizes health care through the tax code by excluding the cost of employer-provided health coverage from taxable income. On a smaller scale, the government encourages use of solar power by providing tax credits for those who install solar panels. Alternatively, the government could encourage solar-power use by directly purchasing solar panels and distributing them to citizens.

Tax expenditures are a vital policy tool. In fiscal year 2014, tax expenditures reduced U.S. federal income tax revenue by over $1.1 trillion, or 6.6 percent of gross domestic product (GDP). That is a lot of implicit spending, roughly equal to all U.S. discretionary spending, which includes all government spending except Medicare, Medicaid, and Social Security.[26] Tax expenditures are also important outside the United States. A 2010 Organisation for Economic Co-operation and Development report found that tax expenditures in seven member countries averaged 5.1 percent of GDP.[27] Canada and the United Kingdom, among others, use more tax expenditures as a percentage of GDP than does the United States.[28]

While macroeconomists pay a good deal of attention to the automatic stabilizing effects of income taxes and direct government spending, they tend to ignore the effects of tax expenditures on aggregate demand. Because tax expenditures are an integral part of fiscal policy, this neglect is troubling. It is yet another cost of separation between law and macroeconomics, and it is not benign. Most important U.S. tax expenditures—such as the deduction for employer-provided health insurance—destabilize the economy automatically.

Most governments subsidize or pay for health care costs. In a direct spending program, government pays for care itself, as with Britain's National Health Service. Or government reimburses private providers, as the U.S. government does with Medicare. In either model, the business cycle does not affect government spending on health care, so long as individual demand for health care does not change with the business cycle.[29]

Another way to subsidize health care costs is through the tax code. In the United States, this is accomplished through Internal Revenue Code Section 105, which excludes employer-provided health insurance from income for tax purposes. In other words, when an employer provides compensation in the form of subsidized health insurance, that compensation goes untaxed. By contrast, if an employer compensated an employee in cash, and the employee purchased health insurance with the money, the compensation would be taxed. In 2014, the value of this subsidy was estimated at $213 billion.[30]

But Section 105 also destabilizes the economy.[31] This is because employment is pro-cyclical. In recessions, unemployment rises, which means fewer workers benefit from Section 105's implicit subsidy. As a result, the government spends less subsidizing health care during recessions and more when the economy is operating at capacity.

Figure 2.1 demonstrates that health care coverage in the United States decreased dramatically during the Great Recession before recovering (in part due to the Affordable Care Act of 2009). With fewer people receiving health care coverage from employers, the U.S. government spent less subsidizing employer-provided health care coverage during the Great Recession than it did beforehand. Moreover, Figure 2.1 understates the decrease in private health insurance coverage. During the Great Recession, many unemployed workers who once had private coverage obtained Medicaid. Private health insurance coverage, the only type that benefits from the Section 105 exclusion, undoubtedly declined by even more than Figure 2.1 demonstrates.

The estimated cost of the Section 105 exclusion, which equals the value of employer-provided health insurance received by employees multiplied by the tax rate that would have applied to this "income" absent Section 105, provides additional evidence that the exclusion leads to more spending when the economy is healthy and less when the economy struggles. In the wake of the Great Recession, the estimated cost of the Section 105 exclusion declined for the first time in memory, dropping from approximately $134 billion in fiscal year 2007 to $131 billion the following year.[32] This decline marked a sharp deviation from a decades-long trend of rapidly increasing costs for the Section 105 exclusion. By the next year, however, the cost of the exclusion resumed its secular upward trend, rising to $144 billion. In total, the rate of increase in the cost of the tax expenditure during the Great Recession was far below its trend during the previous period of economic growth.[33] Given the incredibly high rate of health care price inflation during this period,[34] it is almost certain that the cost of Section 105 would have increased substantially in 2007–2009 in the absence of the Great Recession.

In total, the exclusion of employer-provided health insurance from the income tax presents an extremely destabilizing government program. A direct spending program that did this—that reduced spending on health

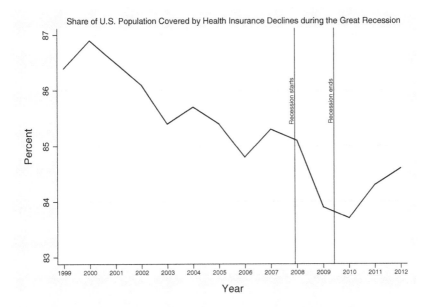

Figure 2.1 The share of the U.S. population covered by health insurance, and thus benefitting from health insurance tax expenditure subsidies, dropped sharply at the beginning of the Great Recession.

Data Source: U.S. Bureau of the Census, "Health Insurance Coverage: Coverage Rate in the United States (DISCONTINUED)" [USHICCOVPCT], retrieved from FRED, Federal Reserve Bank of St. Louis, https://fred.stlouisfed.org/series/USHICCOVPCT.

care when there is greater unemployment—would be almost inconceivable. Yet we have a $200 billion annual implicit spending program doing just that.

The United States' largest tax expenditure destabilizes the economy. So do two other important U.S. tax expenditures—the home mortgage interest deduction and the charitable-giving deduction. Each allows U.S. taxpayers to reduce their federal income tax liability for government-favored spending on home ownership or the provision of charitable services. Kingi and Rozema used household-level spending data to estimate that these two prominent tax expenditures reduce the automatic stabilizing properties of the income tax by 1.13 percent (for the home mortgage interest deduction) and 0.9 percent (for the charitable-giving deduction), relative to an income tax code with both tax expenditures eliminated. In 2016, the home mortgage interest deduction cost the public fisc $75.3 billion and the charitable deduction cost $57 billion. If the mortgage interest deduction and the charitable-giving deduction are typical tax expenditures in terms of their destabilizing effects, then these results suggest that the cumulative $1.5 trillion in tax expenditures in 2016 reduced the automatic stabilizing properties of the income tax by more than 23 percent.[35]

The Destabilizing Tax Cut and Jobs Act of 2017

At the end of 2017, U.S. congressional Republicans, with support from President Trump, transformed the U.S. income tax code by passing the Tax Cut and Jobs Act (TCJA) of 2017. The TCJA limited one important tax expenditure, capping the previously unlimited tax deduction for state and local tax payments at $10,000. Because tax expenditures destabilize the economy, the TCJA's imposition of a cap on the tax expenditure for state and local tax payments enhanced the countercyclical effect of the income tax.

The rest of the bill, however, gutted the U.S. income tax's role as a countercyclical force. The TCJA's reforms to the taxation of business income particularly undermined the automatic stabilizing properties of the income tax.[36]

Corporations derive their income from business profits. Profits equal the difference between revenues and expenses. Although revenues fluctuate with the business cycle, many business expenses are fixed. In booms and in busts, businesses must continue to pay their debt, rent, and pension obligations.

This combination of variable revenues and fixed expenses leaves profits very sensitive to the business cycle. In flush times, revenues may exceed expenses by a large margin, producing fat profits. In 2007, for example, U.S. corporations earned profits of over $1.05 trillion (less losses). In recessions, by contrast, revenues fall while many expenses remain steady, sharply reducing profits. By 2009 (the heart of the Great Recession), U.S. corporate profits fell below $450 billion.[37] Total U.S. income, by contrast, declined only 3.1 percent from 2007 to 2009.

Because it collects a steady proportion of a highly pro-cyclical component of total income, the corporate income tax collects significant revenue in booms and much less in busts. It is a great automatic stabilizer. In 2007, for example, U.S. corporate income tax revenue exceeded $370 billion.[38] If the United States collected corporate income tax at the same effective rate in 2009 as in 2007, then corporate income tax collections would have automatically fallen to $160 billion. (In reality, 2009 corporate tax receipts were $140 billion, which reflects some cuts in the effective corporate income tax rate in that year.) The corporate income tax thus provided an automatic stimulus to the U.S. economy of over $200 billion (in lower tax revenue) in 2009 relative to 2007. For comparison, the 2009 American Recovery and Reinvestment Act (the primary U.S. fiscal stimulus package during the Great Recession) lowered taxes by roughly $100 billion in fiscal 2009.[39]

The signature provision of the TCJA reduced the U.S. corporate tax rate from 35 percent to 21 percent. From a stabilization perspective, this cut is a disaster. In the next Great Recession, we won't enjoy the benefit of a $200 billion automatic stimulus package.[40]

Any tax cut reduces the automatic stabilizing properties of the income tax. But cuts to the corporate tax reduce stability more than tax cuts on other forms of income. Because corporate income fluctuates more in tandem with the business cycle than other types of income, it is a particularly good automatic stabilizer. Even if the revenue losses caused by the cuts to the corporate tax rate are ultimately offset with increases to other taxes, TCJA will have undermined one of the most important automatic stabilizing forces in the economy.

The debate over both tax expenditures and the TCJA illustrates the harm caused by separating law and macroeconomics. While lawyers and economists have devoted countless pages of scholarship to tax expenditures, they have mostly ignored the effect of tax expenditures on stability. Similarly, lawyers and economists spoke loudly and voluminously about the pros and cons of the 2017 TCJA, but both camps ignored the macroeconomic effects of the act. Estimating the macroeconomic effects of tax expenditures or the TCJA requires an understanding of both the nuances of the tax system and the macroeconomic implications of those nuances. Few lawyers or economists have the relevant combination of skills. As a result, the pernicious macroeconomic effects of critical elements of tax policy go largely unheeded.

Matching Grant Programs as Automatic (De)Stabilizers: The Case of Medicaid

In contrast with tax expenditures, means-tested government spending programs automatically stabilize the economy. Spending on these increases when the economy is in recession. In theory, this should increase demand and help the economy recover. But an institutionally realistic analysis of government spending programs complicates this story, too.

Consider Medicaid, which provides health insurance for the indigent in the United States. When incomes go down in recessions, more people qualify for Medicaid, and government spending rises accordingly, offsetting the demand decline that caused incomes to drop. Right? In fact, Medicaid spending is not so simple. It is not just outlays that matter but also the structure of spending—the sort of thing law and macroeconomics pays attention to but which other fields typically ignore.[41]

Medicaid is the largest of many U.S. programs that rely on federal matching grants. It is administered at the state level and funded with state, local, and federal dollars. The federal government reimburses states at varying rates depending on their per capita incomes; in total it covers approximately 60 percent of Medicaid spending.[42] In 2011 federal grants to states totaled 17 percent of U.S. federal spending and 4 percent of GDP.[43]

Matching aid programs, combined with state and local balanced budget requirements, reduce the automatic stabilizing properties of Medicaid. The logic follows a course that, by now, should be familiar. During a recession, state revenues go down. To maintain a balanced budget, states cut spending to match the decrease in revenues. Because programs partially funded by federal matching grants consume a substantial portion of most state budgets—Medicaid alone accounted for "18.9 percent of spending from state general funds" in 2013[44]—cash-strapped states often cannot avoid cutting them. But then the state loses a portion of its federal matching funds, reducing federal spending in tandem with state spending. Thus, reductions in state spending necessitated by balanced budget laws are amplified by reductions in federal spending on matching grants, even though the federal government faces no balanced budget requirement. And the cuts come just when spending is most needed.

Federal matching grant programs to states and localities therefore have a serious macroeconomic cost, which, to date, has not been appreciated. They automatically destabilize the economy relative to federal spending programs that are not linked to state spending, and they introduce the pathologies of state spending into the U.S. federal system. In order to improve the automatic stabilization properties of federal spending, Congress should consider switching matching-grant spending programs to block-grant spending programs, whereby the sum given to states is not determined by the state budget.

The destabilizing effect of matching aid programs also explains the emphasis on non-matching aid to states and localities in the 2009 American Recovery and Reinvestment Act (ARRA), also known as the Obama Stimulus. The ARRA allocated about $140 billion for direct aid to states.[45] Not only does aid to states raise state spending directly, but it also raises federal spending indirectly by increasing matching-grant spending by the federal government. As a result, the ARRA's aid for states may have had a greater stimulus effect than commonly realized.

Government Insurance Programs as Automatic Stabilizers and Destabilizers: The Federal Housing Administration Insurance Fund

Government insurance programs automatically stabilize the economy. The U.S. Federal Housing Administration (FHA), for example, insures mortgage loans in exchange for fees from borrowers. If an insured homeowner fails to repay the mortgage, the FHA repays the bank. When there are few defaults, the FHA collects more in insurance premiums than it pays out. But when defaults multiply in busts, the FHA runs a deficit. If the FHA's reserve fund were added to the federal government's balance sheet, then the combined balance sheet would show larger deficits in recessions and smaller deficits in good times.

The FHA performs an even more important automatic stabilizing role by increasing access to credit during prolonged recessions. When financial institutions and borrowers repair balance sheets, credit is scarce. The FHA uses the U.S. federal government's balance sheet to address the weakness of credit markets in busts.

During the Great Recession, the FHA performed one of the most important stabilizing roles of any government agency or program, as depicted in Figure 2.2. In 2005–2006, when the mortgage lending market overheated, FHA guaranteed less than 2 percent of all mortgage loans used to purchase homes in the United States. In the worst of the housing bust, by contrast, the FHA guaranteed almost 30 percent of home purchase mortgage loans. Many of the home purchases aided by the FHA would have fallen through otherwise. Without the FHA, the housing bust and Great Recession likely would have been much worse.

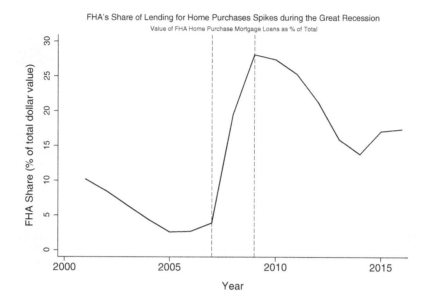

FHA's Share of Lending for Home Purchases Spikes during the Great Recession
Value of FHA Home Purchase Mortgage Loans as % of Total

Figure 2.2 Note the sharp spike in the FHA's share of mortgage lending for new home–purchase mortgages during the Great Recession. The FHA's support to the home-buying market proved essential during the Great Recession.

Data Source: "FHA Single Family Insurance Activity Mortgage Market Share by Dollar Volume, annual data for 1996–2016," at https://www.hud.gov/sites/documents /FHA_SF_MARKETSHARE_2017Q1.PDF at Table 1.

But even as the FHA stabilized the economy, it unconsciously destabilized it as well. Any government insurance program, like the FHA's Mutual Mortgage Insurance (MMI) fund, that avoids minimum or excessive reserves tends to tighten its budgets in the immediate aftermath of bad economic performance, hindering economic recoveries.[46]

When mortgage delinquencies and expected delinquencies rise more than expected (as they did from 2008 to 2010), the MMI fund gets depleted. U.S. law regulates the MMI fund, requiring a ratio of MMI reserves to insured mortgage values of at least 2.0 percent.[47] The MMI ratio fell short of this minimum during the Great Recession, as a result of the surge in delinquencies during the U.S. housing market collapse that helped cause the Great Recession.[48]

In response, the FHA increased insurance rates by more than 50 percent during the Great Recession (see Figure 2.3). This rate increase reduced

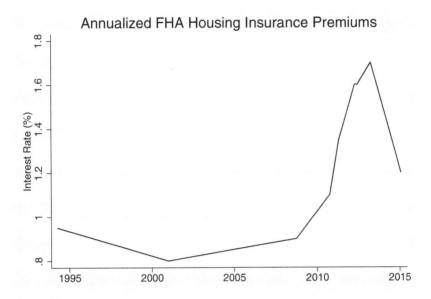

Figure 2.3 FHA annualized insurance premiums increased dramatically during the Great Recession, and then fell back to previous levels as the economy rebounded.

Data Source: Department of Housing and Urban Development, "Actuarial Review of the Federal Housing Administration Mutual Mortgage Insurance Fund Forward Loans for Fiscal Year 2015, Exhibits B-2, B-3, at https://www.hud.gov/sites/documents/AR2015MMIFWDRPT .PDF. Annualized figure created by discounting upfront premium at a 5:1 ratio to annual premium and combining.

the disposable income and spending of the homeowners relying on the FHA to finance or refinance their purchases. Before 2007, annualized FHA mortgage insurance costs for a typical mortgage remained below 1 percent of the total loan value on an annualized basis for more than a decade. After a series of increases in response to the housing bust, mortgage insurance premiums exceeded 1.5 percent annually from 2012 to 2015. Once the housing market recovered, the FHA reduced mortgage insurance premiums again, with annual rates falling below 1 percent by the beginning of 2016 (Figure 2.3).

During the Great Recession and the anemic recovery that followed, FHA mortgage insurance premiums were higher than they were before or afterward, destabilizing the economy. By charging higher fees to new borrowers during the Great Recession, the FHA hindered the recovery of the housing market. The increase in fees also reduced borrowers' discretionary income (relative to keeping insurance fees steady) when spending was already low.

It is remarkable that this action came from an agency founded to stabilize the housing market in response to the Great Depression and heavily criticized during the Great Recession for doing too much to support the housing market.[49] Even when a government insurance program like the FHA is intended to stabilize the economy (and succeeds in doing so), the pressure to replenish depleted reserves leads it to raise premiums and decrease disposable income when aggregate demand is weakest and to lower premiums when aggregate demand is robust.

There are many other examples. U.S. state unemployment insurance funds raised their premiums in response to high layoffs during the Great Recession, holding back employment according to a recent paper.[50] Likewise, the Federal Deposit Insurance Corporation (FDIC) raised its deposit insurance rates in the midst of the Financial Crisis of 2008–2009 in order to replenish its depleted reserves, reducing banks' cash flow precisely when banks were already restricting lending activity.[51]

Ironically, all of these insurance programs (FHA mortgage insurance, FDIC deposit insurance, and state unemployment insurance) are intended to stabilize the economy. And if the destabilizing effects of insurance program premiums are the price to be paid for their primary countercyclical effects, then so be it. We have a more stable economy with the programs than we would without.

But more could be done. Even government insurance programs are designed so that fees rise during recessions and fall during booms. To minimize these destabilizing effects, insurance program reserve funds need to exceed their statutory minimums by considerable margins during good times, giving the programs space to hold down fees during recessions while remaining compliant with regulatory reserve minimums. Alternatively, the government could make minimum reserve ratios sensitive to the business cycle, decreasing them in busts and increasing them in booms. Finally, the reserve ratios could be eliminated entirely. This last option, however, means that badly managed insurance programs can continue running deficits indefinitely.

In this chapter, I demonstrated that the institutional details of income taxation and spending programs affect the stabilizing properties of fiscal policy. Even though discretionary fiscal policy is theoretically attractive, many economists reject it because of its institutional weaknesses. Automatic stabilizers, by contrast, are favored because of their superior design. Ironically, however, the sustained analysis of government spending and taxation programs in this chapter revealed many destabilizing features in programs designed to automatically stabilize. Where possible, these destabilizing features should be eliminated. By highlighting these properties of fiscal policy, I illustrated the value of a law and macroeconomic approach to fiscal policy.

THREE

Law and Monetary Policy When Interest Rates Are Well above Zero

I now engage in a critical review of the institutions of monetary policy. As in Chapter 2 with respect to fiscal policy, my goal here is twofold: to both improve monetary policy by subjecting it to a law and macroeconomic lens; and to set forth the strengths and weaknesses of monetary policy as an alternative to law for making macroeconomic policy. I also highlight law's integral role in enabling a combination of monetary policy control and stable exchange rates via the introduction of legal capital controls.

Monetary Policy Stabilization

In Chapter 2, I discussed the role of the savings market in bringing aggregate demand back to capacity in the restaurant economy. When aggregate demand is low, interest rates decrease as savers outnumber borrowers. The decrease in interest rates encourages borrowers to borrow more and savers to save less, increasing the number of meals purchased from the restaurant and reducing the demand shortage.

This discussion of the savings market ignored the role of money in the economy. Money is a commodity that makes it easier to buy and sell things. Money can be supplied by government fiat (for example, paper currency), but it does not have to be (as when an economy uses a gold standard).

Savings can be held as money or lent to borrowers at interest. Savers must earn an interest rate to get them to lend their funds to others rather than hold money, which is more convenient. If the demand for money exceeds its supply, then the interest rate rises, making holding money, which doesn't earn interest, less attractive relative to lending, which does.

When we introduce money to our restaurant economy, we introduce a second role for the interest rate. The interest rate still brings savings and borrowing into balance. The interest rate also balances the demand and supply of money. But one variable cannot keep two different markets in balance. Instead, two variables, output (of meals) and the interest rate, jointly bring balance to both the market for cash and the savings/borrowing market.

When the government uses a fiat currency, it can increase or decrease the supply of money. As we will see, the government often delegates control over the money supply to an independent central bank. When a central bank increases the money supply, it makes cash more abundant. To accommodate the increased supply of cash, the interest rate needs to decline to induce more people to hold their savings in cash rather than giving them to lenders.

This shift in the interest rate in the money market affects the savings market as well. With interest rates down, borrowers borrow more so that they can buy more meals. In order to accommodate the increased demand for meals, the restaurant produces more meals. Output increases.

An increase in the money supply therefore causes an increase in meal output as well as a decrease in interest rates. The increased abundance of money requires increased production of meals as well as a shift in interest rates in order to bring both the money market and the savings market into balance.

A decrease in the money supply makes cash scarce. Interest rates must rise in order to reduce the demand for cash so that it equals the newly reduced supply. The higher interest rate also moves the savings market, reducing borrowing and therefore reducing demand for meals. Output decreases.

The reasons a central bank might wish to use monetary policy are not unlike those of a legislature attempting fiscal policy: monetary policy can offset the effects of shocks to the demand for meals, hastening the return of output to capacity. If bad weather temporarily reduces aggregate demand below the restaurant's capacity, then the central bank increases the money supply. Interest rates go down, prompting borrowers to borrow more and demand more meals. By dropping interest rates sufficiently, the central bank can stimulate enough additional demand to mitigate the shock caused by bad weather.

In the restaurant economy, central banks control interest rates (and, indirectly, output) because they control the money supply. But the central bank generally does not enjoy perfect control over the money supply and therefore cannot shift the money supply at will. Instead, the central bank controls base money: currency and private banks' reserves held by the central bank. (The amount of base money determines extremely short-term interest rates such as the federal funds rate in the United States.) Base money does affect the broader money supply, but there are other factors at work, such as private bank reserves and the money multiplier.

To illustrate the money multiplier, suppose that the central bank prints $100 in cash and uses it to lend to a restaurant worker. This action raises the monetary base by $100. The consumer then deposits the money with a bank, which holds some of the deposit and lends the rest to someone else. This lending also adds to the money supply. Suppose the bank lends $80 out of each $100 deposited. The bank transfers a credit of $80 to a new borrower's account, along with a debt obligation of $80. The money supply is now $180 larger rather than the original $100. In turn, the new borrower may keep the $80 in the bank for a time. The bank now lends $64 (80 percent of $80) to still another borrower. The money supply is now $244 ($100 + $80 + $64) larger. The process continues until the money supply reaches its limit at a point $500 larger.[1] An initial base-money increase of $100 expands the money supply by $500, so the money multiplier equals five.

Of course, the multiplier is not always five or any other factor. The money multiplier depends on capital requirements, reserve requirements, and bank confidence. Banks will lend more of each additional dollar in deposits when capital and reserve requirements are lower and when those banks are more confident. If reserve requirements are 25 percent, then the banks can only lend $0.75 of each dollar, reducing the money multiplier as compared with a bank lending $0.80 on the dollar. If the bank's leaders are concerned that depositors may demand their money—that is, make a run on the bank—the bank may lend even less, thereby maintaining cash on hand. This also reduces the money multiplier and the money supply.

Although joint causality—meaning that monetary policy both responds to and influences changes in output—makes it difficult to provide precise estimates for the efficacy of central bank monetary policy in stabilizing aggregate demand, a wide variety of econometric methods indicate that what works in theory also works in practice: when central banks tighten monetary policy—when they reduce the money supply—interest rates rise and output declines.[2] Even though central banks don't enjoy exclusive control over the money supply, they retain an imperfect ability to influence interest rates and output with their control over base money.

As with fiscal policy, monetary policy achieves no gains from permanently keeping demand high. The only long-term result of maintaining demand at a point above capacity is higher inflation and queuing. This means the central bank needs to be concerned with not letting the economy overheat. To that end, the central bank raises interest rates when demand for meals experiences a positive shock, such as good weather that induces more spending. Higher interest rates dissuade borrowers from borrowing to purchase meals, bringing demand for meals back into balance with the restaurant's supply capacity.

Monetary Policy Institutions

Who Controls Monetary Policy?

In a democracy, we start with a presumption that the legislature exercises control over policy instruments. If that control proves unwieldy, then legislatures often delegate control to administrative agencies.[3]

In spite of its democratic appeal, direct legislative control over monetary policy would be misguided. Legislators are unlikely to understand monetary policy and the workings of the macroeconomy. Moreover, because shocks constantly buffet aggregate demand, monetary policy needs to respond quickly to many new developments, a requirement that most countries' legislative processes cannot meet. Finally, legislators likely would use their control over monetary policy opportunistically, stimulating the economy by lowering interest rates shortly before elections even when doing so is inappropriate in the longer term. If monetary policy were implemented entirely by legislatures, then it would be a very poor macroeconomic instrument.

Owing to these concerns, all wealthy democracies cede control over monetary policy to central banks with varying degrees of independence. Legislatures establish central banks and provide policy guidelines for them, as they do for all agencies. The Federal Reserve Act, for example, established the Fed and charged it with the pursuit of "maximum employment, stable prices, and moderate long-term interest rates."[4] Article 127 of the Treaty of Maastricht established the European Central Bank (ECB) and charged it with the primary objective of "price stability."[5] Another democratic check is provided by elected leaders, who appoint central bank governors. Finally, central bank chairs testify regularly in front of relevant legislatures.

Beyond these elements of democratic control, however, central banks generally enjoy extraordinary independence compared with other agencies established by legislatures. On core monetary policy decisions, such as setting short-term interest rates, central banks have almost unlimited discretion. Their interest-rate decisions cannot be reversed by courts. Unlike the leaders of many agencies, central bank heads cannot be terminated at will. Instead, they can only be fired for specific causes such as malfeasance. Otherwise, central bank leaders serve long fixed terms—fourteen years, in the case of the Federal Reserve Board—or until they resign. In addition, many central banks, including the Fed and the ECB, control their own budgets; they don't rely on legislative appropriations. Finally, some central banks enjoy explicit protection from legislative interference. The Maastricht Treaty, for example, forbids the ECB from seeking or taking any instructions from any EU or national institutions or governments. The treaty also forbids these governments and institutions from offering such instruction.[6]

The autonomy of monetary policy is especially striking when compared with the nondelegation of fiscal policy, which is formulated by legislatures. Monetary policymaking occurs outside legislative bounds, sacrificing democratic legitimacy for the benefit of technocratic expertise. Conversely, fiscal policymaking is the work of elected leaders, enjoying the ultimate degree of democratic legitimacy without any of the benefits of expertise or independence from legislative opportunism.

Forgoing the Benefits of Monetary Policy Stabilization

Many jurisdictions forgo independent control over monetary policy. Either they lack a central bank charged with using control over the money supply to stabilize the economy, or their central bank's capacity to stabilize is limited by its commitment to other goals.

If a jurisdiction has used control over the money supply poorly in the past (for example, by letting the money supply grow uncontrollably, which leads to hyperinflation), then it may prefer to give up control over monetary policy and adopt a "hard currency." A gold standard, for instance, prevents the state from using money to influence macroeconomic conditions. The supply of gold, rather than policy considerations, determines monetary conditions. Similarly, the adoption of a foreign nation's currency, such as Ecuador's adoption of the U.S. dollar as their national currency, sharply reduces inflation expectations. Adopting a foreign currency, however, disables the use of monetary policy to respond to macroeconomic challenges.

A state might also relinquish monetary policy control to promote trade.[7] Shared currencies facilitate trade by removing exchange-rate risks and reducing transaction costs associated with trade, such as the costs of exchanging currencies. If these benefits are large enough, then jurisdictions may choose to share a currency, at the cost of losing control over monetary policy. Anticipating these trade-enhancing benefits, the members of the Eurozone have done precisely this. Likewise, U.S. states belong to a currency union (the dollar)[8] that eliminates exchange-rate risks and costs from interstate trade at the price of each state's ability to respond to macro conditions using monetary policy. If a jurisdiction within a currency union needs to bring its economy back into balance, it will have to turn to other macroeconomic policy tools, such as fiscal policy (often barred by balanced budget requirements) or the expansionary legal policy I develop in Part II.

Most jurisdictions either enter currency unions that facilitate trade but forgo monetary policy or allow their currencies to "float" in order to retain monetary-policy control. Indeed, the "impossible trinity" of international macroeconomics demands some policy tradeoffs: a jurisdiction cannot simultaneously have all three of (a) fixed exchange rates and low trading costs, (b) control over monetary policy, and (c) free capital flows.

To understand the impossible trinity, suppose that the central bank of a jurisdiction with a currency peg and free capital flows raises the jurisdiction's interest rates above the prevailing world rate in order to inhibit the economy in the face of a positive shock to aggregate demand. The increase in local interest rates encourages capital to flow into the jurisdiction. As foreigners move capital into the jurisdiction to take advantage of the higher interest rates, the jurisdiction's exchange rate should appreciate. In order to prevent appreciation and keep its fixed exchange rate, the jurisdiction needs to defend its exchange rate by using currency reserves. But it cannot do so indefinitely. Alternatively, the jurisdiction could restrict entry of capital by law, relieving the pressure on the currency in spite of the difference between world and local interest rates. This, however, violates the free capital-flow prong of the trinity. Finally, the jurisdiction could keep its interest rate equal to prevailing world rates. This enables the jurisdiction to maintain a stable exchange rate and allow capital to flow freely, but it means that the jurisdiction loses control over local interest rates, which are now determined by global conditions. A jurisdiction can have any two elements of the impossible trinity but never three.

To benefit from a currency peg, jurisdictions must either forgo control over monetary policy or restrict the flow of capital to and from other jurisdictions. Wedded to the notion of free capital flows, many jurisdictions therefore allow their currencies to float rather than lose the ability to use monetary policy to facilitate macroeconomic adjustments.

Capital Controls: Law Enabling Macroeconomic Policy

In *The Globalization Paradox,* Dani Rodrik argues against a binary choice between currency unions and currency-flotation regimes. Instead, Rodrik argues for capital controls, the often-overlooked third prong of the impossible trinity. With capital controls, jurisdictions get the benefits of monetary policy and the benefits of stable exchange rates. Jurisdictions lose the benefits of free international flows of capital, but Rodrik asserts that these benefits are smaller and more uncertain than commonly perceived.

Rodrik's capital-control regime, with its starring role for law, is not in vogue among industrialized democracies. But this wasn't always the case. Recall the Bretton Woods agreements negotiated in the aftermath of the Great Depression and World War II. These imposed capital controls managed by the IMF, newly established to promote trade and prosperity.[9] If capital controls harmed the economy during the Bretton Woods era (1944–1971), then their negative effect is hard to spot. This was a golden era for Western economic growth. Today, China enforces capital controls. It weathered the Great Recession better than any other large economy, growing throughout at unmatched rates.

Law and macroeconomics assumes a much more important role in a fixed exchange-rate/capital-control regime than it does when currencies float or jurisdictions have a shared currency. Capital controls are legal instruments, imposed by governments and implemented by regulators and judges. Under a capital-control regime, the most important interaction between law and macroeconomics is independent of managing aggregate demand directly. Instead, asking more of law enables policymakers to combine two invaluable macroeconomic instruments—monetary policy and stable exchange rates—that would otherwise be jointly unachievable.

The capital controls of the Bretton Woods regime pervaded law. IMF Article VIII.2(b), for example, obliged member countries to make "unenforceable" any foreign-exchange dealings that violated another member country's capital controls. According to the IMF legal department, this meant that "the courts in members' territories must not lend their assistance to implement the obligations of such contracts" that violated another member's capital controls.[10] Maintenance of capital controls was so critical to the international macroeconomic system that it superseded the ordinary enforcement of contracts—one of the fundamental commitments of most legal systems. Bretton Woods thus entailed an important change in law to facilitate macroeconomic ends.

Many economists assume that capital controls are doomed to failure because they are subject to "evasion and circumvention."[11] The critique proves too much: every law is subject to evasion and circumvention. Government control over the money supply also can be evaded and circumvented. When people counterfeit currency, they undermine monetary policy. Likewise, fiscal policy depends on the government's ability to raise and lower taxes, which may be evaded. But we don't give up on monetary policy because of counterfeiters or on fiscal policy because of tax evaders. Instead, we ban counterfeiting and tax evasion and rely on criminal law to enable governments to keep a lid on scofflaws.

Capital controls can also be protected, through legal regimes that reduce incentives to send capital across borders. It may be true that capital controls are easier to evade, are more costly to enforce, or provide less benefit than the regimes that protect monetary and fiscal policy. But legal experts, not just economists, need to help make this determination. Such a legal-economic partnership has happened before—with Bretton Woods. Today, unfortunately, legal experts rarely take part in this discussion because they don't know the macroeconomic stakes well enough to balance the costs of enforcing capital controls against the benefits.

Monetary Policy versus Fiscal Policy

When a jurisdiction relinquishes control over monetary policy to enter a currency union, there is no choice between monetary and fiscal policy as macroeconomic tools. The jurisdiction must instead choose between fiscal policy and simply allowing macroeconomic fluctuations to run their course. In these circumstances, the legal policy options described in Part II will be especially desirable.

When monetary policy is an option, however, most economists conclude that it offers a better stabilization policy instrument than fiscal policy—when interest rates are well above zero. Even some ardent proponents of expansionary fiscal policy in depressed economies, such as former Treasury Secretary Larry Summers, concede that there is "no space for expansionary fiscal policy as a stabilization policy tool" in "normal times."[12] In this section, I explore this consensus, linking legal institutions with monetary policy's efficacy.

The Advantages of Monetary Policy over Fiscal Policy

Fiscal policy is enacted by politicians who mostly lack macroeconomic expertise. By contrast, monetary policy is carried out by experts chosen by heads of state. Two recent chairs of the Federal Reserve, Ben Bernanke and Janet Yellen, were esteemed researchers and teachers at elite university economics departments. Before becoming chair, each gained experience as a lower-ranking board member of the Fed, as did the Fed's current chair, Jerome Powell. The current chairs of the European Central Bank and Bank of Canada, Mario Draghi and Stephen Poloz, respectively, possess doctorates in economics and extensive central banking experience. Both the head of the Bank of Japan, Haruhiko Kuroda, and the head of the Bank of England, Mark Carney, led important international financial institutions before assuming their current positions.

That central bankers know their stuff does not mean they will always get macroeconomic policy right. But they are in a better position to do so than are politicians, most of whom know little about managing economies.

Much of monetary policy's perceived superiority to fiscal policy stems from the former's quicker responsiveness to developments in the economy. After all, macroeconomic policy materializes only after policymakers recognize that there is some change in aggregate demand that needs addressing. That recognition is hastened by expertise. Because monetary policy is set by knowledgeable men and women who employ large staffs to analyze macroeconomic data, monetary policymakers should diagnose shocks to demand before fiscal policymakers do. But even with expertise, there may be long lags in identifying demand shocks. In the restaurant economy, it is hard to know if a one-day decline in demand for meals is the harbinger of a secular decrease in demand for meals or just an idiosyncratic event. While we may reasonably hope that the experts can tell the difference before the typical legislator can, we should still expect some delay in the identification of important changes to demand.

The big advantage in speed comes after the need for new policy becomes clear. At this point, legislators may enter into lengthy and often-fruitless periods of debate over the appropriate response. In contrast, central banks have well-developed avenues for formulating responses. They meet regularly—approximately every six weeks—and their board members vote on measures at each meeting. Central banks are also free to alter monetary policy in between meetings if they feel it is necessary. Of course, as previously noted, the delays constraining fiscal policy depend on the structure of lawmaking, with parliamentary systems moving rapidly. Thus, the argument for monetary policy is generally stronger in the United States than in, say, Canada or the United Kingdom, where legislative action faces fewer hurdles.

Although it may be easier to enact monetary than fiscal policy, monetary policy's effects on aggregate demand materialize more slowly. If interest rates drop as a result of monetary policy, it may still be a while before investment and consumption decisions change and spending increases. Indeed, the economy's sensitivity to monetary policy declined over the last several recessions.[13] It takes longer for output to respond to a decline in interest rates than it used to, meaning that monetary policy's putative advantage over fiscal policy has diminished.

The Role of Law in the Sensitivity of Output to Monetary Policy

Law plays an important role in the lag between changes in monetary policy and in spending. Law may also help explain why the economy has become less sensitive to monetary policy.

Consider the construction industry, one of the most important channels through which lower interest rates raise demand. Because construction activity is both highly variable and very sensitive to interest rates, one of the most important effects of a change in interest rates is their effect on construction.[14] Construction is a notoriously cyclical component of the economy, accounting for a much larger amount of total fluctuations than would be

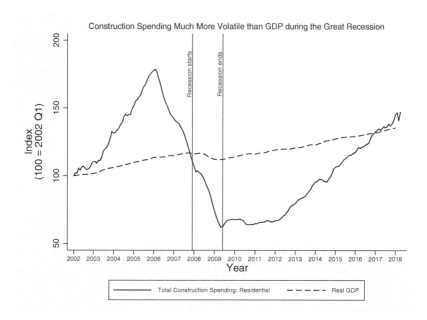

Figure 3.1 Construction spending increased much faster than the economy as a whole from 2003 to 2007 and then collapsed during the Great Recession.

Data Source: U.S. Bureau of the Census, "Total Construction Spending: Residential" [TLRESCONS], retrieved from FRED, Federal Reserve Bank of St. Louis, https://fred .stlouisfed.org/series/TLRESCONS; U.S. Bureau of Economic Analysis, "Real Gross Domestic Product [GDPC1]," retrieved from FRED, Federal Reserve Bank of St. Louis, https://fred.stlouisfed.org/series/GDPC1.

expected from its share of the economy. Before the Great Recession, U.S. construction boomed more than the economy as a whole; during the recession, construction crashed more dramatically (see Figure 3.1)

Law affects the sensitivity of construction to interest rates. For instance, in many areas of the United States and elsewhere, development projects must satisfy layers of zoning and environmental reviews, judgments, and appeals before construction begins. These legal proceedings take time, dampening the industry's sensitivity to monetary policy by ensuring that demand for construction does not respond to a change in interest rates until the proceedings are through. Imagine if there were a one-year delay in purchasing meals in the restaurant economy. In that case, a drop in interest rates today would not be felt until a year from now. Zoning and land-use laws may have similar effects on the real economy. If it takes two years to get shovels in the ground once a developer begins a project, then a decrease in interest rates will take two years to stimulate construction spending.

Legally imposed lags are not just a theoretical concern, as the state of New Jersey showed during the Great Recession. At the beginning of the housing bust, many developers halted construction projects. This raised the specter of lost approvals: each of these projects underwent the usual required course of permitting, but if those permits expired while sites remained fallow, the construction recovery would be long in coming even if economic conditions improved. In response, New Jersey passed the Permit Extension Act of 2008. This act extended many state, county, and local permits and approvals through 2015 and sometimes 2017, an effort to reduce the delays caused by zoning and land-use law.[15]

Zoning and land-use lags are a relatively new development. Before the 1970s, they were not commonly thought of as obstacles to development.[16] But zoning and land-use laws have changed, creating much more lag. They may thus offer a partial explanation for the economy's diminished sensitivity to monetary policy. One of monetary policy's primary mechanisms—promotion of construction spending via lower interest rates—simply no longer works as well as it used to.

Monetary Policy Offsets Fiscal Policy

Thus far I have mostly discussed monetary and fiscal policy as though they were alternatives to choose between. But both might be enacted at once. Indeed, this is plausible, because central banks and legislators both seek to correct the same problematic demand conditions. When this happens, monetary policy offsets fiscal policy, assuming interest rates are well above zero.[17] This is another source of the consensus behind the superiority of monetary policy: if monetary policy nullifies fiscal policy with the same ends, why pursue fiscal policy in the first place? Let's see how it works.

Say there is a sharp decline in the demand for meals in the restaurant economy. Thanks to its expertise and independence, the central bank will probably respond first, lowering interest rates in order to stimulate demand. If the legislature then decides to respond on its own with fiscal policy—government purchases of meals—the demand stimulus may prove excessive, leading to restaurant lines and higher prices. Now the restaurant economy has an inflation problem, so the central bank reverses course, raising interest rates. This bump offsets the fiscal stimulus to demand. One might say that, on net, fiscal policy changes not demand but monetary policy.

Conventional wisdom in economics therefore holds that discretionary fiscal stabilization is not worth the effort: it compromises other goals of fiscal policy—redistribution and spending of public goods—without stimulating demand. Thus, it is better to stabilize with monetary policy alone when interest rates exceed zero.[18]

Reinterpreting the Consensus in Favor of Monetary Stabilization over Fiscal Stabilization

Economists tend to favor monetary over fiscal stabilization when interest rates exceed zero. But their position is more tenuous than they care to admit.

Simply put, it makes little sense to promote monetary policy when many jurisdictions—such as members of a currency union or users of a currency peg—lack that lever of power. Even if aggregate demand proves inadequate, these jurisdictions cannot raise the money supply to lower interest rates and stimulate demand. In these jurisdictions, there is no choice between monetary and fiscal policy. They get fiscal policy or nothing. (In Part II, I argue that law offers an alternative macro tool for these jurisdictions.)

Even where jurisdictions retain control over monetary policy, the consensus in its favor reflects more of a legal and political calculation than an economic one. Monetary policy is not preferred to fiscal policy because it is better at offsetting fluctuations in aggregate demand. As a matter of both theory and empirics, both monetary and fiscal policy stabilize aggregate demand. Rather, the consensus favors monetary policy because it is institutionally superior: the province of expert, responsive, and politically independent central banks, while fiscal policy remains in the hands of slow-moving legislatures.

If the institutions of fiscal policy were identical to those of monetary policy, then there would be no reason to favor the latter. If we let a central bank or some equally independent and expert administrative agency control fiscal policy, then monetary policy would have no obvious advantage. Because interest-rate changes often take time to translate into aggregate-demand changes, fiscal policy may actually be a superior stimulus instrument, even when interest rates exceed zero.

Of course, modern democracies do not allow central banks, or any other agencies, to control fiscal policy. As described in the previous chapter, such a fundamental democratic power cannot be responsibly outsourced. By contrast, delegation of monetary policy to central banks is widely accepted. What the perceived superiority of monetary policy really means is that monetary policy is less important to democracy than fiscal policy and so can be assigned to unelected experts.

This is a valid reason to support monetary policy over fiscal policy, and I have no desire to undermine the consensus surrounding it. But delegation of monetary policy should not be taken for granted. As the *Economist* emphasized in 2017, "The power of central banks ebbs and flows."[19] Indeed, as recently emphasized by ex-central banker Paul Tucker,[20] economists should be careful to avoid tempting fate by arguing for increasing empowerment of central banks, lest they court popular backlash. U.S. central banks have twice lost their mandates from Congress. We are told that, in our febrile political environment, "Populism Is Shaking the Edifice of Central Bank Independence."[21] In the United States, calls to "audit the Fed" or otherwise restrict its discretion grow more urgent;[22] and in Europe, German politicians criticize the independent ECB for enabling the rise of the populist Alternative für Deutschland party.[23]

In particular, central banks need to be sure to avoid exceeding their authority. While their powers over the money supply and interest rates seem accepted by the public, unconventional policies are on shakier ground. Negative interest rates, for example, have spawned considerable anger in Germany.[24] Likewise, one sponsor of legislation to reform the Fed justified his initiative by explaining that the "Federal Reserve [has] more power and responsibility than ever before."[25] It is foolhardy to think that the consensus in favor of monetary policy as a stabilization mechanism continues to apply when monetary policy is used in unconventional ways. Unconventional policies risk criticism that threatens central banks' cherished independence. Even if unconventional monetary policies are effective—a contention that, as discussed in Chapter 5, is debatable—they threaten central bank independence.

In this chapter, we've seen that exclusive reliance on monetary policy for macroeconomic stabilization works only when jurisdictions control their own currencies. When monetary policy is not available because of trading imperatives, we cannot rely on monetary stabilization and must look elsewhere for macroeconomic help. Yet, even where monetary policy is available, it is not necessary effective. In the next two chapters, I show that, at the zero lower bound on interest rates, monetary policy loses efficacy. In a liquidity trap, the need for alternative macro policy tools—such as expansionary fiscal policy or even expansionary legal policy—becomes urgent.

FOUR

The Painful Costs of Prolonged Recessions: Evidence and Theory

The case for expansionary legal policy (see Part II) or institutional reform of fiscal and monetary policy depends on the stakes. If recessions don't cost that much, then we don't really need to expand our macroeconomic policy options with law.

In this chapter, I first document the grievous economic and political costs of the Great Recession. If deep recessions cause harms of this magnitude, threatening the fabric of the social order, then allowing them to run their course should not be an acceptable option. We should be open to any policy that mitigates harms, even if these policies require sacrifices.

I then discuss theoretical accounts of the Great Recession and other prolonged recessions. These accounts differ from the accounts of recessions provided in Chapters 1, 2, and 3. I focus on the related explanations of the liquidity trap and "secular stagnation," both of which highlight the role of the zero lower bound on interest rates. The theory of liquidity traps emphasizes how short-term declines in aggregate demand get prolonged by zero interest rates while secular stagnation emphasizes longer term factors, such as an "imbalance resulting from an increasing propensity to save and a decreasing propensity to invest" that make episodes of zero interest rates more likely in general.[1]

At the zero lower bound, interest rates cannot fall even if aggregate demand falls short of the economy's capacity. With interest rates stuck, the economy loses its adjustment mechanism. Aggregate demand and output can fall short of capacity for extended periods. In addition, conventional monetary policy loses traction at the zero lower bound—expanding the money supply at the zero lower bound cannot lower interest rates, meaning that monetary policy becomes impotent.

I also provide a parallel account of deep recessions—the theory of debt supercycles—that emphasizes the importance of financial frictions rather than constraints on interest rates. I argue that the difference in accounts of prolonged recessions makes little difference for the role of law and macroeconomics.

The Economic and Social Costs of the Great Recession

The Great Recession affected just about every sector of the global economy, but it began in the realm of finance. In 2008, large institutions such as Bear Stearns, Lehman Brothers, and the Royal Bank of Scotland foundered. Even those that did not collapse sputtered. In spite of heroic central bank efforts, financial markets panicked. In the aftermath of the financial crisis, demand plummeted, output sank, and unemployment skyrocketed. Long after the financial crisis dissipated, output, employment, and growth rates remained well below expectations.

The Great Recession imposed enormous costs. A 2013 study by the Dallas Federal Reserve estimated the cumulative loss of output at $6–30 trillion in the United States, relative to potential.[2] Other economies suffered at least as much. These costs were also distributed unequally. Those who lost their jobs suffered grievously, while those who kept their jobs suffered far less, if at all.

What is more, the costs have lingered. With low annual growth of 1–2 percent the new norm, it took the Euro area some eight years to return to its 2008 level of output.[3] Indeed, the Great Recession appears to have permanently lowered growth rates, thanks to the lengthy terms of unemployment it imposed. A large body of research demonstrates that unemployment lasting more than one year has long-lived effects.[4] Those unemployed for long periods often leave the labor force or accept underemployment. Workers who accept jobs that don't take advantage of their skills may permanently damage their own growth prospects, collectively harming the economy as a whole. And labor-force participation rates in the United States and Europe, which dropped dramatically during the Great Recession, have yet to fully recover.

Economists term this long-term shadow of a recession—reduced potential output in the long run—*hysteresis*. There is good evidence to suggest

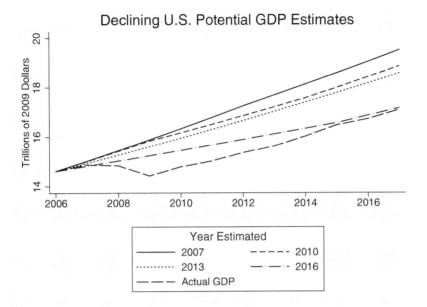

Figure 4.1 Estimates of potential GDP in the United States declined sequentially as the Great Recession progressed. By 2018, the gap between what the United States actually produced in 2018 and what the United States projected in 2007 that it would produce in 2018 was over $2 trillion.

Data Source: Potential GDP estimates from the Congressional Budget Office's annual Budget and Economic Outlook report; U.S. Bureau of Economic Analysis, "Real Gross Domestic Product [GDPC1]," retrieved from FRED, Federal Reserve Bank of St. Louis; https://fred.stlouisfed.org/series/GDPC1.

that hysteresis has set in since the Great Recession. The Great Recession technically has ended, yet growth rates in many developed economies have not returned to pre-recession trends. Instead, growth rates look to be permanently lower. Although estimates of potential long-run output are as likely to be too high as too low, in the United States and Eurozone they have consistently been revised downward, reflecting the consistently disappointing performance of these economies, relative to pre-recession expectations (see Figures 4.1 and 4.2).[5]

The economic costs of hysteresis are staggering. If the United States had continued to grow at its potential rate as estimated in 2008, then the economy would have surpassed its actual 2016 output by $2.5 trillion. Similarly, if the Eurozone had grown as forecast in 2008, then its actual 2015

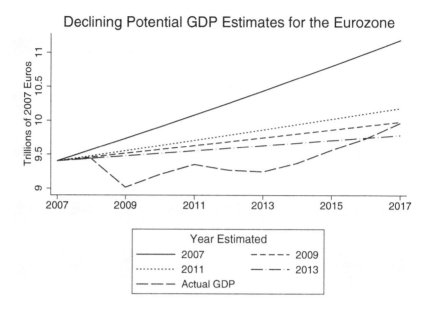

Figure 4.2 Estimates of potential GDP in the Eurozone declined sequentially as the Great Recession progressed. By 2017, the gap between what the Eurozone actually produced in 2017 and what the European Union projected in 2007 that it would produce in 2017 was over €1 trillion.

Data Sources: Nominal GDP from Eurostat, "Gross Domestic Product at Market Prices," at https://ec.europa.eu/eurostat/tgm/refreshTableAction.do?tab=table&plugin=1&pcode =tec00001&language=en. GDP deflator data from Organisation for Economic Co-operation and Development, "Main Economic Indicators," at https://stats.oecd.org/Index.aspx?QueryId =61354; potential output growth forecasts from Robert Anderton et al., "Potential Output from a Euro Area Perspective," European Central Bank Occasional Paper Series No. 156 (2014), charts 1 and 5, at https://www.ecb.europa.eu/pub/pdf/scpops/ecbop156.en.pdf.

output would have been €1.5 trillion greater. With each passing year, the gap between forecast and realized output is growing. If the Great Recession permanently lowered growth rates, then even a $30 trillion cost in the United States may prove to be an underestimate.

The effects of the Great Recession extend beyond the straightforwardly economic. The recession also undermined the political orders of many industrialized democracies, which should further inspire policymakers to try new tools of macroeconomic stabilization that might be more successful than existing forms of monetary and fiscal policy.

The source of these social shifts has been populism, which has thrived in many Western nations since the Great Recession. In the United States, Donald Trump garnered the Republican nomination and eventually the presidency in 2016, despite rejecting many party orthodoxies, such as openness to trade. Bernie Sanders, a self-declared democratic socialist, nearly won the Democratic primary. Whatever happens during the Trump presidency, most observers agree that his election reflects a dramatic break from the status quo in U.S. politics.

While Trump was marching toward the GOP nomination, the United Kingdom was experiencing its own social and political convulsion. The vote for Brexit—the British retreat from the European Union—upended earlier commitments to the free movement of goods, services, capital, and people throughout Europe. It was in effect a vote for national control over immigration and regulation, on the basis of a populist challenge to the global liberal order. Similar populist challenges grew stronger in many other European countries during and after the Great Recession.

It would be hard to argue that the Great Recession was the only, or even primary, cause of this populist wave. But deep recessions and financial crises have a history of boosting the populist right in particular. The Great Depression, for example, helped to undermine Germany's Weimar Republic and lay the groundwork for Nazism, as well as fascism in many other countries. Indeed, a recent empirical study of Europe between 1870 and 2014 found that, after an economic crisis, "polarization rises. . . . Voters seem to be particularly attracted to the political rhetoric of the extreme right, which often attributes blame to minorities or foreigners. On average, far-right parties increase their vote share by 30% after a financial crisis."[6]

If deep recessions cause harms of this magnitude, threatening the fabric of the social order and harming long-run growth through hysteresis, then allowing them to run their course should not be an acceptable option. We should be open to any policy that mitigates harms, even if these policies require sacrifices along other dimensions.

Three Explanations of Prolonged Recessions: Liquidity Traps, Secular Stagnation, and the Debt Supercycle

In order to avoid another Great Recession, we need to understand why the Great Recession and other prolonged recessions differ from the ordinary recessions described in the previous chapters. In this section, I explore accounts of prolonged recessions based on liquidity traps, secular stagnation, and the debt supercycle. These are related, differing in points of emphasis but not in their causal diagnosis: persistently weak aggregate demand underlies prolonged recessions. Most macroeconomists subscribe to a combination of the three accounts, each of which has implications for law and macroeconomics.

Liquidity Traps

Liquidity traps begin with a sharp decrease in aggregate demand. In many cases, including the Great Recession, a financial crisis is the trigger.[7] A liquidity trap, however, is more than just a drop in demand. Alone, even a large drop shouldn't cause deep recessions, because when demand falls far short of capacity, savings become plentiful and interest rates decrease in response. Lower interest rates tempt potential spenders to buy more and savers to save less. Demand ultimately recovers and so does output and employment. Expansionary monetary policy, raising the money supply to lower interest rates, hastens this fall in interest rates and subsequent recovery.

Liquidity traps emerge when very low interest rates persist. The Great Recession is emblematic. At the beginning of the Great Recession, short-term interest rates fell to zero; they were pinned there for the better part of a decade in most of the Group of 7 (G7) club of large industrialized democracies (see Figure 4.3). Long-term interest rates also fell to historically low rates, with ten-year government bond yields falling below 2 percent per year in each G7 country. (Long-term rates need to be above short-term rates to compensate savers for the additional risk associated with locking in savings at low rates over an extended period.)

In a liquidity trap, the zero lower bound on interest rates impedes the usual macroeconomic adjustment process. Once interest rates hit zero, they cannot fall further in order to bring the economy into balance. The macroeconomy's natural equilibrating mechanism—the interest rate—ceases to function. Figure 4.3 depicts the zero lower bound in action. Although short-term government interest rates moved fluidly between 2 and 15 percent between 1990 and 2008, they hit a floor at or near zero in 2008. We observe many years after 2008 in which government interest rates equal zero but almost none in which interest rates are negative, and they are never substantially negative (that is, below −1.0 percent).[8]

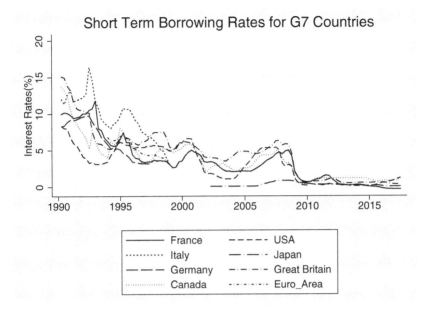

Figure 4.3 Short-term government borrowing rates declined precipitously in all G7 countries from 1990–2015. By 2010, they had hit the zero lower bound in each of the seven countries.

Data Source: Organisation for Economic Co-operation and Development, "Short-Term Interest Rates," at https://data.oecd.org/interest/short-term-interest-rates.htm. Custom search for G7 countries from 1990–2017.

If no one wants to borrow and spend even when the interest rate is zero, then why doesn't the interest rate just keep declining and go negative until the market for saving is in balance? In other words, why is there a zero lower bound on interest rates?

The reason is that the interest rate plays two roles: it balances the markets for both money and saving. Savers hold their reserves either in the form of money or by lending to borrowers. Money is more convenient than lending because money facilitates purchases. Money also returns an interest rate of zero and no lower. Thus, when interest rates on lending are well below zero, there is no benefit on saving through loans as opposed to directly storing away cash. Cash is more convenient—more liquid—and yields a better interest rate. To induce savers to lend rather than hold money, the interest rate must be at least zero—money's rate of return.[9]

In the restaurant economy, an interest rate of zero means that savers hold on to their extra money instead of lending it to borrowers. With the lending market frozen, additional meal purchases by spenders cannot offset a decrease in purchases by savers. The decline in spending caused by savers cutting back translates entirely into a fall in meals produced.

Thus, when interest rates get stuck at zero, interest rates can no longer be reduced in an effort to revive aggregate demand and bring it into balance with capacity.[10] Output alone, rather than a combination of interest rates and output, continues to decrease in response to weak aggregate demand. Without a falling interest rate to help demand recover, declines in output linger for much longer than they would in an economy with no constraints on interest rate adjustment.

Liquidity traps are often accompanied by deflation or very low inflation, which further exacerbates the lack of demand. If people expect prices to decrease in the future, then they reduce spending in the present in anticipation of cheaper purchases later.

Secular Stagnation

Like the liquidity-trap account of prolonged recessions, the theory of secular stagnation emphasizes the role of the zero lower bound in exacerbating recessions. The difference here is that secular stagnation focuses on long-term causes of very low nominal interest rates.[11] The concern is that if there is a long-term excess of savings relative to investment, then real and nominal interest rates go down in both good times and bad. Lower interest rates raise the likelihood of liquidity traps whenever aggregate demand slumps. Excess savings also raise the likelihood of asset bubbles, as savers chase after new investment opportunities. Anemic growth becomes a chronic condition, as deficient demand impedes growth in the long and short terms.

The economic history of Japan in the late twentieth and early twenty-first century offers a cautionary tale of the risks of liquidity traps and secular stagnation. From the end of World War II until the 1980s, Japan enjoyed one of the fastest-growing rich economies. That growth came to an end when a real estate asset bubble burst. Thereafter, most expected Japan to struggle through at most a few years of slow growth before resuming its heady rates. But it was not to be. Instead, Japan fell into a "lost decade"—now approaching three—of anemic growth, falling behind the economies of many other Western countries. Japanese short-term interest rates have been near zero since 1995, and the country has suffered many years of deflation. In an effort to prop up demand and jump-start the economy, Japan financed public spending by accumulating unprecedented levels of public debt. But private spending remains depressed, as evidenced by high savings rates. The state's ability to continue propping up demand with public spending is limited by debt.

Unfortunately for other industrialized democracies, the threat of secular stagnation and repeated episodes of the liquidity trap looms large. As interest rates and inflation expectations have tumbled over the last thirty years, the likelihood of zero nominal interest rates constraining macroeconomic adjustment has risen. A 2017 paper estimated that the zero lower bound may constrain interest rates as frequently as 30–40 percent of the time if recent savings and investment behavior persist.[12] The zero lower bound may be the most common background condition for coping with future recessions.

Debt Supercycle

The debt supercycle account emphasizes the role of the financial sector in prolonging, as well as precipitating, deep recessions.[13] The financial sector mediates the movement of savings from savers to borrowers. But the financial sector faces crucial impediments. Financial institutions are inherently unstable. If most investors believe financial institutions are sound, then they are indeed sound and can lend as usual. This is a good equilibrium. But when people grow concerned that such institutions are vulnerable, a crisis may follow in the form of a run on bank deposits and other short-term liabilities (such as "repo" agreements). Because every financial institution lends some of its funds to other borrowers, none has enough liquid assets to repay all short-term investors, and any might fail if enough short-term investors demand their money. While it is hard to explain exactly what triggers shifts from the good equilibrium of stable financial institutions to the bad equilibrium of widespread bank runs (animal spirits?), both states are possible.

For a variety of reasons, in late 2008, people assumed that financial institutions might fail rather than continue with business as usual, deepening the downturn that had begun almost a year earlier.[14] As confidence in financial institutions fell, asset values plunged. The collapse in asset values triggered the negative-leverage cycle described in Chapter 1. With asset values lower, many people chose to save rather than spend in order to repair their balance sheets, decreasing aggregate demand. And even those willing to spend faced grave difficulty obtaining loans. Shaky financial institutions were reluctant to lend to spenders whose withering assets no longer served as adequate collateral. The result was a further fall in spending. Thus did the bad equilibrium in the financial sector induce a bad equilibrium in the whole economy.

According to the debt supercycle theory, the economy continues to underperform long after a financial crisis because it takes many years for savers to repair their balance sheets and begin borrowing again. Similarly, financial institutions need time to repair their balance sheets so that they can restart lending. Until the deleveraging process is complete, aggregate demand will be reduced, limiting output. After deleveraging ends, the positive phase of the debt supercycle begins. Spenders start borrowing and spending again, driving up asset values and bolstering aggregate demand and output. With collateral values rising, spenders enjoy even greater access to capital. They spend still more, and the economy and asset values continue booming until financial instability brings the positive phase of the debt supercycle to an end.

Law and Macroeconomics and the Theory of Prolonged Recession

The liquidity trap, secular stagnation, and debt supercycle theories all blame demand deficiencies for prolonged recessions. Policies that promote aggregate demand, whether through law or via fiscal or monetary policy, should therefore mitigate prolonged recessions. I mostly emphasize accounts focusing on the zero lower bound (liquidity traps and secular stagnation), but even if this emphasis is misplaced, and the debt supercycle theory offers a superior account of prolonged recessions, the policy thrust of this book—finding new tools to stimulate aggregate demand—applies with equal force.

Still, it does matter which theory we adopt, because each implies a differently structured stimulus program. A liquidity trap calls for short-term fiscal stimulus. If the government spends enough, then interest rates escape the zero lower bound, economic growth returns to normal, and the liquidity trap ends. The secular stagnation theory, by contrast, calls for long-term increases in government spending. With demand deficient over the long run, short-term fiscal stimulus does not suffice to escape the zero lower bound.

In theory, private stimulus would also be an effective policy response to either liquidity traps or secular stagnation. Other than tax cuts, however, macroeconomists have not devoted sustained attention to policies that increase private, rather than public, spending. As I discuss in later chapters, law and macroeconomics offers a new set of private stimulus tools that expand the stimulus options available.

The debt supercycle theory turns a more skeptical eye toward government debt and public spending. Debt supercycle theorists fear government debt because of a greater concern for the risks of financial crises. Governments need the ability to borrow in order to mitigate crises and so shouldn't exhaust their borrowing capacities in order to finance spending.

The debt supercycle theory also rejects the premise—essential to the liquidity trap and secular stagnation accounts—that savings are abundant during deep recessions. Even if government borrowing rates are zero, the financial constraints faced by many borrowers during deep recessions suggest that capital may be scarcer than it appears. If savings are not abundant, then the argument for increased government spending weakens. Government spending no longer puts idle resources to work but instead displaces other forms of economic activity. As a result, governments should avoid incurring massive debt to raise spending. Because the debt supercycle eventually turns and ends a prolonged recession, it may be better for governments to ignore prolonged recessions than to engage in wasteful debt-funded spending.

What matters most in debt supercycle accounts is the health of financial institutions. Such accounts therefore recommend strengthening the financial sector in order to mitigate prolonged recessions. This was the thinking behind the massive government bailouts of financial institutions during the Great Recession, such as the U.S. Troubled Asset Relief Program (TARP) and the British Bank Recapitalisation Fund. These bailouts aimed to quickly repair financial institutions' balance sheets. With healthy balance sheets, financial institutions could continue allocating funds from savers to spenders, bolstering aggregate demand. The success of these bailouts was questionable, though. They prevented the demise of the largest financial institutions and a worldwide depression but failed to stanch the Great Recession.

The debt supercycle theory also supports policies that channel funds to spenders cut off from capital. If the financial system no longer allocates funds to spenders, then government policies should find other means, such as debt relief, of moving funds to spenders who lack access to capital. By improving spenders' access to capital, these policies raise spending, stimulating a moribund economy.

Law and macroeconomics can play an important role here. Debt relief, for example, can be facilitated by fiscal policy, but it must be accomplished through the legal system. And bankruptcy and contract law provide legal mechanisms for repairing spenders' balance sheets, regardless of whether public funding is available for debt relief (see Chapter 11). More generally, law and macroeconomics emphasizes the role of private stimulus rather than government spending in mitigating prolonged recessions.

Because the different accounts of prolonged recessions make little difference for law and macroeconomics, I use the terms "zero lower bound" and "liquidity trap," not the "contractionary phase of the debt supercycle," as shorthand for when expansionary legal policy should be triggered. This shorthand enables focus on the novel aspects of law and macroeconomics without adjudicating between different but overlapping macroeconomic accounts of prolonged recessions. Readers who find the debt supercycle account most compelling can still apply law and macroeconomics ideas but will simply look for a different trigger (a financial crisis rather than zero short-term interest rates).

The Great Recession's grave costs show the urgency of mitigating prolonged recessions under any account of the business cycle. In Chapter 5, I describe the failure of monetary and fiscal policy—the standard tools of recession mitigation—during the Great Recession.

FIVE

Law, Monetary Policy, and Fiscal Policy in a Liquidity Trap

Good macroeconomic policy eases the burden of recessions by stimulating inadequate aggregate demand. Unfortunately, our conventional macroeconomic policy tools—expansionary monetary and fiscal policy—prove inadequate in the prolonged recessions in which they are most urgently needed, as I explain in this chapter. If our conventional macroeconomic tools are ineffective, then we desperately need alternatives like law and macroeconomics to mitigate future prolonged recessions.

In addition to preventing ordinary interest rate adjustments, the zero lower bound on interest rates constrains monetary policy. Monetary policy usually stimulates demand by lowering interest rates, which becomes impossible at the zero lower bound.

In response to the impotence of conventional monetary policy during the Great Recession, central bankers adopted a number of unconventional monetary policies that I describe in this chapter. In doing so, central banks assumed a much larger role in the economy than they traditionally occupied. In response, central banks experienced backlash, threatening their legitimacy and cherished independence. Indeed, some ECB monetary actions violated the simplest reading of the Treaty of Maastricht and became the subject of extremely high-stakes constitutional litigation.

Moreover, unconventional monetary policy proved only moderately effective. In spite of expanding their role in the economy by a factor of five or more, central banks' unconventional policies could not prevent the painful costs imposed by the Great Recession. And central banks' most powerful unconventional policy tool—"helicopter money"—requires such a radical economic intervention that central banks are understandably wary of even mentioning it.

Given the constraints on monetary policy, macroeconomists (including central bankers) emphasize the importance of expansionary fiscal policy at the zero lower bound on interest rates. But the flaws of fiscal policy described in Chapters 3 and 4 don't go away just because expansionary fiscal policy assumes a more salient macroeconomic policy role. As I describe here, balanced budget requirements, political paralysis, and fears of excessive debt burdens limit the scope of expansionary fiscal policy in response to prolonged recessions.

The inadequacy of monetary and fiscal policy at the zero lower bound explains why many believe that the best answer to the question "are we ready for the next recession?" is "no." As a result, it is imperative to consider alternative macroeconomic policy tools such as expansionary legal policy.

Monetary Policy in a Liquidity Trap

In ordinary recessions, central banks follow a slump in demand and output with expansionary monetary policy. With money abundant, interest rates fall and demand and output go up. The zero lower bound, however, means that expansionary monetary policy no longer lowers short-term interest rates, rendering it powerless. Alternative monetary policies are desperately needed, and many such alternatives were debated or implemented during the Great Recession.

Raising Inflation Targets

One popular monetary-policy recommendation during liquidity traps is to raise inflation targets.[1] An inflation target is a central bank's goal for inflation rates. If inflation targets are increased, then inflation expectations should rise as well, assuming central banks can be trusted to hit their targets.

The idea is that, if the nominal interest rate is stuck at zero, then raising inflation expectations lowers the real interest rate—which equals the head-line "nominal" interest rate minus the rate of inflation—and thus stimulates investment. If people expect inflation of 2 percent, and the nominal interest rate is zero, then the real interest rate is –2 percent per year. If inflation expectations can be raised to 4 percent by raising the inflation target to 4 percent, then real interest rates are effectively lowered to –4 percent per year, even though nominal rates remain zero because of the lower bound. Because investment depends on real, rather than nominal, interest rates, raising inflation expectations should stimulate investment. With a high enough inflation target, achieved with the stroke of a pen, the zero lower bound becomes less of a problem.

Of course, such a policy involves trade-offs. Many central bankers oppose raising inflation targets even if they feel that higher targets are economically warranted, because they worry that they will lose their hard-won credibility. Credibility matters because inflation expectations actually can determine inflation, even with no expansion of the money supply. If the public expects high inflation, then they will insist on wage and price increases, leading to inflation. These inflation expectations, in turn, depend upon the central banks' credibility. A credible central bank means that the public can expect inflation to equal the target. But a central bank that periodically changes its target is less credible. And if the public no longer trusts the central bank when thinking about inflation, then the central bank's ability to achieve any inflation target may be undermined.

It is not only inflation hawks who cite credibility grounds in opposing increased inflation targets. As Alan Blinder, vice chair of the Fed in the Clinton administration and a central banker not known for inflation paranoia, explains, "Central bankers have invested a lot and established a great deal of credibility on their 2 percent inflation target, and I think they're right to be very hesitant to give it up. If you change from 2 percent to 3 percent, how does the market know you won't change 3 to 4?"[2]

Looking at this concern from an institutional design perspective suggests a solution: have some other body, not the central bank, raise the inflation target. Central bank credibility depends on adherence to the official target, not on the value of the target itself. If the central bank unilaterally raises its inflation target from 2 to 4 percent, then it violates its previous commitment. If some other body raises the inflation target, then the central bank breaks no commitments.

However, charging another institution with changing inflation targets is no panacea. If the second institution alters the target enough, then monetary policy loses predictability and consistency even if the central bank faithfully pursues the goals assigned to it. Although the central bank retains credibility, this credibility matters little because the credibility of monetary policy as a whole has been diminished.

To mitigate this concern, inflation targets might be changed by the legislature. The difficulty of legislative change mitigates the credibility problem associated with allowing changes in inflation targets. Because it is so hard to change laws, a legislative change in the inflation target should not cause widespread fears of further changes.

But legislative adjustment to a central bank's inflation target may be impossible—or at least very difficult. In the Eurozone, the ECB's goal of price stability is set constitutionally by the Treaty of Maastricht. This goal could be changed only by an amendment to Maastricht or by a change in the interpretation of the treaty adopted by the governing board of the ECB. In the United States, a dysfunctional Congress raises the risks of relying on the legislative process to fine-tune inflation targets.

If changing inflation targets by legislative decree is impossible, then central banks should develop procedures to formally review inflation targets or other monetary policy goals at preset periodic intervals. This would enable revision of the inflation target when necessary without opening the floodgates to repeated, unpredictable change. A formalized system of this kind has been in place in Canada since 1991.[3] The Bank of Canada's inflation target is subject to review every five years, allowing predictable adjustment. At the same time, the long fixed interval and regularized renewal procedure reduces the harm that a change in the inflation target might cause to the Bank of Canada's credibility.

Quantitative Easing, Negative Interest Rates, and Helicopter Money

In spite of inflation retargeting's theoretical appeal at the zero lower bound, no G7 country—not even Canada—raised its target during the Great Recession. Instead, many central banks pursued unconventional monetary policies, most prominently, quantitative easing. Under a quantitative-easing program, a central bank attempts to boost aggregate demand by purchasing assets it normally shuns, such as long-term bonds, in an effort to bring down long-term interest rates directly. The central bank creates money in order to purchase these assets. By reducing long-term interest rates, the central bank can raise investment spending, even if the short-term interest rate cannot go lower than zero.[4]

Quantitative easing should also raise inflation expectations, as the public expects that the expanding money supply will ultimately translate into higher prices. With higher inflation expectations, real interest rates go down, stimulating investment even if nominal rates are stuck at zero.

Because quantitative easing enables the central bank to buy many more classes of assets, central bank assets increase. Before the Great Recession, central bank assets increased slowly. With aggregate demand roughly in proportion to capacity, central banks were just as likely to contract the money supply by shedding assets as expand it by buying assets. But during the Great Recession, central bank policies changed dramatically. As Figure 5.1 indicates, the Federal Reserve tripled the size of its balance sheet in a period of a few months in 2008–2009. By 2016, the Federal Reserve, the ECB, and the Bank of Japan had all introduced quantitative easing and held many more assets than they had before the Great Recession. That is to say, the monetary policy response to the Great Recession was extremely aggressive, perhaps unprecedentedly so.[5]

Central banks did not turn to quantitative easing because they liked the idea. It is decidedly a second-best policy, instituted because expansionary fiscal policy, which typically dominates unconventional monetary policy at the zero lower bound, was itself dormant owing to the obstacles of the legislative process. As Paul Krugman explained:

> Here we are, with anything resembling first-best macroeconomic policy ruled out by political prejudice, and the distortions we're trying to correct are huge—one global depression can ruin your whole day. So we have quantitative easing, which is of uncertain effectiveness, probably distorts financial markets at least a bit, and gets trashed all the time by people stressing its real or presumed faults; someone like me is then put in the position of having to defend a policy I would never have chosen if there seemed to be a viable alternative.[6]

The trash talk Krugman refers to includes predictions of runaway inflation. After all, quantitative easing involves a massive increase in the money supply (technically, in base money). But inflation did not ensue. As described above, at the zero lower bound, additional money gets held as an asset rather than triggering more economic activity or inflation.[7] (Indeed, the failure of this massive monetary expansion to cause inflation is one of the most striking and successful predictions of the liquidity trap account of the Great Recession.)

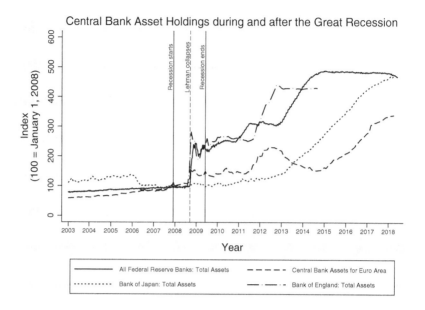

Figure 5.1 Central bank assets increase many-fold in the wake of the collapse of Lehman Brothers, implying a much greater role for central banks in the economy.

Data Source: European Central Bank, "Central Bank Assets for Euro Area (11–19 Countries) [ECBASSETS]," retrieved from FRED, Federal Reserve Bank of St. Louis, https://fred .stlouisfed.org/series/ECBASSETS; Board of Governors of the Federal Reserve System, "All Federal Reserve Banks: Total Assets [WALCL]," retrieved from FRED, Federal Reserve Bank of St. Louis, https://fred.stlouisfed.org/series/WALCL; Bank of Japan, "Bank of Japan: Total Assets for Japan [JPNASSETS]," retrieved from FRED, Federal Reserve Bank of St. Louis, https://fred.stlouisfed.org/series/JPNASSETS.

How did this aggressive monetary response to the Great Recession affect the economy? As the *Economist* summarized in 2015:

> The jury is still out on QE [that is, quantitative easing]. Studies suggest that it did raise economic activity a bit. But some worry that the flood of cash has encouraged reckless financial behaviour and directed a firehose of money to emerging economies that cannot manage the cash. Others fear that when central banks sell the assets they have accumulated, interest rates will soar, choking off the recovery. [In 2013], when the Fed first mooted the idea of tapering [long-term bond purchases], interest rates around the world jumped and markets wobbled. Still others doubt that central banks have the capacity

to keep inflation in check if the money they have created begins circulating more rapidly. Central bankers have been more cautious in using QE than they would have been in cutting interest rates, which could partly explain some countries' slow recoveries.[8]

From the perspective of 2018, quantitative easing looks a bit more effective. Industrialized economies finally are growing robustly. Inflation remains in check. And Mario Draghi's 2012 promise to "do whatever it takes" to keep European government bond yields down, including quantitative easing, appears to have reduced pressures on the Eurozone that might have led to its breakup.[9] But even if quantitative easing can yield benefits, and even if it may be better than doing nothing, it entails considerable risk.

In response to quantitative easing's inability to decisively expand aggregate demand, some central banks have tried even more aggressive monetary interventions. Among these is the negative interest rate. While expanding the money supply won't turn interest rates negative, the central bank can charge banks for deposits. Negative interest causes deposits to lose value over time, which encourages spending now. In theory, that boosts aggregate demand.

One might wonder how it is possible to obtain a loan at negative interest. After all, savers and institutions are loath to lend at a rate that loses them money when they can hold cash instead. But there is a caveat. Savers may prefer to receive negative interest rates than to hoard cash or find some other way to effectively earn a zero return on assets, such as paying income taxes in advance. Even so, interest rates can't go too negative without causing inefficient behavior. Hoarding cash, for example, is an unwieldy and dangerous way to save. And slightly negative interest rates have, as Ben Bernanke summarized in a 2016 review, only "modest benefits."[10] The advent of negative interest rates in much of Europe and Japan was not associated with a rapid improvement in macroeconomic conditions.

If paper money were abolished, then an important asset class offering an implicit interest rate of zero would be eliminated. The abolition of cash should therefore enable interest rates to move further into negative territory, stimulating economies formerly stuck at the zero lower bound. Although unconventional, the policy has prominent supporters, such as Kenneth Rogoff.[11] But the abolition of cash would have regressive effects. Those without access to the banking system, who are typically poorer, would find it more difficult to buy and sell things, while those with access to cash alternatives, such as credit cards and checking, would be less affected. The abolition of cash is also risky and has not fared well in the few test cases. For example, when India eliminated high-denomination bills in 2017, chaos and economic slowdown followed.

Another radical option, which received a "flurry of attention" in 2015–2017, is so-called helicopter money.[12] With helicopter money, additional spending is financed by currency debasement. Instead of requiring the treasury to issue new debt to finance additional government spending, the central bank prints money and uses it to pay for the fiscal expansion. In the extreme, Milton Friedman half-jokingly suggested, newly printed cash should be dropped from helicopters, enabling greater spending by whoever happens to be in the flight path.

If helicopter money sounds outlandish, that's because it is. There is no wonder it is untested: economists and policymakers are wary of the great risk of hyperinflation. Print enough money, and inflation, in both consumer prices and asset values, will follow, even if we are not sure exactly when. Still, Bernanke writes, "Under certain extreme circumstances—sharply deficient aggregate demand, exhausted monetary policy, and unwillingness of the legislature to use debt-financed fiscal policies—[helicopter money] may be the best available alternative."[13]

But the greatest concern surrounding helicopter money—and, to a lesser extent, quantitative easing and other assertive forms of monetary intervention—may be political: few would accept such a forceful policy intervention by an unelected central bank.

Unconventional Monetary Policy, Central Bank Independence, and Law

Helicopter money is no technocratic exercise. It gives central bankers the "power of the purse" ordinarily left to legislatures. Allowing an unelected and relatively unaccountable central bank to risk hyperinflation by printing money and influencing how the money will be spent strains the limits of democratic government.

Central bankers know this, and they approach helicopter money with understandable trepidation. Lawmaking bodies have also taken steps to prevent such usurpation of political prerogatives by central banks. In the Eurozone, helicopter money is likely illegal, a violation of the Maastricht Treaty's prohibition on "monetary financing"—that is, paying for government spending with newly printed money.[14] Even less intrusive versions of unconventional ECB monetary policy tread uncomfortably close (at best) to this monetary financing prohibition. One of the ECB's most important quantitative easing programs, Outright Monetary Transactions (OMT), which enabled the ECB to buy Eurozone members' long-term public debt on secondary markets, was challenged as a Maastricht violation. Critics declared that OMT was "fiscal policy, not monetary policy"[15]—in other words, the province of legislatures, not central banks.

Germany's Federal Constitutional Court largely agreed with this assessment. In a suit brought by German plaintiffs, the high court concluded, "It is likely that [OMT] is not covered by the mandate of the European Central Bank" because "it does not constitute an act of monetary policy, but a predominantly economic-policy act."[16] It is hard to disagree. OMT explicitly sought to decrease the long-term bond yields of countries—such as Italy, Spain, Portugal, and Ireland—with relatively high debt levels or stagnant economies. This certainly sounds like economic policy.

However, the Federal Constitutional Court did not rule on the constitutionality of OMT, instead referring the question to the European Court of Justice (ECJ), which sided with the ECB.[17] The Court of Justice found that the quantitative-easing program was monetary policy, not financing through monetary means. The policy was justified because the ECB's ability to control interest and inflation rates using standard monetary policy had been disrupted during the Great Recession (that is, by the zero lower bound). The bank therefore was granted latitude; it could, the court decided, take extreme measures in an effort to reestablish the control over the macroeconomy it had lost.[18]

As a textual matter, the plaintiffs have what appears to be the stronger argument. As the German ruling articulates, buying the long-term sovereign debt of some Eurozone nations but not others with money created by the central bank is just about the definition of monetary financing. OMT "envisages a targeted purchase of government bonds of selected Member States" by the ECB even though the "prohibition of monetary financing prohibits the suspension of the independence of the national budgets which relies on market incentives."[19] The ECJ dismissed this argument on a technicality, explaining that the ECB is "entitled to purchase government bonds indirectly, on secondary markets" even if the ECB is prohibited by the Maastricht Treaty from purchasing government bonds "directly" from issuing governments.[20]

In ordinary times, courts should reject arguments that permit otherwise illegal actions so long as funds are laundered through third parties. But these were not ordinary times. Arguably, the ECJ's expansive reading of the Maastricht Treaty can be justified as a necessary response to exigent circumstances. The constitutional structure of the Maastricht Treaty, which likely prevented OMT, was failing when the program was announced. The ECB and the ECJ faced a stark decision: either functionally "amend" the monetary financing prohibition of the Maastricht Treaty by enabling OMT, or allow the Euro currency union possibly to fail. The ECB and the ECJ chose to "amend" the treaty.[21]

At a desperate time, OMT worked—more decisively than any other unconventional monetary policy intervention of the Great Recession. OMT's 2012 announcement sharply lowered bond yields for many struggling Eurozone nations, as market panic subsided after the promise of ECB intervention. If the ECJ or the German Constitutional Court had prohibited OMT, then the Eurozone might have disintegrated. If the purpose of the Maastricht Treaty was to enable a single currency while requiring prudent fiscal policy and preventing hyperinflation, then OMT probably fostered the aims of Maastricht more than it violated them. It was the best resolution of a failing constitutional arrangement.

The same technical reading of the prohibition against monetary financing applied by the ECJ could be applied to versions of helicopter money. So long as the ECB does not directly buy government bonds with the money it has created, helicopter money does not appear to violate the ECJ's understanding of the Maastricht Treaty's prohibition on monetary financing.

But the ECB should not continue on this journey into the legal netherworld. Even if the ECJ's functional amendment to Maastricht was justified with respect to OMT as a necessary response to a crisis, the ECB and ECJ should be extremely reluctant to extend the maneuver. Enabling helicopter money would effectively repeal, rather than simply amend, Maastricht's protections against spendthrift fiscal policy and hyperinflation. The protections would remain on the books, but they would amount to nothing in substance. Such a complete change in Maastricht's meaning requires formal amendment of the Maastricht Treaty rather than creative judicial interpretation in response to exigent circumstances. Helicopter money, if implemented or even just approved, also would push the ECB still further into a governance role, bolstering the already-potent anti-democratic critique of the European Union.[22]

The ECJ's final ruling speaks to the power and the peril of law as an enabler of macroeconomic stimulus. In response to the Great Recession, the law of central banking changed in a way that allowed the ECB to flex its macroeconomic muscles, to good effect. The ruling also shows that the legal system can parse central bank powers finely. But even such an expansive reading of Maastricht should not be interpreted to allow the ECB to implement helicopter money at will. Indeed, it would have been much better for the rule of law in the Eurozone if the ECB had never felt obligated to pursue OMT.

Instead of borderline unconstitutional pursuit of unconventional monetary policy at the zero lower bound, why couldn't central banks (and the judiciary) rely on expansionary fiscal policy to stimulate the economy? Indeed, most macroeconomists advised a turn toward expansionary fiscal policy during the Great Recession.

As I document below, fiscal policy fell short during the Great Recession in spite of its theoretical and empirical desirability, leaving monetary policy as the "only game in town."

Fiscal Policy in a Liquidity Trap

As we saw in Chapter 3, lowering taxes and increasing spending can stimulate demand. True, fiscal policies are difficult to implement and produce many inefficiencies. But at the zero lower bound, when demand cannot be effectively stimulated through interest-rate cuts, fiscal policy has often been a popular alternative. I first consider the theory underlying the deployment of fiscal policy in a liquidity trap and then assess the wisdom of such policies.

The Restaurant Economy

In the restaurant economy, fiscal stimulus (government purchases of meals) becomes more attractive at the zero lower bound than in ordinary times because zero interest rates indicate a lack of demand for meals. People must be saving, which drives interest rates to their lowest possible level. A surplus of savings is associated with inadequate demand for meals. Increasing demand will raise output. Even better, expansionary fiscal policy at the zero lower bound raises output without raising interest rates and replacing private meal purchases. Instead, expansionary fiscal policy induces savers to lend rather than holding money, increasing output rather than raising interest rates. By bringing output closer to capacity, expansionary fiscal policy also reduces the risk of harmful price deflation.

Perceived Advantages of Fiscal Policy in a Liquidity Trap

Fiscal policy is also most effective at the zero lower bound because here monetary policy does not offset it. Recall (from Chapter 3) that when fiscal policy contracts demand, decreasing output below capacity and lowering interest rates, the central bank typically responds with monetary expansion, further lowering the interest rate and bringing output back to capacity. And when fiscal policy stimulates demand and brings output above potential, the central bank will probably tighten monetary policy, raising interest rates and bringing output back to potential. Fiscal policy thus has a limited macroeconomic effect above the zero lower bound.

In a liquidity trap, there is no offset. With output below capacity, the central bank wants to stimulate the economy by lowering interest rates, but the zero lower bound prevents it from doing so. The central bank therefore welcomes fiscal stimulus as an acceptable alternative and will not try to offset.

Timing is another concern that dissolves at the zero lower bound. As we have seen, fiscal policy moves slowly. By the time fiscal stimulus has been implemented, the need for stimulus may have passed. But in the wake of financial crises, periods of slow or negative growth and zero interest rates can last more than a decade, far longer than ordinary recessions.[23] As a result, timing problems that typically plague fiscal stimulus are less damaging in liquidity traps.

How Effective Is Fiscal Policy at the Zero Lower Bound?

If fiscal stimulus in fact has a greater effect on output at the zero lower bound than it does in ordinary times, then we should be able to detect this in the fiscal multiplier—the amount by which output increases after a $1 increase in government spending (also known as the "government spending multiplier"). With respect to fiscal policy, this number should be higher at the zero lower bound than it is when interest rates are well above zero. That is, the fiscal multiplier should be greatest during liquidity traps.

A significant, but not unanimous, empirical literature supports this proposition. A 2017 survey of papers estimating fiscal multipliers when there is little monetary offset of fiscal policy (a condition that characterizes the zero lower bound) gives a consensus multiplier estimate of 1.8.[24] By contrast, the IMF pegs the fiscal multiplier around 0.5 during ordinary economic times.[25] The IMF's own research also distinguishes between multipliers when interest rates exceed zero and multipliers at the zero lower bound, observing that "multipliers have actually been in the 0.9 to 1.7 range since the Great Recession."[26] The report went on to conclude, "This finding is consistent with research suggesting that in today's environment of substantial economic slack" and with "monetary policy constrained by the zero lower bound . . . multipliers may be well above 1."[27] A later IMF working paper summarized the empirical evidence:

> Fiscal multipliers are generally found to be larger in downturns than in expansions. This is true both for fiscal consolidation and stimulus. . . . Multipliers can potentially be larger, when the use and/or the transmission of monetary policy is impaired—as is the case at the zero interest lower bound (ZLB). Most of the literature focuses on the effect of temporary increases in government purchases and finds that the multiplier at the ZLB exceeds the "normal times" multiplier by a large margin.[28]

When multipliers exceed one, spending causes a positive externality. Spending at the zero lower bound doesn't just affect buyers and sellers. It also benefits third parties. When the buyer spends, she raises the seller's income. In turn, the seller spends, benefiting people who had no connection to the first transaction. Such "downstream" third-party effects are a classic externality, and the literature demonstrating high multipliers at the zero lower bound testifies to the importance of this externality.

There is also reason to believe that fiscal stimulus at the zero lower bound reduces hysteresis effects, thereby reducing long-run budget deficits. This is counterintuitive; after all, fiscal stimulus costs the treasury money and so should increase deficits. But when conducted at the right time, fiscal stimulus can increase output in the long run, helping to grow the economy. By limiting the number of the long-term unemployed and the resultant loss of human capital, fiscal stimulus in a liquidity trap raises long-term output. This in turn means lower long-term deficits at a given tax rate. Thus, fiscal stimulus at the zero lower bound may be deficit neutral or even reduce budget deficits. Delong and Summers conclude that this theoretical possibility likely came to fruition during the response to the Great Recession.[29]

Consensus Favors Fiscal Policy at the Zero Lower Bound

Because monetary stimulus is relatively ineffective and risky at the zero lower bound, and because fiscal stimulus is more effective than usual, macroeconomists overwhelmingly prefer the latter. The vast majority of prominent economists polled in a 2014 survey, 97 percent of them, agreed that U.S. deficit spending in 2009–2010 decreased unemployment.[30] Even Martin Feldstein—noted deficit hawk, head of the Council of Economic Advisers under Ronald Reagan, and leading adviser to 2016 U.S. Republican Party candidate for president Jeb Bush—conceded that fiscal policy can be useful "when the economic downturn is expected to be deep and long" and that "those conditions prevailed in the recession that began at the end of 2007."[31]

This consensus holds among policymaking institutions and their leaders, too. In 2015, the IMF titled a publication on fiscal policy "Now Is the Time" and concluded, "Fiscal policy has an essential role to play in both building confidence and sustaining aggregate demand."[32] In late 2016, ECB chair Mario Draghi asserted that unconventional monetary policy "cannot be the only game in town" and stressed instead that "fiscal [stimulus] and structural policies are needed to reinforce growth and make it more inclusive."[33] As Fed-chair Bernanke observed in 2014:

> Excessively tight near-term fiscal policies have likely been counterproductive. Most importantly, with fiscal and monetary policy working in opposite directions, the recovery is weaker than it otherwise would be. But the current policy mix is particularly problematic when interest rates are very low, as is the case today. Monetary policy has less room to maneuver when interest rates are close to zero, while expansionary fiscal policy is likely both more effective and less costly in terms of increased debt burden when interest rates are pinned at low levels. A more balanced policy mix might also avoid some of the costs of very low interest rates, such as potential risks to financial stability, without sacrificing jobs and growth.[34]

In a late 2016 address, Jason Furman, chair of the U.S. Council of Economic Advisers, summarized the "new view" of fiscal policy as follows:

1. Fiscal policy is often beneficial for effective countercyclical policy as a complement to monetary policy.
2. Discretionary fiscal stimulus can be very effective and in some circumstances can even crowd in private investment. To the degree that it leads to higher interest rates, that may be a plus, not a minus.
3. Fiscal space is larger than generally appreciated because stimulus may pay for itself or may have a lower cost than headline estimates would suggest; countries have more space today than in the past; and stimulus can be combined with longer-term consolidation.
4. More sustained stimulus, especially if it is in the form of effectively targeted investments that expand aggregate supply, may be desirable in many contexts.
5. There may be larger benefits to undertaking coordinated fiscal action across countries.[35]

Backers of this consensus are not blind to the disadvantages of fiscal stabilization, in particular the trade-off between stabilization and the other core functions of fiscal policy—redistribution and provision of public goods. What these economists are saying is that, given the pain inflicted by deep recession, we should be prepared to accept the costs of disruption to other aims of fiscal policy.

Fiscal Stimulus in Practice: The Case of the Great Recession

Much theory and some evidence support the use of fiscal stimulus at the zero lower bound. But during the Great Recession, when industrialized democracies had the chance to put theory to the test, the consensus behind fiscal policy broke down.

At the outset of the financial crisis, fiscal stimulus was widely supported. In November 2008, the G20 group of nations agreed to "use fiscal measures to stimulate domestic demand to rapid effect," and almost all of them followed through.[36] But enthusiasm waned quickly. The vast majority of EU states adopted austerity plans.[37] The United States did, too. Looking back in early 2014, Bernanke wrote,

> Federal fiscal policy was expansionary in 2009 and 2010. Since that time, however, federal fiscal policy has turned quite restrictive; according to the

Congressional Budget Office, tax increases and spending cuts likely lowered output growth in 2013 by as much as 1 to 1.5 percentage points.[38]

A 2016 IMF publication decried the political success and macroeconomic failure of austerity, concluding:

> Austerity policies . . . hurt demand—and thus worsen employment and unemployment. . . . Episodes of fiscal consolidation have been followed, on average, by drops rather than by expansions in output. On average, a consolidation of 1 percent of GDP increases the long-term unemployment rate by 0.6 percentage point.[39]

Why was fiscal policy contractionary, in spite of a consensus favoring stimulus? The reasons vary by jurisdiction.

Deficit Restrictions

As discussed in Chapter 3, many governments must balance their budgets every year. This impeded stimulus during the Great Recession, when tax revenues fell. In response, governments bound by deficit restrictions raised taxes and cut spending so as to meet balanced budget requirements. In the United States, a large proportion of state governments were forced to pursue contractionary policy, making it even harder for the federal government to appreciably stimulate the economy as a whole. Not only was it fighting the recession, it was doing so hampered by retrenchment at the state level.

Deficit restrictions also limited fiscal stimulus in Europe. While the Eurozone's Stability and Growth Pact allows violations of deficit targets in "periods of severe economic downturn," this flexibility is limited by the interpretations of the European Commission (the European Union's executive arm) and European Council (composed of the heads of the EU member states, the head of the Commission, and a single executive "president").[40] If the Commission finds that a country is violating the rules of the pact, then the Commission can compel the country to adopt austerity measures. In practice, the European Union's most powerful creditor nation, Germany, supported austerity. As a result, most Eurozone countries were restricted in their ability to apply fiscal stimulus. As the director general of the Commission's Economic and Financial Affairs division admitted in 2016, "From a purely macroeconomic perspective, the fiscal stance was at times too restrictive during the crisis."[41]

Political Paralysis

During most of the Great Recession, the legislative and executive branches in the United States were controlled by different parties. Divided government induced political paralysis. In these conditions, passing any form of fiscal stimulus, let alone a package sufficient to overcome the contractionary drag of state and local policy, proved difficult. The initial federal stimulus was passed when Democrats controlled both branches. When Republicans took control of Congress in 2010, federal policy turned toward reduced deficits. In particular, the "sequester" of 2010 curtailed government spending during the middle of the Great Recession.

Lack of Fiscal Space

Fiscal stimulus demands state borrowing at reasonable interest rates. But countries in very bad economic shape may be effectively barred from public debt markets. In these countries, fiscal stimulus is not a viable policy option; such countries are said to lack "fiscal space." Thus, the IMF's 2015 call for fiscal stimulus left out two EU states: Greece and Cyprus. Suffering from high debt and borrowing costs, neither could get affordable loans and therefore neither had the fiscal space to stimulate demand.[42]

When there is no fiscal space, fiscal multipliers should be small, or even negative. Increased government spending may exacerbate fears of a debt crisis and reduce private spending.

The Flawed Idea of Expansionary Austerity

In addition to these institutional and practical impediments, fiscal stimulus faces an intellectual obstacle. Although the case for fiscal stimulus is strong, and most policy experts are convinced of its value in downturns, during the recession a vocal minority successfully pressed for austerity on the theory that it can have expansionary effects. The idea is that debt reduction fosters business confidence, triggering an increase in overall demand even as government demand drops. If the fiscal multiplier is negative rather than well over one, then a decrease in government spending expands output rather than decreasing it. This theoretical argument for austerity to reduce public debt burdens received theoretical support from an article indicating that countries with public debt burdens in excess of 90 percent of output grew very slowly relative to countries with more fiscal space.[43] This empirical finding was subsequently debunked.[44]

Especially in 2010 and after, expansionary austerity was the official position of the government in the United Kingdom and in Germany and, through German pressure, in much of the Eurozone. This turn to austerity came despite the pleas of many prominent central bankers, including the chairs of the Federal Reserve, the ECB, and the Bank of England, for more fiscal stimulus.

After an initial increase due to the American Recovery and Reinvestment Act, U.S. government spending also decreased during the Great Recession. Figure 5.2 shows real U.S. government investment and employment numbers before and after the Great Recession. Real investment (new investment minus depreciation of existing investment) plunged, rather than increased, from 2010 to 2016, while government employment decreased slightly over the same period.

As predicted by the central bankers and many other macroeconomists, austerity had harmful consequences for output and unemployment. During and after the Great Recession, growth in countries that pursued austerity lagged growth in countries that stuck to a more relaxed fiscal posture. As the IMF's World Outlook from October 2012 observed, "[Economic] activity has disappointed in a number of economies undertaking fiscal consolidation."[45]

Unconventional Fiscal Policy When There Is No Fiscal Space

Fiscal stimulus that increases aggregate demand and raises public debt is not the only fiscal policy that can stimulate at the lower bound. Unlike fiscal stimulus, "unconventional fiscal policy" does not increase public debt or government spending. Instead, it aims to increase private sector spending by using tax policy to adjust price expectations. Because unconventional fiscal policy does not increase debt levels, it can be implemented by governments that lack the fiscal space or constitutional license to increase their debt levels or erroneously perceive that they lack the fiscal space to pursue conventional fiscal stimulus.[46]

Unconventional fiscal policy raises inflation expectations by setting forth a schedule of sales or consumption tax increases. After the government announces the tax increases, people expect prices to rise in the future. This lowers the real interest rate at the zero lower bound, increasing spending

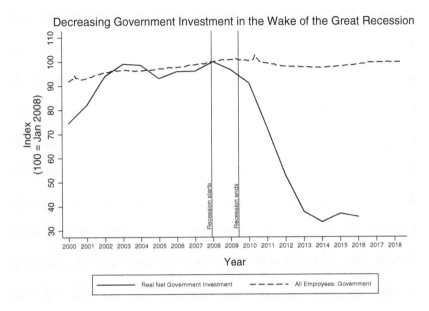

Figure 5.2 Real net government investment decreased dramatically with the onset of the Great Recession and remained below its pre-Great Recession norm through 2016. This policy response is the polar opposite of the Keynesian recommendation of fiscal stimulus during deep recessions.

Data Source: U.S. Bureau of Economic Analysis, "Real Net Government Investment [A889RX1A020NBEA]," retrieved from FRED, Federal Reserve Bank of St. Louis, https://fred.stlouisfed.org/series/A889RX1A020NBEA; U.S. Bureau of Labor Statistics, "All Employees: Government [USGOVT]," retrieved from FRED, Federal Reserve Bank of St. Louis, https://fred.stlouisfed.org/series/USGOVT.

today. Of course, the increase in taxes also lowers disposable income, potentially reducing consumption. But this effect can be offset by a deficit-neutral decrease in income taxes, which will increase disposable income by the same amount as the consumption tax increase lowered disposable income. The end result is a policy combination that raises inflation expectations and spending without increasing government deficits.

Unconventional fiscal policy suffers from many of the flaws that plague ordinary fiscal policy. Political paralysis will make it difficult to pass a series of consumption tax increases accompanied by deficit-neutral income tax decreases. In addition, this legislative two-step demands considerable expertise and communication skills that may be out of the reach of legislatures—unconventional fiscal policy works by increasing inflation expectations and then delivering on these expectations. As a result, unconventional fiscal policy should be attempted only by expert and nimble legislatures that cannot pursue ordinary fiscal policy due to restrictions on their borrowing capacity.

Are We Ready for the Next Recession?

Although fiscal policy is the expert's choice for stimulus at the zero lower bound, it failed to stimulate aggregate demand during the recession, largely for political and institutional reasons. As late as early 2017, much of Europe was still mired in high unemployment despite zero interest rates, yet fiscal policy remained largely off the table. Japan also remains mired at the zero lower bound with low growth rates, yet its historically unprecedented government debt burden makes additional fiscal stimulus risky.

With conventional monetary stimulus ineffective at the zero lower bound and fiscal stimulus politically and institutionally unfeasible, central banks implemented new "unconventional" monetary policy tools. Most macroeconomists did not believe that unconventional monetary policy was the best response to the Great Recession. Instead, it was the only tool available in the face of fiscal policy's failure. But unconventional monetary policy proved partially effective (and very risky) at best. Even so, central bankers may consider even more radical forms of unconventional monetary policy, such as helicopter money, in the future.

When policymakers are implementing unconventional monetary policy and considering unconventional fiscal policy, it is past time to revisit our macroeconomic policy toolkit still further and consider other unconventional policy tools. Otherwise, the next recession may well be as harmful as the Great Recession. Broadly, there are two macroeconomic policy options to mitigate future episodes of the zero lower bound. First, reform fiscal policymaking so that governments can use their powers of spending and taxation to provide effective stimulus during the next recession. Second, develop new macroeconomic policy tools that can significantly stimulate demand.

Law is essential to the reforms that will enable fiscal stimulus in times of deficient demand. I discuss relevant proposals in Chapters 6 and 7. I also argue that administrative agencies, such as the Internal Revenue Service (IRS) in the United States, should use their lawful discretion over policy to stimulate the economy at the zero lower bound. Although this sometimes entails an aggressive interpretation of agencies' roles, recall that central banks such as the ECB have been adopting even more aggressive interpretations of their legal roles in order to support policies of questionable efficacy.

Law also offers means to support aggregate demand directly. Indeed, expansionary legal policy is well within our power today, but this power has not been exercised. This is the subject of Part II.

SIX

Institutional Reform of Fiscal Policy

Most economists agree that fiscal stimulus was urgently necessary during the Great Recession. Yet it was, for the most part, unavailable, and the fiscal stimulus that was attempted was inadequate for the scale of the problem. Automatic stabilizers kicked in, which meant that public spending and deficits rose during the Great Recession. But the demand boost wasn't nearly enough. Indeed, government employment actually fell during the Great Recession in several countries.

As we have seen, discretionary fiscal policy faces great hurdles to enactment and implementation. Many governments are constitutionally required to maintain balanced budgets or keep deficits small. Fiscal policymakers often lack expertise in macroeconomics, making it easier for them to be led astray by ideas like "expansionary austerity." And fiscal policy must be implemented through the legislative process, which is often clunky. Monetary policy is much nimbler, a product of expert central bank decisions made through routine votes decided by simple majorities. But because the zero lower bound undermines monetary policy, the benefits of that nimbleness are lost.

The failure of fiscal policy during the Great Recession wasn't caused by irremediable flaws in the economic effects of fiscal policy itself. It was a result of the failure to try those policies. The trouble lies in the institutional design of fiscal policymaking, which does much to limit policymakers' ability to respond to economic duress. In this chapter, I explore institutional reforms that would unshackle fiscal policy to the point where it could provide the stimulus required in a liquidity trap. These include amendments to constitutional balanced budget requirements, new administrative agencies and legal tools to better implement fiscal policy stabilization, and educational reforms to convey to fiscal policymakers the urgency of macroeconomic policy.

The question, then, is how to inject lumbering fiscal policy institutions with some agility, so that they can respond adequately when demand is low and interest rates are at the zero lower bound. What procedures offer a good-enough balance between enabling states to formulate optimal fiscal policy on the fly and maintaining the democratic accountability that legislatures require?

Repeal Balanced Budget Requirements

Balanced budget requirements force governments to cut spending in recessions, reducing aggregate demand at the worst time. Yet, even though these requirements automatically destabilize the economy, most U.S. states have them in some form. So do most units of local government. These requirements don't prevent any kind of government debt; covered entities can issue debt for capital expenditures, such as road construction, and some off-budget items, such as obligations for future pension or health care payments, may not be included under balanced budget requirements.[1] But ongoing expenses must be met with current revenues. On the whole, research suggests that balanced budget requirements curtail public spending by U.S. state and local governments.[2]

Deficit restrictions impose less macroeconomic harm in Europe, but they still constrain spending. At the supranational level, European Commission spending, equal to about 1 percent of EU GDP,[3] is subject to a balanced budget requirement.[4] EU member states themselves are limited by article 126 of the Treaty of the European Union (Maastricht Treaty), which reads, "Member States shall avoid excessive government deficits."[5] EU institutions interpret this provision to limit annual deficits to 3 percent of GDP or less during ordinary times (though enforcement of this limitation is often half-hearted).[6] Higher deficits may be permitted during "severe economic downturns."[7] Moreover, the European Union evaluates budget deficits under Maastricht by emphasizing the "cyclically adjusted" or "structural" deficit rather than the actual deficit.[8] A cyclically adjusted budget calculates surpluses and deficits by assuming output equal to potential and un-

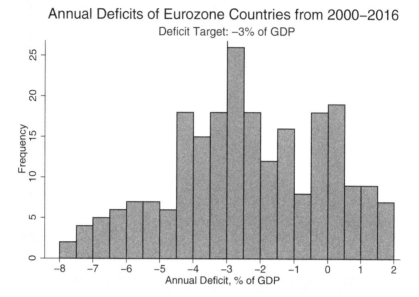

Figure 6.1 Note the relative frequency of annual government budget deficits just under –3 percent (the EU deficit target). This bunching implies that countries change their behavior (either reducing deficits directly or fiddling with the numbers) in response to the target.

Data Source: Organisation for Economic Co-operation and Development, "General Government Deficit, Total, % of GDP, 2000–2016." Customized search for European Union Countries (28), years 2000–2016, at https://data.oecd.org/gga/general-government-deficit .htm.

employment at its normal rate. A government running a small deficit during a recession will not violate the European Union's deficit guidelines if its cyclically adjusted deficit remains in balance, with the deficit being attributed to the business cycle rather than a structural imbalance.

In theory, these allowances for economic downturns provide some macroeconomic flexibility to EU budgets. But the deficit restrictions still seem to constrain budgets. EU member countries typically have budget deficits of 2.5–3.0 percent of GDP (see Figures 6.1 and 6.2, histograms showing that EU nations' annual deficits cluster in the range of –2.5 to –3.0 percent).[9] This was true even during the Great Recession, when the "severe economic downturn" clause took effect and the difference between the structural deficit and the reported deficit should have been considerable. European recovery was feeble, yet actual (that is, not structural) member-state budget

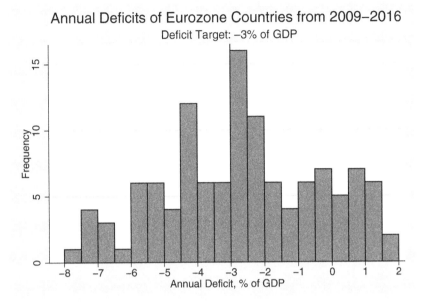

Figure 6.2 Bunching of EU annual government deficits just above −3% of GDP continued through the Great Recession, even though the EU's deficit target was ostensibly less strict during this period.

Data Source: Organisation for Economic Co-operation and Development, "General Government Deficit, Total, % of GDP, 2009–2016." Customized search for European Union Countries (28), years 2000–2016, at https://data.oecd.org/gga/general-government-deficit .htm.

deficits after 2008 have continued to cluster at the same 2.5–3 percent of GDP (see Figure 6.2). At the very least, this clustering of deficits just below −3.0 percent of GDP is circumstantial evidence that treaty obligations have some effect on European national budgets, if only as norms guiding policy choices.

Since the Great Recession, many have called for the abolition of balanced budget requirements, to prevent them from automatically destabilizing economies.[10] I agree with these reformers. Upholding balanced budget requirements in downturns means renouncing fiscal policy stabilization, incapacitating an essential macroeconomic tool vital for coping with the zero lower bound.

One argument against repealing balanced budget requirements is that shortsighted politicians will take the opportunity to run excessive deficits. However, this problem can be mitigated by tweaking current requirements.

Instead of scrapping budget requirements entirely, we can replace them with cyclically adjusted versions, as the European Union's Stability and Growth Pact already does. Jurisdictions subject to a cyclically adjusted balanced budget requirement therefore achieve budget balance when output equals potential, run deficits when downturns produce tax shortfalls, and run surpluses in booms.

Because cyclical adjustment does not force spending cuts in response to unexpectedly low revenues, it does not automatically destabilize the economy. This allows better fiscal policy from a macroeconomic perspective. At the same time, as long as estimates of potential output are reasonably accurate, cyclical-adjustment requirements should constrain deficits. When output is at or above potential, a government that runs deficits violates budget rules. In order to return to compliance with the cyclically adjusted balanced budget requirement, the government needs to raise revenues or cut spending. Cyclical adjustment is therefore almost as effective as an ordinary balanced budget requirement in terms of restraining deficits when they aren't needed to stimulate demand.

It is true that an opportunistic government could violate the spirit of a cyclically adjustment requirement by using overly optimistic estimates of the jurisdiction's economic capacity. For this reason, the jurisdiction's potential output should be estimated by an independent body, such as the central bank, not by the legislative or executive branches. Helpfully, institutions like the IMF already calculate cyclically adjusted deficits for most countries and publish the methodologies they use for doing so.[11] By relying on established methodologies implemented by third parties such as the IMF, jurisdictions could continue to enjoy the institutional check of the balanced budget requirement in ordinary times, while ensuring that officials can run bigger deficits only when macroeconomic stimulus is a pressing need.

Raise Investment Spending

Another way to rescue an economy from a liquidity trap is through capital spending. Yet, even though such spending is not subject to balanced budget requirements—governments can spend more than they raise in tax revenue in order to build long-lived assets, such as highways and school buildings—capital investment is hardly a given during recessions. During the Great Recession, governments could have done a great deal more capital spending. With interest rates near zero and plenty of construction capacity waiting to be used, costs of infrastructure investment were at record lows.[12] Even infrastructure projects with meager rates were cost-justified under these conditions, especially given the risks of hysteresis. As we saw in the previous chapter (see Figure 5.2), however, real net government investment plunged during the Great Recession. When interest rates were zero, government infrastructure spending went down by almost 50 percent when it should have gone up.

There is good reason to be cautious about capital spending: in a rush to stimulate aggregate demand, politicians may binge on bad infrastructure projects. But this concern can be mitigated by better preparation for liquidity traps. When planning infrastructure projects, authorities should not limit themselves to those that would be funded in ordinary economic times. Instead, they should devote some resources to planning projects that would be funded only in a liquidity trap. Should a liquidity trap arise, governments won't be in the position of selecting dubious projects for the sole purpose of speed. Instead, they can turn to those already approved under more sanguine circumstances. Given the costs of liquidity traps and their relative frequency, some investment in this kind of preparation appears justified.[13]

Such preparedness also improves the prospects for effective fiscal stimulus during liquidity traps. Even legislators receptive to fiscal stimulus in a liquidity trap may reject it in practice out of concern for the waste associated with stimulus. But since liquidity-trap preparedness mitigates waste in another spending arena—capital investment—legislators may be more willing to support fiscal stimulus than they otherwise would be.

Design Fiscal Rules Sensitive to the Business Cycle

If automatic fiscal stabilizers work better than discretionary ones, then we should amp up the effects of automatic stabilizers. The simplest way to enhance automatic stabilizers is to increase government spending and income tax rates. If government spending is insensitive to the business cycle or even countercyclical, then a high share of government spending means that a higher proportion of aggregate demand doesn't fluctuate with the business cycle. Similarly, if progressive income taxes dampen economic shocks by reducing the sensitivity of after-tax income, then higher and more progressive income tax schedules stabilize the economy by more than a smaller and flatter income tax burden. During the Great Recession, scholars concluded that European automatic stabilizers were much stronger than U.S. automatic stabilizers.[14] The superiority of European automatic stabilizers reflected government's greater role in the economy in Europe and decreased Europe's need for discretionary fiscal stimulus.

Big government, however, is not the only means of enhancing automatic stabilizers. Governments can also institute fiscal rules that make taxation and spending more sensitive to the business cycle at any given government size. One approach would be to tether taxation and spending levels to the interest rate, unemployment rate, or both.[15] If the interest rate is sufficiently low and the unemployment rate sufficiently high, then fiscal rules can mandate lower tax rates and more spending. For example, the U.S. Congress could pass a law cutting payroll tax rates by some agreed-upon percentage whenever three-month treasury bills yield less than 0.25 percent interest and the unemployment rate at midyear exceeds 150 percent of the previous three-year average. The same conditions could be used to trigger additional allocations for spending on infrastructure and scientific research.

Indeed, such procedures are already the norm with respect to certain social welfare programs. In the United States, spending on unemployment insurance rises with the unemployment rate. When a state's unemployment rate exceeds 120 percent of the previous two-year average, the federal government funds up to twenty additional weeks of unemployment insurance for benefit recipients, leading to greater overall spending.[16] There is no reason other fiscal policies can't also be contingent on the unemployment rate, allowing governments to take fuller advantage of automatic stabilizers and avoid the obstacles involved in discretionary fiscal policy.

Although more automatic countercyclical fiscal policy would be helpful during a recession, business cycle–sensitive spending rules are no panacea. Statutory trigger mechanisms are only as useful as the measurements they are based on, but these may be rendered obsolete by economic changes or simply prove over time to be inaccurate or otherwise unhelpful. For example, using the unemployment rate as a trigger can be tricky because the rate goes down when people leave the labor force. This occurred in large numbers during the Great Recession, artificially dropping the official unemployment rate and therefore any automatic stabilization mechanisms triggered by it.

Thus, a major challenge inherent to automatic stabilization is that the trigger won't be a perfect proxy for economic conditions. Just because the law places the interest rate trigger at, say, 0.1 percent, that doesn't mean an economy with a 0.2 percent short-term interest rate doesn't suffer from a liquidity trap. And a sudden increase in the ratio of population to employment may be the result not of a demand deficiency but rather of a social shift (for example, baby boomers begin retiring). If stimulus were needlessly applied under such conditions, the result would be higher inflation and deficits, with no appreciable reduction in the unemployment rate.

Empower Fiscal Policy Agencies

Automatic fiscal policy overcomes some of the challenges facing discretionary policy but brings problems of its own. One alternative that might account for deficiencies in both approaches would be to delegate fiscal policy to an agency that can respond decisively to liquidity traps while retaining the discretion needed to prevent automatic stabilizers from overheating the economy. This agency would in some respects mirror a central bank, which quickly and flexibly makes macroeconomic policy. Not surprisingly, in the wake of the Great Recession, some have revived long-standing calls for such an agency.[17]

How would it work? Fiscal policy agencies would have to be established by legislatures, which would set their goals and decide on their appropriate sphere of policy action. (Fiscal councils with advisory but not regulatory power already exist in many countries.[18]) The legislature might reasonably dictate the following: whether the cyclically adjusted deficit must be positive or negative (and to what extent), or whether it should be zero; what the average cyclically adjusted tax and spending rates should be; how to allocate this spending across different priorities (for example, defense, social welfare, infrastructure); and how the response to business-cycle conditions (the change from the average level) should vary across tax and spending priorities—that is, whether deficit increases should come from lower tax rates, higher spending, or both.

With this legal framework, the agency, staffed by fiscal policy experts, would be positioned to decide how to respond to economic conditions as needed. Just as central banks adjust monetary policy in response to macro conditions, so too would the fiscal policy agency adjust taxes and spending.

During liquidity traps, it would lower tax rates or raise spending, or both, as the guidance demands. In boom times, it would raise tax rates and lower spending. And when the economy is producing at capacity, the agency would aim to maintain the cyclically adjusted deficit stipulated by the legislature.

A fiscal policy agency offers many benefits. Because it is independent of the legislative process, it makes discretionary fiscal policy more reliable. Such an agency also can take a finer-grained approach to fiscal policy. After all, some types of spending and tax cuts stimulate more than others. An expert agency will be able to advance and emphasize the more effective stimulus options, while a legislature will be beholden to interests that may prevent it from making the most effective choices.

But delegating fiscal policy to an agency is itself troublesome because doing so removes a core democratic function from the legislature. Fiscal policy is not a technocratic exercise. It structures the government's role in the economy, public spending priorities, and efforts at redistribution. Even if the legislature retained some control by specifying guidelines for taxation and spending, the agency would assume an unusually central role in national life. It would make decisions for which democratic legitimacy is essential, even though it lacks any strong claim on that legitimacy.

We urgently need better fiscal policy, but not at the cost of betraying core democratic values. The authors of the U.S. Constitution did not have the advanced understanding of economics that today's social scientists can claim, but they understood that giving over fiscal power to a few unelected officials was inherently unwise. That is why the Constitution reserves the "power of the purse" for the legislative branch, the most democratic branch of government.[19]

Establish an Office of Fiscal and Regulatory Affairs

Although an agency charged with making fiscal policy arrogates too much power from the legislature, space remains for agencies that rationalize countercyclical fiscal policy. If every U.S. agency considered the short-term fiscal impact of its discretionary actions, then U.S. fiscal policy would become more effective. Governments should therefore establish an Office of Fiscal and Regulatory Affairs (OFRA) to coordinate fiscal policy (and legal policy) stabilization. OFRA would enjoy supervisory authority over administrative decisions with fiscal effects, but it would not be endowed with the power of the purse. The power of the purse would remain with Congress or with the diffuse administrative agencies to which Congress has delegated limited components of this power. OFRA's authority would be supervisory.

A model for this sort of office already exists in the United States, where government often confronts new policy problems by establishing supervisory offices. For example, in the late 1970s and early 1980s, U.S. legislators concluded that regulators needed to pay more attention to the costs of their regulations in addition to the benefits. Congress created the Office of Information and Regulatory Affairs (OIRA) to address this concern.[20] Subsequently, President Reagan issued Executive Order 12291 instructing that "regulatory action shall not be undertaken unless the potential benefits to society from the regulation outweigh the potential costs to society." In addition to requiring regulators to consider costs of regulation, Executive Order 12291 instructed OIRA to oversee cost–benefit analysis of all significant regulations. (Many other countries have since instituted agencies with similar tasks.) In practice, this means that, say, if the Environmental Protection Agency (EPA) overemphasizes environmental protection over costs, then OIRA will insist that the regulation be altered. Through cost–benefit analysis, OIRA institutionalizes a microeconomic perspective on law, even though most regulators do not have microeconomic expertise.

Fiscal stabilization policy in the United States and elsewhere needs something similar to OIRA. An OFRA that examines the macroeconomic effects of fiscal and regulatory actions and of proposed laws would reduce the risk of ill-advised pro-cyclical fiscal designs. OFRA should be staffed by experts in macroeconomics as well as by experts in law and regulation. In a recession with zero short-term interest rates and fiscal multipliers well above one, OFRA should instruct every agency with implicit authority over fiscal policy to analyze the macroeconomic effects of its fiscal and regulatory actions with an eye toward stimulating spending. OFRA should also supervise these analyses to make sure that they are developed competently and consistently.

To bolster its legitimacy, OFRA should be established by Congress. Once OFRA is established, executive orders from the president can guide its function, much as executive orders have shaped OIRA.

A new office to coordinate macroeconomic policy enjoys historical precedent. Indeed, OIRA itself has macroeconomic origins. Congress created the first regulatory coordinating agency, the Council on Wage and Price Stability, in 1974.[21] The Council was authorized to review the decisions of all

U.S. agencies in a (failed) effort to control inflation. (See Chapter 10 for a discussion and critique of the U.S. experience with price controls.) To compel regulators not concerned with macroeconomics to consider the effects of their rulings on inflation, President Gerald Ford required that "major proposals for legislation, and for the promulgation of regulations or rules by any executive branch agency must be accompanied by a statement which certifies that the inflationary impact of the proposal has been evaluated."[22] President Ford also instructed the chairman of the Council, among others, to develop criteria for developing and evaluating these "inflation impact statements."[23] When OIRA was founded in 1981, it absorbed the economists formerly employed by the Council to evaluate these inflation impact statements.[24] There is thus a long history in the United States of requiring regulators to consider the macroeconomic implications of their decisions and enabling a centralized office to review these evaluations.

Teach Lawyers Macroeconomics

Effective fiscal policy stabilization in a democracy requires policymakers to have some macroeconomic literacy. In particular, legislators and members of the executive branch of government need to be attuned to the business cycle and to recognize when the zero lower bound constrains monetary policy and requires fiscal stimulus. To improve fiscal policy stabilization, we therefore need to consider not just how fiscal policy is crafted and implemented but also who is responsible for the crafting and implementation and whether they have the requisite expertise to make good policy. If they don't, then we have to think about what sort of changes would improve the economic knowledge base in legislatures.

There is good reason to believe politicians don't have the expertise necessary to make the sound countercyclical policy we need from them. Many legislators simply lack the training to do so. They are, for the most part, not economists, but lawyers. Twenty-five of the forty-five U.S. presidents (56 percent) have been lawyers. What is true for executives is also true for legislatures. In the 114th U.S. Congress (2015–2016), for example, 159 members of the House (36 percent) and 54 members of the Senate (54 percent) held law degrees. And in 2010, approximately one-third of the German Bundestag's members were lawyers.[25]

These future politicians don't study macroeconomics in law school. In the United States, microeconomics is pervasive in legal education, but macroeconomics is almost nowhere to be found. In introductory courses on federal income taxation, for example, law students learn a great deal about how taxation distorts incentives with respect to savings and the labor supply—the province of microeconomics. But prominent tax casebooks rarely discuss macroeconomic stability as a goal of tax policy, much less explain how tax policy might usefully change at the zero lower bound. One reason politicians failed to pass and implement adequate fiscal stimulus during the Great Recession may be that many of them never learned why a stimulus package would be desirable when interest rates are zero. And even if they did learn macroeconomics at some point, its importance wasn't emphasized or even mentioned during their most important training period before assuming an important role in public policy.

Happily, we can change this: we can teach macroeconomics to lawyers and others whose backgrounds make them ripe for political careers, such as master of business administration students. They, too, are primarily focused on microeconomics. Lawyers and others considering political careers need not be macro experts; they just need to realize the urgency of stimulus during prolonged recessions.

Macroeconomic education, like improved fiscal policy institutions, should improve fiscal policy in future episodes of the zero lower bound on interest rates or other constraints on monetary policy. But the hard slog of institutional reform is not the only way law and macroeconomics can improve fiscal policy. A macroeconomic lens reveals many existing opportunities for fiscal stimulus that were overlooked during the Great Recession.

SEVEN

Expansionary Fiscal Policy by Administrative Agencies

We do not necessarily need significant institutional reforms such as those discussed in Chapter 6 for agencies to play a larger role in fiscal policy. In many cases, a change of attitude from the administrators will suffice. If political inefficiency, rather than a lack of fiscal space, limits discretionary fiscal policy, then regulators and administrators should apply some of the discretion they already exercise over fiscal policy to stimulate the economy at the zero lower bound on interest rates.

Although most agencies do not enjoy the discretion over policy exercised by central banks, they invariably enjoy considerable discretion over important policy dimensions. So long as the agency does not "abuse" its discretion, it enjoys very wide latitude in making decisions. When the IRS instructs employers to withhold a certain amount of income taxes from employees making a given amount of money, for example, its choice of withholding amounts is effectively discretionary. Unless the taxpayer can show evidence of improper behavior within the agency, courts leave the choice of withholding amounts to the IRS, much as they leave the choice of short-term interest rates to the Federal Reserve.

To this point, contemporary administrative agencies outside the central bank have rarely taken macroeconomic conditions into account when making decisions affecting fiscal policy. If agencies instead used their discretion to stimulate demand during liquidity traps, they could do much to recharge an economy in recession, without any legal change.

Recall that the Obama administration recognized the need for short-term fiscal stimulus, as demonstrated by its successful 2009 push for the American Recovery and Reinvestment Act (ARRA) and repeated requests for further stimulus measures thereafter. But the administration was unable to induce Congress to pass additional stimulus measures after ARRA, even as the Great Recession and its painful aftermath lingered. In other moments of congressional resistance, the Obama administration turned to aggressive administrative action. When Congress failed to pass a law on climate change, the administration developed the Clean Power Plan. When immigration reform was stymied, the administration put forward Deferred Action for Childhood Arrivals, a more aggressive interpretation of executive authority than any that I will present here. It is striking that the Obama administration did not turn to its discretionary authority when Congress refused to enact economic stimulus. To the extent that executive authority can be used to stimulate the economy, it should be.

To ensure that expansionary fiscal policy by administrative action does not run amok, I then propose limiting principles for expansionary fiscal policy by administrative action. First, regulators and administrators cannot break the law in pursuit of fiscal expansion at the zero lower bound. Instead, they should stimulate spending in a liquidity trap only when the law already grants the agency discretion over two options, one of which raises spending more than the other. Second, expansionary fiscal policy by agencies needs the coordinating hand of macroeconomic experts. The Office of Fiscal and Regulatory Affairs discussed in Chapter 6 should direct agencies in their pursuit of expansionary fiscal policy.

Fiscal Stabilization via the IRS

In the United States, Congress delegates significant authority over income tax laws to the IRS, which has issued thousands of pages of regulations and other administrative guidance explaining which tax laws apply to whom and under what circumstances. When a new IRS regulation or guidance results in greater tax collection, fiscal policy effectively tightens. When IRS decisions decrease government revenue, aggregate demand is effectively stimulated. But the IRS does not currently make macroeconomic effects a serious aspect of its deliberation on these decisions. Here, I offer two suggestions for how it might, so that the IRS can use its legitimate statutory authority actively to stimulate demand in liquidity traps. Tax authorities in other jurisdictions should enjoy similar stimulus opportunities.

Offers in Compromise

The IRS has considerable discretion to work with people unable to pay their tax liability. This is known as "offers in compromise." As the IRS explains, "An offer in compromise allows you"—the taxpayer—"to settle your tax debt for less than the full amount you owe. It may be a legitimate option if you can't pay your full tax liability, or doing so creates a financial hardship. We consider your unique set of facts and circumstances: Ability to pay; Income; Expenses; and Asset equity."[1] In 2015, the IRS accepted payments of $205 million in exchange for forgiving liabilities worth an undisclosed amount but likely much more than $205 million.[2]

Tax collectors could and should use this discretion over offers in compromise to stimulate an economy stuck in a liquidity trap. At the zero lower bound, the IRS should adopt a laxer standard for accepting offers in compromise from individuals unable to pay their full tax liability. This will cause tax revenues to fall over the long run, but taxpayers unable to pay their bills will have more disposable income and have resolved an important source of economic uncertainty. If they consume more as a result, aggregate demand will rise. Because the IRS also possesses the authority to set its own standards vis-à-vis offers in compromise, it can use this power to stimulate demand without any changes in law.

During the Great Recession, however, the IRS accepted fewer offers in compromise. The value of IRS accepted offers-in-compromise reached a twenty-year nadir in 2010. Instead of accepting more offers to quickly resolve financial uncertainty during the Great Recession, the IRS continued with business as usual. It thereby passed up an opportunity for fiscal stabilization.

It is possible that taxpayers would abuse this system by delaying paying taxes when times are good, in hopes that they can secure a better deal on their obligations during a liquidity trap. This is a real risk, and the IRS should reject offers from taxpayers who appear to be using the program opportunistically. But the risk should not be exaggerated. Liquidity traps are unpredictable events; a taxpayer would be ill advised to delay a settlement in the expectation that the economy will deteriorate.

Withholding Schedules

While the offers-in-compromise program offers an illustrative but relatively small example of the IRS's unused capacity for fiscal stimulus, the IRS's pivotal role in the administration of the income tax system means that its capacity for discretionary fiscal stabilization policy is quantitatively significant. For example, the IRS could provide a multibillion-dollar stimulus to aggregate demand by adjusting the tax-withholding schedule provided to employers.[3] The schedule, listed in Publication 15, dictates how much tax an employer must withhold from an employee given the employee's income and family status. The withholding amount for each employee changes each year with the publication of a new schedule in Publication 15, even if the employee never changes his or her tax information about dependents and exemptions. At present, the schedule prescribes over-withholding for the vast majority of employees, and the value of excessive withholding is refunded to taxpayers when they file their returns. The value of over-withholding is economically significant, with the IRS issuing over $315 billion in refunds in 2016.[4] For some taxpayers, this doesn't make much difference. But among the cash-strapped, over-withholding delays consumption, reducing demand.

Excessive withholding can therefore be destructive during a liquidity trap. In these conditions, the IRS should adjust the withholding schedule so that it culls less from each paycheck. With more income in their pockets, employees will have opportunities to spend just when the economy is in a liquidity trap. This is a desirable policy because it prevents hysteresis, which becomes more damaging the longer aggregate-demand deficiencies linger. In other words, escaping a liquidity trap now is better than escaping it later. Moreover, some evidence suggests that taxpayers are more likely to save from a large refund check than to save from weekly earnings, which means that lower withholding may not just change the date of consumption but may also expand it.[5]

Because Congress has delegated to the IRS discretion over compiling the withholding schedule (for example, the IRS offers employers more than one method for calculating withholding amounts),[6] the agency can move spending forward without breaking any laws or testing democratic legitimacy. Indeed, in 1992, the IRS did just this without congressional approval: it reduced withholding rates with the aim of providing economic stimulus.[7] Unfortunately, the IRS refrained from this sort of activism during the Great Recession, even though the need for stimulus was much greater than in 1992.

In addition to lowering withholding to boost aggregate demand at the zero lower bound, the IRS can raise withholding to delay spending and increase saving when excessive aggregate demand causes rising inflation. To the degree that contractionary fiscal policy is needed, the IRS could provide it without running into the sorts of problems legislatures face, such as dithering and political opportunism. The IRS also possesses a good measure of expertise, employing many professional economists and policy experts in its Office of Research, Applied Analytics, and Statistics.

IRS Notice 2008-83

During the Great Recession, the IRS generally avoided using its discretion over tax administration to stimulate the economy—with one giant exception, IRS Notice 2008-83. With this Notice, the IRS increased the tax-shelter value of money-losing assets—an incredibly valuable change given the ubiquity of impaired assets during the 2008 Financial Crisis. According to some early reports, Notice 2008-83 increased projected deficits by as much as $140 billion.[8] Congress subsequently overrode the Notice's guidance. Congress's decision reflected a widely held perception that Notice 2008-83 involved a strained interpretation of the law and that a "Notice"—a relatively informal form of administrative action—was an inappropriate procedure for such a momentous and ill-founded change.[9]

Notice 2008-83 represents expansionary fiscal policy by administrative agency taken too far. Instead of putting all its eggs in one illegitimate form of expansionary fiscal policy by regulation, the IRS should have trained its attention to areas where its discretion was better established and the non-macroeconomic merits of its rulings more ambiguous.

Notice 2008-83 provides a cautionary tale about the dangers of expansionary fiscal policy by administrative agency. But the Notice also demonstrates the IRS's discretionary power over federal revenues. If this discretionary power were exercised to stimulate the economy in more legitimate ways, then the IRS could become a powerful agent of fiscal stimulus.

Agency Discretion over Spending and Stimulus

Tax authorities can use their discretion only over one side of the fiscal policy equation: revenue collection. But we can turn to other agencies to exercise discretion over explicit and implicit spending decisions. In a liquidity trap, they should use this discretion to stimulate the economy.

Spend What's Allocated

Even if a legislature has appropriated money for spending, agencies are in many cases in charge of the spending. Agencies unfamiliar with the urgency of fiscal stimulus can stymie fiscal stimulus explicitly authorized by the legislature. During the Great Recession, Congress made several attempts to assist homeowners by reducing the value of mortgage obligations. The Troubled Asset Relief Program (TARP) of 2008, for example, authorized over $45.6 billion in spending for "housing support programs" that would help struggling homeowners reduce debts.[10]

This makes perfect sense: deficit-financed spending increases output during a liquidity trap. But the appropriated money was not spent. As of the first quarter of 2017, only $23.7 billion had been spent.[11] By contrast, the more famous part of TARP—a $204.9 billion appropriation to support financial institutions through capital purchases—was spent in its entirety.

If there was $45.6 billion in funding, why wasn't there $45.6 billion in debt forgiveness? According to scholars and policymakers familiar with the issue, the problem was administrative and legal.[12] Just as money for shovel-ready infrastructure projects ran into obstacles to implementation, so did the money for debt relief.

Part of the failure can be blamed on the Federal Housing Finance Administration (FHFA), a government agency that guarantees and owns mortgage loans via its control over the nationalized credit and investment firms Fannie Mae and Freddie Mac. Through 2012, the FHFA refused to forgive any principal on mortgages it owned, even though this forgiveness was subsidized by TARP funds appropriated for the "reduction of loan principal."[13] This decision was momentous. By putting more than half of the mortgage market off limits for principal forgiveness, the FHFA dramatically curtailed the scope of systematic debt forgiveness.

The FHFA was the worst offender, but it was not the only agency whose obstructionism prevented the expenditure of congressionally appropriated funds for debt relief. The Treasury Department also deserves, and has received, blame for the flaws in its mortgage-adjustment effort, the Home Affordable Modification Program (HAMP). As Neil Barofsky, the Special Inspector General for TARP, explained:

> Treasury's bungling of HAMP and its refusal to heed our warnings and those of the other TARP oversight bodies resulted in the program harming many

of the people it was supposed to help. . . . Treasury had failed to ensure that the [loan] servicers had the necessary infrastructure to support a massive mortgage modification program. . . . Worse, though Treasury provided various "directives" to the servicers, they shifted constantly, making compliance all but impossible. Documentation guidelines, for example, were changed routinely, exacerbating a quickly emerging problem with the servicers' incompetent handling of borrower documents.

Another big problem was that Treasury kept changing the terms by which servicers had to evaluate borrowers for modifications. These terms were called the Net Present Value (NPV) test. . . . Under HAMP, if the NPV test for a particular loan was positive, the servicer was required to offer a modification. But Treasury couldn't figure out the right formula for the test, which was at the heart of its entire program, changing it nine times in the first year alone.[14]

Others believe HAMP failed because of a lack of commitment on the part of government officials. Sheila Bair, head of the Federal Deposit Insurance Corporation, lays blame at the feet of Obama's top economic advisor, Larry Summers, and Tim Geithner:

HAMP was a program designed to look good in a press release, not to fix the housing market. Larry and Tim didn't seem to care about the political beating the president took on the hundreds of billions of dollars thrown at the big-bank bailouts and AIG bonuses, but when it came to home owners, it was a very different story. I don't think helping home owners was ever a priority for them.[15]

If these assertions are correct, then it is not surprising that the funds appropriated for debt relief were not spent. Administrative incompetence and weak commitment will sink almost any program, no matter how well funded.

Administrative incompetence is inevitable, and some policies, when put in practice, are revealed to have bugs. But these problems can be overcome. If a policy enjoys high priority, then it is more likely to be administered by energetic and competent staff who can surmount obstacles. During a liquidity trap, fiscal stimulus policies deserve priority. Obstacles to government spending programs need to be overcome quickly to revive demand before hysteresis and political instability ensues.

The Administration of Social Welfare Benefit Programs and Take-up Rates

Just as tax guidance implicitly determines fiscal policy, so does the administration of social welfare programs. This is clear in the low "take-up" rates that bedevil such programs in the United States. Of those eligible for benefits at any given time, only a fraction sign up. Many housing benefit programs, for example, have take-up rates below 50 percent, and even a widely taken up program like the Earned Income Credit (EIC) enjoys take-up rates below 90 percent.[16]

Low take-up rates reduce government spending. In 2010, the U.S. state and federal governments spent over $900 billion on public benefits programs aside from Social Security and Medicare. A 5 percent increase in take-up rates would therefore translate into a spending increase of tens of billions of dollars.

One cause of low take-up is the approval procedure used to decide who gets which benefits. For instance, agencies may require in-person interviews in order to vet potential beneficiaries. This will reduce the number of fraudulent beneficiaries, but it will also reduce take-up among eligible individuals, who may not be able to interview for any number of reasons, including work obligations. Vetting is therefore a balancing act and sometimes a cruel one. Deserving recipients of social welfare programs may lose access to programs because they cannot get through the hoops designed to prevent false take-up. But no agency disburses social welfare funds without undertaking some form of vetting, implying that this trade-off is thought to be a necessary one.

As long as welfare agencies vet applicants for social welfare programs, eligibility should depend on the business cycle. At the zero lower bound, providing a benefit to the indigent yields a greater social benefit than it would in ordinary times because the increase in indigent spending is subject to a greater multiplier effect than in ordinary times. At the zero lower bound, higher take-up rates raise aggregate demand and output. In ordinary times, by contrast, higher take-up leads to higher inflation and interest rates without raising output. If we assume that the costs of false take-up are constant across the business cycle, then agencies should aim for higher take-up in liquidity traps. The balance tilts toward comparatively high true and false take-up rates at the zero lower bound and toward lower true and false take-up rates during more robust economic times. Agency vetting procedures for social welfare programs should adjust accordingly.

But what about the concern about accountability reflected in the tight legislative control over fiscal policy in most democracies? If administrators use their discretion over policy to expand fiscal stimulus at the zero lower bound, then legislators lose some of their control over fiscal policy. As a result, doesn't the fiscal stimulus proposed in this section threaten core democratic values?

We should be concerned about administrative encroachment into fiscal policy. But the recommendations presented in this chapter do not arrogate a new power to bureaucracies. Agencies already exercise considerable discretion with respect to income tax withholding rules or procedures to qualify for public benefits. The fiscal stimulus recommended in this section uses this existing discretion toward a new end—macroeconomic policy—rather than unilaterally increasing administrative power. Moreover, expansionary fiscal policy diffuses the administrative response to inadequate aggregate demand across agencies, a more legitimate solution than concentrating macroeconomic power in a single agency such as a central bank or a fiscal agency with the power of the purse.

Which Spending Programs?

If social welfare programs always spent a fixed amount, then higher take-up rates induced by administrative discretion redistribute government spending rather than increasing it. As a result, agencies should not use their discretion to expand spending in "discretionary" spending programs, which are subject to fixed annual budgets. But many social welfare programs are "entitlements." An entitlement program (for example, Medicare) guarantees benefits to all members of a group without regard to budgetary limits. When more people take up an entitlement program, the government spends more. Aggregate demand therefore rises when agencies use their discretion to raise take-up rates in entitlement programs, as they should do in liquidity traps.

The suggestion that administrative agencies use their discretion to expand eligibility for social welfare programs at the zero lower bound assumes that higher spending on social welfare programs increases aggregate demand. Some disagree with this assertion with respect to specific programs. In *The Redistribution Recession*, Casey Mulligan argues that, by extending unemployment-insurance eligibility beyond the usual period of twenty-six weeks after termination to as long as one year, the U.S. government incentivized unemployed people to stay out of work. This led to a needlessly prolonged bout of high unemployment.[17]

Mulligan's view—that extending unemployment benefits increases unemployment and reduces output—is widely disputed. The best recent empirical study suggests that increases in the duration of unemployment benefits neither raise nor lower the unemployment rate.[18] As a result, Mulligan's claims about unemployment insurance are unsubstantiated (as are claims that unemployment benefits lower unemployment by increasing aggregate demand). But even if we accept Mulligan's argument entirely, it does not apply to all social welfare programs. Although some social welfare programs, like unemployment insurance and disability insurance, plausibly reduce labor supply, other programs, like the Earned Income Credit in the United States, increase labor force participation. As a result, even those who reject fiscal interventions that encourage leisure should support expanding eligibility for the EIC at the zero lower bound. Expanding the EIC raises employment incentives and stimulates aggregate demand at the zero lower bound.

Limiting the Scope of Expansionary Fiscal Policy by Administrative Action

Using the power of the regulatory state to stimulate the economy offers macroeconomic benefits, but it also creates risks. If agencies implement expansionary fiscal policy haphazardly, then we may get opportunistic or excessive fiscal stimulus. In this section, I consider how to mitigate these risks.

Expansionary Fiscal Policy Actions Cannot Exceed Preexisting Bounds on Administrative Discretion

Expansionary fiscal policy by administrative action introduces the risk of rogue administrators. If an IRS administrator, for example, thinks that the government collects too much tax revenue, then the administrator may use the excuse of expansionary fiscal policy to implement these idiosyncratic preferences.

To mitigate this risk, expansionary fiscal policy should be restricted to an agency's legitimate preexisting discretion. In delegating authority to an agency, the legislature specifies a set of policies that are mandatory for the agency, a set of policies that are prohibited, and a set of policies that are left to the agency's discretion. Alongside these formal requirements, agencies develop norms regarding what policies are mandatory, prohibited, or discretionary. Expansionary fiscal policy uses this third, discretionary, set of policies to stimulate the economy. We have seen it done: in the early 1990s, the IRS used its discretion to tweak withholding rates, stimulating the economy. This act was within the bounds of existing norms. Agencies cannot and should not implement fiscal stimulus by pursuing policies prohibited by the legislature or by existing norms, but when they stay in bounds, they can achieve useful results. With this restriction, expansionary fiscal policy by legislative agency introduces no additional risk of rogue administrative behavior.

Where officials are already pushing the limits, they can go no further—another reason we need not be concerned about rogues. Consider that IRS officials who think the government collects too much tax already exercise their discretion over tax policy to reduce collections.[19] If these officials already exercise their discretionary authority in favor of taxpayers, then they will have no scope for expansionary fiscal policy at the lower bound. Law and norms confine these administrators from overreaching, regardless of whether stimulus is a concern.

Indeed, IRS Notice 2008–83 demonstrates how law and norms constrain agencies in their attempts to pursue expansionary fiscal policy. When the IRS violated norms in its pursuit of expansionary fiscal policy, law intervened. Congress overturned the notice at the same time it enacted a massive fiscal expansion.

Only administrators who do not already use their discretion to the limit enjoy leeway to implement expansionary fiscal policy at the zero lower bound. As a result, expansionary fiscal policy by administrative agency does not expand the scope of administrative discretion. Instead, it directs this preexisting discretion in a new way.

Coordinating Expansionary Fiscal Policy by Administrative Agency

Restricting expansionary fiscal policy to actions within agencies' preexisting discretion limits the scope for rogue behavior. But it does not ensure that agencies implement expansionary fiscal policy wisely. Agencies do not employ macroeconomic experts. Left to their own devices, each agency may put a different weight on the imperative to stimulate, leading to inconsistent and less effective stimulus.

A law and macroeconomics "czar," such as my proposed OFRA, reduces these risks. When OFRA's experts determine that aggregate demand is inadequate and that fiscal multipliers are well above one, they should instruct agencies to use their discretion over spending and revenue collection to stimulate.

OFRA should also facilitate consistent application of expansionary fiscal policy by administrative agencies. By publishing official estimates of policy-relevant fiscal multipliers and reviewing agencies' use of these estimates, OFRA would ensure that all agencies use consistent and sensible macroeconomic estimates in pursuing expansionary fiscal policy.

In doing so, OFRA would do for macroeconomic externalities—spending multipliers greater than one—what OIRA now does for the externalities associated with climate change. Almost every regulation issued by a government agency affects carbon emissions, but most agencies have no expertise in estimating the harm associated with such emissions. To calculate a consistent "social cost of carbon," OIRA convened an interagency expert working group. Once the working group figured out its cost estimates, all government agencies were instructed to use them when evaluating proposed regulations for their effect on climate change. OIRA thereby facilitated consistent climate change policy across regulatory agencies.[20] OFRA should do something similar with respect to macroeconomic externalities by calculating a "social benefit of spending," which estimates fiscal multipliers during prolonged downturns.

Wrapping up Part I

Throughout this chapter and indeed Part I, we have seen the vanishingly small boundary between monetary policy, fiscal policy, and law. If unconventional monetary policy potentially violates the EU constitutional order and the interpretation and administration of tax laws alters fiscal policy, then the line between monetary policy, fiscal policy, and legal policy cannot be neatly identified.

We also saw that government agencies generally failed to take advantage of myriad opportunities for fiscal stimulus. This failure to act reflects the absence of law and macroeconomics from the policy discussion. If macroeconomic policy is the province of legislators and central bankers but not lawyers and other administrators and regulators, then we should not be surprised when these other actors miss chances to improve macroeconomic policy at the zero lower bound. By emphasizing the interaction between law and macroeconomics, I hope to enable more effective fiscal and monetary stabilization policy in the future. Opportunities for fiscal stimulus abound, but we need a law and macroeconomic lens in order to see them.

Having explored the role of law, regulation, and administration in fiscal policy and monetary policy, I turn in Part II to law's potential for stimulating demand through private channels—without directly altering government spending or revenue generation. I begin with the case of the Keystone oil pipeline in 2010–2011, a moment when expansionary policy was badly needed and when law could have provided it.

The Pros and Cons of Expansionary Legal Policy

EIGHT

Expansionary Legal Policy:
The Case of the Keystone Pipeline

The partial interchangeability of law and fiscal policy is plain to see. For example, when governments want to protect the earth from climate change, they could turn to regulation (law), but they may prefer taxation and government spending (fiscal policy). Most countries use a combination of both law and fiscal policy to address the threat of climate change or other "externalities" that result from economic behavior. In the United States, government spending supports research into carbon mitigation technologies, such as improved batteries. Gasoline taxes reduce consumption of oil. Tax expenditures subsidize usage of solar panels, electric cars, and energy-efficient appliances. These provisions use fiscal policy to mitigate carbon emissions. On the legal and regulatory side, the United States (or parts thereof) imposes fuel-efficiency standards on cars and introduced the Clean Power Plan to cap carbon dioxide emissions from power plants. (The Trump administration issued proposed rules that rescinded the Clean Power Plan regulations in 2018.[1])

Economists and lawyers debate the microeconomic merits of taxation and regulation. Each type of policymaking offers a number of conspicuous strengths and weaknesses. For our purposes, this debate is beside the point. What matters is that governments use law and fiscal policy as substitutes for implementing environmental policy and in many other policy domains.

As with environmental policy, so too with macroeconomic policy. Just as economic behavior causes climate change externalities that justify regulation, so too does spending generate "aggregate demand externalities" at the zero lower bound that call for legal or regulatory intervention. The outsized spending multipliers that characterize the zero lower bound on interest rates capture the size of these aggregate demand externalities.

As we saw, during the Great Recession, legislative ineffectiveness and fears of public debt limited expansionary fiscal policy. The zero lower bound on interest rates rendered conventional monetary policy ineffective. In these circumstances, policymakers should have turned to legal and regulatory tools, just as they often do in other areas of policy.

When governments use law and regulation specifically to stimulate flagging aggregate demand, I call this expansionary legal policy. Expansionary legal policy expands the scope of the response to inadequate aggregate demand. Instead of relying on one or two stimulus instruments, like monetary and fiscal policy, expansionary legal policy offers multitudes: if almost every legal decision affects spending, then almost every legal decision offers an opportunity to make macroeconomic policy.

The restaurant economy offers a simple example of how expansionary legal policy operates. Say the restaurant economy suffers a negative shock, so people buy fewer meals. The government might respond by enacting a mandate—backed up by penalties—requiring every consumer to purchase additional meals. An appropriately designed mandate can bring demand for meals back into balance with supply.

Like expansionary fiscal policy, expansionary legal policy raises demand for goods and services—at least in theory. In reality, expansionary legal policy, like expansionary monetary and fiscal policy, faces a number of institutional obstacles. In this chapter and the next, I explore the virtues and vices of expansionary legal policy by focusing on the regulatory approval process surrounding the Keystone oil pipeline from 2005 to 2018.

The Keystone Pipeline and Law and Macroeconomics

In 2005, TransCanada, an energy company based in Alberta, proposed building a pipeline to bring oil from Western Canada's "oil sands" to the U.S. Gulf Coast.[2] Because the pipeline crossed the U.S.–Canada border, the pipeline required approval from the U.S. Department of State, which the company formally sought in 2008.[3] Executive Order 13337, issued to interpret the State Department's role in implementing several laws passed by Congress, charged the State Department with determining whether the pipeline was in the "national interest," a "determination that includes

economic, environmental, national security and foreign policy implications."[4] At first, it looked like the State Department would sign off on
the proposal, but the department dithered after 2010. Congress intervened and, in late 2014, passed a law approving construction, which President Obama then vetoed. Soon after, sixty-two senators voted to overturn
the veto, just shy of the margin needed. Meanwhile, the State Department
process continued, and in late 2015, President Obama announced that the
proposal had been rejected, "ending a seven-year review that had become
a symbol of the debate over his climate policies."[5] Shortly after his inau-
guration in 2017, President Trump issued a memorandum calling for re-
consideration of the denial.[6] This time, the State Department approved
construction.[7]

Why We Need Law and Macroeconomics: The Inadequacy of Conventional Cost–Benefit Analysis

The Keystone pipeline proposal sparked enormous and continuing contro-
versy because it demanded trade-offs among important goals of the legal
and regulatory systems.[8] On the one hand, the pipeline offered many benefits, including the provision of reliable oil supplies for the United States
(before the "shale oil" revolution), 40,000 new temporary jobs, promotion
of good relations between the United States and Canada, and the efficiency
gains of transporting oil from a location where it was relatively cheap to one
where it was relatively expensive.[9]

On the other hand, there were several noteworthy harms. Because fuels
from the Canadian oil sands emit more carbon dioxide per unit than other
types of oil, the construction of the pipeline would have hastened climate
change caused by excessive carbon dioxide in the atmosphere. Although additional emissions associated with Keystone would have been less than
1 percent of total U.S. emissions, the pipeline nonetheless reflected new investment in the fossil-fuel economy of the sort that climate activists opposed. Pipeline construction also created risk of oil leaks that could damage
the fragile and unique ecosystems of the Nebraska Sandhills and Native
American Tribal Lands near the pipeline.

Conventional cost–benefit analysis—the kind typical of law and
economics—evaluates important features of projects such as Keystone.[10] On
this view, approving Keystone produces benefits for oil consumers and pro-

ducers. The difference in dollar value between oil in the Canadian oil sands and oil on the U.S. Gulf Coast, multiplied by the amount of oil Keystone transports, constitutes the primary benefit of Keystone. In addition, Keystone approval yields diplomatic benefits with Canada. These benefits are hard to quantify, but cost–benefit analysis requires that they be quantified. Keystone's costs include construction, the environmental harm caused by additional carbon-dioxide emissions, and the cost of mitigating and cleaning up oil spills. These costs are also difficult to quantify, but they are given a dollar value nonetheless (in spite of strident criticism).[11]

Conventional cost–benefit analysis ignores job creation and friction in the labor market.[12] Workers and capital are treated as the costs of a given project, and it is assumed that any worker or capital not devoted to that project will be put to (slightly less) productive use elsewhere.[13]

Law and macroeconomics enhances our understanding of costs and benefits by accounting for friction in the labor market. But ignorance of labor-market frictions is just one symptom of a more general problem. Conventional cost–benefit analysis overlooks macroeconomics entirely. Any cost–benefit analysis that fails to consider a policy's effect on aggregate demand is at best incomplete. Macroeconomic variables such as unemployment and output deserve consideration.

Keystone's Potential Effect on Aggregate Demand

In 2011, the State Department described Keystone's short-run effects:

> During construction, there would be temporary, positive socioeconomic impacts as a result of local employment, taxes on worker income, spending by construction workers, and spending on construction goods and services. The construction work force would consist of approximately 5,000 to 6,000 workers, including Keystone employees, contractor employees, and construction and environmental inspection staff. That would generate from $349 million to $419 million in total wages. An estimated $6.58 to $6.65 billion would be spent on materials and supplies, easements, engineering, permitting, and other costs.[14]

With a zero lower bound multiplier estimate of 1.7, this construction, in turn, would produce another several billion in additional third-party spending—positive aggregate demand externalities from the initial spending.

Approval of Keystone would have increased aggregate demand by a considerable amount for just one project. For comparison, the Congressional Budget Office estimated that the ARRA added 750,000 jobs to the economy in the second quarter of 2012,[15] when construction of Keystone would have been in full swing. Approving Keystone alone would therefore have been associated with a short-run employment stimulus, including jobs indirectly created, equal to 5 percent of the effect of the primary U.S. fiscal response to the Great Recession.

The Macroeconomic Cost–Benefit Analysis of Keystone

Positive effects on aggregate demand do not, alone, mean that Keystone should have been approved. The macroeconomic consequences of Keystone ought to be one consideration among many. Moreover, the effect of Keystone on output and employment is not immutable. It depends on the state of the economy. At certain times, an aggregate demand boost is helpful and at other times not.

During ordinary economic conditions, with interest rates well above zero, effects on aggregate demand should play little role in the cost–benefit analysis of projects such as Keystone. When the economy is running at or near capacity, infrastructure investments do not translate into large increases in output. Instead, they shuffle production from one project to another, such that one is built at the expense of another. The outcome is higher interest rates and higher prices rather than higher output. Under these circumstances, it is reasonable to assume, as conventional cost–benefit analysis does, that most workers and capital will find alternative uses. Thus, when interest rates are well above zero, cost–benefit analysis should largely ignore aggregate demand—as it currently does.

Say the restaurant economy is operating at capacity, yet some worker-consumers petition the government for permission to smoke cigarettes in the restaurant, which are currently banned. Smoking in the restaurant gives smokers $100 worth of pleasure but creates externalities—secondhand smoke—that cause harms worth $150 to other diners. Approval of the petition means that people who want to smoke in the restaurant just would buy meals in place of people who would buy them in the absence of secondhand smoke. Because smoking in the restaurant harms third parties more than it benefits smokers and does not affect output, the government should deny the petition.

But if there is excess capacity in the restaurant—for instance, at the zero lower bound—the government should consider allowing smoking because the increased purchases of meals will use up that excess capacity and increase aggregate demand. A comparison of the benefits of smoking to smokers with the harms imposed by smoking on third parties no longer settles the issue. Instead, the government also needs to consider the effects of the petition on aggregate demand. Allowing smoking in the restaurant probably changes aggregate demand for meals. Demand for meals from smokers increases while demand for meals from nonsmokers decreases. If the net effect is to increase demand for meals, then approval for the petition increases output and employment, providing benefits to workers and restaurant owners. The government still needs to compare the benefits of allowing smoking to workers with the harm caused by smoking, but macroeconomic conditions dictate that the effects of the petition on aggregate demand also deserve consideration.

In the case of Keystone, the government effectively rejected the smokers' application while restaurant tables went empty. Deferring approval in 2010–2011, when interest rates were zero and unemployment high, meant construction workers who would have been employed sat idle. Other resources, too, were mothballed; they weren't put to good use elsewhere.

Construction purchases also create an indirect "aggregate demand externality" at the zero lower bound on interest rates, which they don't have in ordinary economic conditions.[16] When a private purchaser such as TransCanada buys labor and capital, the income that results has important multiplier effects as the workers that TransCanada employs to build the pipeline increase their own purchases, sending output and employment still higher. These effects are an external effect of TransCanada's purchasing decisions that TransCanada does not internalize. This multiplier is highest at the zero lower bound because inadequate aggregate demand (reflected in the zero rate of interest), and not capacity constraints, limits output and employment. When we take this business cycle–sensitive externality into account, our cost–benefit analysis changes, as it would if we took any other externality into account. Constructing Keystone may be efficient—with benefits exceeding costs—in a liquidity trap because the positive aggregate demand externalities associated with construction at the zero lower bound exceed the negative externalities that decide the issue in ordinary times.

Robert Haveman and coauthors, among others, have done just such a cost–benefit analysis, analyzing a generic construction project with macroeconomic outcomes in mind.[17] They find that, under plausible assumptions, the total costs of construction of a project like Keystone at full employment are reasonably well approximated by the nominal costs of construction, which assume no change in employment. In other words, building Keystone in 2018's robust economic conditions has little discernible macroeconomic effect. In a liquidity trap with high unemployment—the conditions of 2009–2015—they estimate that the total cost of constructing a project may be less than 50 percent of the nominal cost.[18] The results suggest that Keystone, given its negative externalities, was probably not worth approval during the Trump administration. But the social costs of Keystone in 2011 were much less than the costs in 2017, suggesting that the project should perhaps have been approved earlier.

The State Department was unable to provide such an estimate because its work assumes that the economic effect of a project does not vary over time.[19] As we saw throughout Part I, however, this assumption is often wrong. In a liquidity trap, output capacity exceeds the output demanded. Supply exceeds demand, so an increase in demand will be accommodated, and demand multiplier effects are high. At full employment, by contrast, inputs and capacity constrain output. Increases in demand do not raise overall output but rather reallocate output from one source of demand to another. Demand multiplier effects are low.

A better and more macroeconomically sensitive economic impact analysis of Keystone accounts for these time-varying effects. Haveman's research provides what the State Department doesn't. He uses estimates of the likelihood that employees hired for a project will avoid unemployment, which allows the cost–benefit analysis to adjust with the business cycle. According to Haveman's estimates, the state of the business cycle is an enormously important determinant of the true costs and benefits of regulations. To ignore the state of the business cycle when deciding on Keystone would be as imprudent as ignoring Keystone's effects on the environment.

Empirical Evidence for the Effectiveness of Expansionary Legal Policy

On the basis of the State Department's analysis, we can be reasonably sure that, during a liquidity trap, the proximate effects of Keystone's construction on aggregate spending would be positive. But uncertainty persists with respect to secondary effects.[20] For instance, a concern for any demand stimulus proposal is business and consumer confidence. When the government uses fiscal policy to increase spending, citizens may worry about deficits and reduce consumption and investment in response. Similarly, expansionary legal policy may make consumers and investors nervous. If the resulting reductions in consumption and investment exceed the increase in spending, then stimulus will fail. We must account for confidence and a range of other factors if we are to be reasonably sure that good policy is in the offing.

At present, we don't have good empirical evidence about such indirect effects of legal policy on aggregate demand. But we do have empirical evidence about the size of indirect spending effects in another context—the fiscal multiplier. As we saw earlier, an ample literature shows that, under liquidity trap conditions, increases in government spending translate into significant increases in output, even accounting for "confidence" and other indirect effects. If this is true of spending directly transacted by the government, then it is also likely to be true of spending induced by the government via its regulatory authority. In the absence of contrary evidence, we should assume that the multiplier on spending induced by legal action equals the government spending multiplier. This would be so with respect to Keystone and any other project requiring government approval.

Indeed, we have reason to believe that the legal spending multiplier should be higher than the government-spending multiplier. When the government runs a deficit, consumers should anticipate higher tax obligations in the future and reduce consumption in response, limiting the positive impact on demand and output. Empirical evidence supports this hypothesis, finding particularly high multipliers when an increase in spending is not accompanied by a future obligation to repay, something that occurs when spending is funded by a much larger jurisdiction (for example, U.S. states spending federal money or regional-development spending in EU countries funded from the EU budget).[21] Spending induced by a decision to approve Keystone also would not raise future public debt or tax obligations, so it should result in a high multiplier.

Expansionary Legal Policy Does Not Mean Deregulation

Rejection of Keystone can be framed as the imposition of an infinite tax on the pipeline's construction. After all, regulation is often thought of in the same way as taxes: both impose costs that make it more difficult to consume and invest. As a general matter, lower taxation is expansionary, increasing disposable income and thereby encouraging consumption and production.[22] Reasoning by analogy, we might assume that deregulation, like lower taxation, stimulates the economy. Expansionary legal policy, then, is another term for deregulation to combat deficient demand at the zero lower bound.

But this is not actually how regulation or expansionary legal policy works. Regulation is not in all cases equivalent to a tax. Instead, a considerable amount of regulation imposes spending mandates. A mandate resembles a hybrid program of taxation and spending. The government imposes a tax that equals the costs of complying with the mandate and then spends the receipts to bring the regulated party into compliance. Although this process is deficit-neutral, it has a positive effect on aggregate demand because taxes paid from savings are spent. Thanks to regulation, money that otherwise would languish at the zero lower bound is put to productive use.

This principle could have been applied to Keystone as well. Instead of simply banning or approving Keystone, the State Department could have approved the pipeline under conditions that further increase aggregate demand. Indeed, it sought to do so, before the project was scuttled. In 2011, the State Department negotiated for higher building standards than those prescribed in the original Keystone application. The heightened standards would have reduced the risk of environmentally damaging pipeline spills, providing, according to the State Department, "a degree of safety over any other typically constructed domestic oil pipeline."[23] TransCanada agreed, saying it would "adopt 57 project-specific special conditions for design, construction, and operations." These included improved monitoring systems, expanded pipeline testing, and enhanced construction requirements. Complying with these conditions entailed hiring more labor and using more capital than an unconditional approval of the original pipeline application would have. The conditions therefore increased aggregate demand.

The value of the added construction mandates depended on the business cycle. To evaluate construction mandates, we compare the direct costs they impose with the environmental benefits they offer. At the zero lower bound, the true costs of production may be as little as half of the headline costs, as construction utilizes spare labor and capital. Therefore, the mandates' benefits are more likely to exceed their costs at the zero lower bound than at other times.

As with Keystone, so too with many other regulatory mandates. During the Great Recession, for example, the EPA formulated a regulation requiring power plants to install costly pollution scrubbers to minimize mercury and other harmful emissions. The EPA estimated that the pollution regulation would create 46,000 jobs in the short run but very few in the long run.[24] This regulation was especially desirable when interest rates were constrained by the zero lower bound, as they were during the Great Recession.

At the zero lower bound, we need to consider the effects of regulatory decisions on aggregate demand. Regulatory interventions that increase spending, like the approval of the Keystone pipeline conditional on heightened environmental safety requirements, become more desirable at the zero lower bound because they increase output and employment by bringing idle productive capacity back online. The business cycle–dependent value of legal policy parallels the business cycle–dependent value of fiscal policy. The optimal fiscal policy changes with the business cycle, with programs that increase aggregate demand, such as government infrastructure investment, becoming more valuable at the zero lower bound than at other times. If we change our evaluation of fiscal policy with the business cycle, then we should also change our evaluation of regulation—unless, that is, the problems we introduce by tying law with macroeconomics exceed the benefits (a condition that applies to expansionary fiscal policy as well as to expansionary legal policy). Chapter 9 therefore explores the difficulties of incorporating macroeconomic considerations into the regulatory evaluation of Keystone.

NINE

The Costs of Expansionary Legal Policy

J ust because we can stimulate aggregate demand through the regulatory process doesn't mean we should. Like monetary and fiscal policy, legal decisions require tradeoffs. One desirable goal may be achieved at the sacrifice of another. Our legal institutions also are not optimized for the purpose of implementing expansionary legal policy; certain weaknesses make them imperfect vehicles for stimulus. The Keystone pipeline, again, provides a case in point. Approval would have been economically useful during the recession, yet obstacles got in the way. These point to potential challenges of using law for macroeconomic ends.

In this chapter, I explore a range of objections that might be raised to expansionary legal policy. All reflect realistic concerns, but some ought to be taken more seriously than others.

Macroeconomics and the Goals of Law

When regulatory decision makers consider macroeconomic effects, they may be unable to avoid compromising on other goals of law. I consider three of these: microeconomic efficiency, justice, and equity.

Does Expansionary Legal Policy Compromise Microeconomic Efficiency?

Let us begin with the heroic assumption that all the costs and benefits of Keystone can be quantified, so that we can express all goals of approval using a single metric, such as dollars.[1] Assume further that the best analysis suggests that, in ordinary macroeconomic times, the costs of Keystone exceed their benefits. Might we not reasonably argue, then, that Keystone ought never be built? What the cost–benefit analysis tells us is that Keystone fails the test of microeconomic efficiency—specifically, "Kaldor-Hicks efficiency" (which associates efficiency with the largest economic pie).[2] In other words, those made better off by building Keystone aren't so much better off that they could, in theory, compensate those left in worse shape. Some win from Keystone, but the size of the whole economic pie shrinks.

It seems, then, that Keystone is microeconomically inefficient. And because we generally assume that microeconomics does not depend on macroeconomic conditions (otherwise, microeconomics would no longer be microeconomics), a decision to approve Keystone at the zero lower bound should also decrease the size of the economic pie.

But this is only the case if we hew to a time-invariant Kaldor-Hicks definition of efficiency. We need not. Law and macroeconomics revises what we mean by efficiency—making efficiency depend on macro conditions. At the zero lower bound, maximizing the size of the economic pie entails different policies than what would be called for in ordinary economic conditions. Indeed, Hicks (the efficiency definition's second namesake) himself emphasized that "classical" economics does not apply at the zero lower bound. Instead, Keynesian economics applies, meaning that policies that maximize the size of the economic pie at the zero lower bound differ from the efficient policy under ordinary circumstances. Adjusting our cost–benefit analysis to account for the differential economics of liquidity traps brings us closer to Kaldor-Hicks efficiency, properly understood, than the assumption that efficiency is time invariant.

Of course, if Keystone is inefficient in ordinary times, it may still be inefficient during a liquidity trap. Law and macroeconomics doesn't render the cost–benefit analysis that would apply in a better-functioning economy erroneous, merely incomplete. Everything that matters in a healthy economy matters at the zero lower bound. If the environmental harms associated with Keystone are sufficiently grave, then even lower construction costs associated with a liquidity trap will be insufficient to make the project efficient. Macroeconomic considerations simply alter cost–benefit analysis on the margin. Using law and macroeconomics to inform cost–benefit analysis favors decisions that enhance spending at the zero lower bound but does not necessitate them.

Still, the marginal effects of macroeconomic considerations can be very important, such that a degree of microeconomic inefficiency would be acceptable. Gauti Eggertsson argues that liquidity traps may require, and have at times required, legal interventions that appear egregious from a classical microeconomic perspective:

> Can policies that are contractionary according to the neoclassical model, be expansionary once the model is extended to include [macroeconomic considerations]? For example, can facilitating monopoly pricing of firms and/or increasing the bargaining power of workers' unions increase output? . . . The answer is yes under the special "emergency" conditions that apply when the short-term nominal interest rate is zero and there is excessive deflation. . . . These special "emergency" conditions were satisfied during the Great Depression in the United States.[3]

The microeconomic cost of scrapping antitrust restrictions against collusion, restrictions that are almost universally acknowledged to be efficient in ordinary times, is far higher than that of approving a much-debated pipeline project. If even antitrust restrictions can be sacrificed at the zero lower bound, then surely the microeconomic inefficiencies of borderline projects can be endured.

Eggertsson also argues that the microeconomic inefficiencies caused by regulatory changes at the zero lower bound are probably less costly than feared. Microeconomic inefficiencies limit supply capacity, but the costs of this limitation may be irrelevant in a liquidity trap because the economy is not producing at capacity. So long as the reduction in supply does not bring capacity below aggregate demand, then only a policy's aggregate-demand effects—not its microeconomic effects on supply—matter for efficiency.

Another microeconomic-efficiency problem stems from bad incentives. Varying law according to the business cycle will encourage investors to sit on controversial proposals such as Keystone and submit them at the zero lower bound. Should this happen, law and macroeconomics might deliver many unwanted projects.

Regulators need to be cognizant of these possible incentive effects, but they are unlikely to be very costly. For one thing, even if regulators ease up on approvals at the zero lower bound, the precise regulatory regime they impose will not inevitably ensure better returns for investors. Regulators may pair their approvals with spending mandates they would omit in ordinary times because the additional spending associated with the mandates has desirable aggregate-demand influences at the zero lower bound. These mandates may reduce, rather than increase, the returns earned on some projects.

Another factor mitigating the incentive to delay is the unpredictability of liquidity traps. Although there is good reason to believe that the zero lower bound will become more common in the future, forecasting liquidity traps with precision is not possible. Investors waiting for them may find themselves long delayed. Finally, if there is incentive for investors to defer until liquidity traps, that actually may be socially desirable. Investing when the economy is at full capacity raises prices, producing inflation and destabilizing the economy. By contrast, investing during a liquidity trap reduces the costs of unused capacity, stabilizing the economy. Business cycle–sensitive regulation induces the private sector to choose the stabilizing route.

In total, introducing law and macroeconomics into the policy equation may complicate the search for efficient laws and regulation, but it does not abandon Kaldor-Hicks efficiency, the primary criterion of microeconomics. Instead, law and macroeconomics refines our understanding of Kaldor-Hicks efficiency so that efficient policies depend on the business cycle.

Challenges to Justice and Deontological Goals of Law

If all costs and benefits of Keystone can be expressed in dollar terms, then the pipeline's environmental harms can be calculated and weighed against other considerations. But many argue that deontological goals defy quantification. According to this view, it is a mistake to put a price on environmental conservation, justice, and other goods protected by law.

This is a powerful criticism, but it is not limited to macroeconomics. Any economic efficiency perspective on law must balance deontological goals with the goal of increasing the size of the pie. So long as we continue to use economics to evaluate policy with tools like cost–benefit analysis, there is a role for law and macroeconomics in improving the evaluation.

Moreover, the critique goes too far. Part of the legal and regulatory process is balancing between competing values and interests. Quantification imposes some rigor on this process. While the critics are right that any dollar value we put on justice or environmental conservation should not be taken too seriously, they are wrong to argue that this implies that quantification should never be attempted. Rejecting quantification does not eliminate the necessity of balancing deontological objectives in making policy decisions. Instead, it makes the same trade-offs less explicit, weakening the decision-making process.

Fears of Inequality under the Law

At least in theory, law prizes equality. Similarly situated people should be treated the same way under law. The same goes for proposals seeking approval. If law were sensitive to the business cycle, it would seem to violate the principle of equality under the law. How can it be fair that Keystone gets approved at the zero lower bound on interest rates but an otherwise identical project gets denied in periods of normal economic activity?

I submit that there is actually no inequality here, because the two proposals are not the same. Keystone developed during a liquidity trap differs from Keystone developed at other times. While the project itself may look the same, its social cost differs dramatically between zero interest rates and ordinary times. There is nothing inherently inequitable about favoring a proposal that uses an economy's spare capacity over a proposal that merely reshuffles that capacity.

Imperfect Policy for Hard Times

Earlier, I observed that fiscal-policy stabilization may come at the expense of other goals of fiscal policy. When governments introduce fiscal stimulus, they upset a delicate balance between the costs of taxation and the benefits of public goods and redistribution. Yet even ardent critics of discretionary fiscal policy in ordinary times, such as James Buchanan, agree that when "the economy is caught in a liquidity trap," "the creation of a deficit in the government's budget seems clearly to be dictated by rational policy norms, requiring only the acknowledgment that full employment and expanded real output are appropriate objectives."[4]

Expansionary legal policy similarly upsets a delicate balance between many competing goals of law. At the zero lower bound, however, there are no good options. Either we upset other policy goals or the economy remains mired in a terrible slump, with potentially disastrous long-term political and economic consequences. Given the stakes, it makes no less sense to consider law for macroeconomic purposes than to call on fiscal policy for the same ends.

Institutional Weaknesses of Expansionary Legal Policy

The potential of expansionary legal policy is great, and the downsides seem no more discouraging than those of our major stimulus tools, as long as each is used under proper conditions. But given the realities of policymaking, can law and macroeconomics actually deliver? Can our institutions successfully provide expansionary legal policy, or are they capable only of monetary and fiscal stimulus?

Below, I evaluate law and regulatory policy on institutional grounds mostly familiar from my earlier discussions of fiscal and monetary policy, including (1) monetary offset, (2) expertise, (3) uncertain effects, (4) time lags, (5) risks of political opportunism and arbitrariness, (6) democratic legitimacy, (7) spillovers, and (8) coordination problems. I then compare these three kinds of macroeconomic policy in institutional terms.

Although the obstacles are considerable, I argue that the case for business cycle–sensitive laws and regulations remains compelling in some contexts, such as Keystone's 2010–2011 proposal. In other cases discussed in later chapters, I reach the opposite conclusion—that law and regulation are not well suited to macroeconomic policy. For example, I argue that law—in the form of price and wage controls—was the wrong institutional mechanism for coping with the high inflation of the 1970s. At the zero lower bound, however, with monetary policy impotent and fiscal policy potentially constrained by gridlock or fear of excessive debt, some forms of expansionary legal policy are justified.

Monetary Offset

In ordinary economic times, the aggregate demand stimulus associated with approving projects such as Keystone will raise inflation. In response, the central bank will raise interest rates, curtailing the demand-fueled increase in output caused by approval. However, if expansionary legal policy is confined to the zero lower bound, there is no risk of monetary policy offset. The central bank will accommodate the increase in aggregate demand associated with a regulatory decision that increases spending because the economy is producing below its potential and the stimulus brings output closer to capacity and reduces deflationary pressures. Thus, expansionary regulatory policy at the zero lower bound will not suffer from monetary offset.

Expertise

Lawyers, administrators, and regulators generally have little expertise in macroeconomics. Macroeconomics is not taught in law schools, nor is it a focus of students of public policy. After law school, lawyers rarely confront macroeconomic policy questions. Attorneys and regulators often argue about whether a legal outcome is microeconomically inefficient, unfair, inequitable, or morally wrong. They seldom, if ever, consider the macroeconomic effects. Compared with central bankers who regularly consider the macroeconomic effects of policy, the State Department officials and administrators making the decision about Keystone were macroeconomic naifs.

But when compared with fiscal policymakers—that is, legislators—administrators and regulators, in the State Department and elsewhere, look much better. The State Department's 2011 review of Keystone was informed by more than twenty U.S. federal and state administrative agencies. The report contained expert analysis of Keystone's effects on, among other things, "Environmental Justice, Greenhouse Gas Emissions, Geology and Soils, Water Resources, Wetlands, Terrestrial Vegetation, Fisheries Resources, and Socioeconomics."[5] Keystone's proposal may not have reached the desks of any macroeconomists, but it was scrutinized by more experts than a legislature could practically attend to.

The lack of macroeconomic expertise brought to bear on Keystone doesn't reflect institutional weakness; it is correctable. If the Office of Fiscal and Regulatory Affairs (OFRA) proposed in Part I deployed its macroeconomic expertise to inform the Keystone cost–benefit analysis, then the debate over Keystone would have been more macroeconomically informed than most policy decisions. At the moment, the experts called in to the regulatory decision-making process—from agencies such as the EPA, which advised the State Department on Keystone—are rarely macroeconomists.[6] This reflects priorities, not institutional structures. If agencies were supported by supervisory agencies like OFRA to consider the macroeconomic effects of regulations, then they could easily find macroeconomists to advise their policy calculus.

The problem of expertise is also mitigated by the narrow application of expansionary legal policy to liquidity traps. Liquidity traps are clearly indicated by zero short-term interest rates. Only when central bankers, constrained by the zero lower bound, can no longer make conventional monetary policy would regulators be in a position to consider legal stimulus. It should therefore be fairly easy for regulators to identify when the time for macroeconomic considerations is at hand.

Uncertain Effects

Which laws and regulations increase or decrease spending? This question has to be answered on a case-by-case basis because law's effects on spending depend on the conditions of each legal ruling. Imposing mandates on the construction of Keystone increases spending so long as TransCanada accepts the added costs. If the mandates become so onerous that the pipeline is not worth building, then the mandates diminish spending.

In the case of Keystone, the direct effects of the regulatory decision are relatively straightforward. Permit approval increases construction spending, relative to denial. Secondary effects of approval could undo the direct effects, but only if these secondary effects are strongly negative. Thus, even in the absence of empirical evidence, "armchair empiricism" may be enough to support permitting Keystone during a deep recession. We don't need perfect certainty to embrace 42,000 jobs, the State Department's estimate, at a time when the economy needed them. Confidence in Keystone's macroeconomic impact was also enhanced by the conditions attached to approval. These conditions, which would have increased spending while curbing leaks, might have imperiled stimulus by making the project too expensive for TransCanada to take on. But the company agreed to them.

We cannot always be so certain about the aggregate-demand effects of regulatory decisions. But this is a reason to approach expansionary legal policy with caution, not an excuse for law and regulation to ignore aggregate demand altogether. In conventional law and economics, armchair empiricism in the face of uncertain effects is common. When we don't have a reliable, empirically driven estimate of law's effects on microeconomic efficiency, conventional law and economics calls on legal actors to casually predict those effects; but this has not prevented us from using microeconomics to evaluate law. Indeed, intuitions about the effects of a law on overall spending will often be clearer than the law's effects on efficiency, which depend on trading off several possibly offsetting effects. If we can build a field—law and economics—around evaluating law from a microeconomic perspective, then, given the stakes, we should not shrink from exploring law and macroeconomics as well.

Nor should we discard law and macroeconomics over some false certainty regarding monetary and fiscal policy. They, too, can be unpredictable. For example, during the "taper tantrum" of 2013, Fed policy was far more contractionary than intended. A small decrease in quantitative easing was accompanied by a very large and unexpected increase in long-term interest rates. Likewise, the impact of fiscal policy is not guaranteed. During the recession, advocates of expansionary austerity argued sincerely that reduced deficits would so inspire confidence that fiscal contraction would actually stimulate the economy. Reality proved otherwise.

Monetary and fiscal policy comes with no guarantees, yet few economists and policymakers argue these policy tools should therefore be discarded. Likewise, the mere fact of uncertain macroeconomic effects should not preclude the use of law and regulation for macroeconomic purposes.

Time Lags

As we have seen, one of the most significant obstacles to good fiscal policy is timing. Legislation moves so slowly that it often can't keep up with fluctuations in aggregate demand. Legal policy faces the same obstacle. Demand shocks may be too short-lived for legal policy to provide an effective response. Many recessions last for only six months or a year, while changes in law and regulation often come at a much slower pace. The decision on Keystone's approval, for example, was delayed for six years. And even if Keystone had been approved in 2011, construction would have continued until 2013.[7] If a recession ends before the effects of a legal decision on aggregate demand are realized, then law and regulation offer an inadequate tool for responding to macroeconomic fluctuations.

What does this mean for expansionary legal policy? Outside of the zero lower bound, it means that legal intervention is not a wise approach to macroeconomic policy. Regulators should not be asked to account for macroeconomic conditions that will change significantly during the life of a project.

Regulation's lengthy lags are not as serious a problem when intervals of inadequate aggregate demand last many years, an outcome we can reasonably anticipate at the zero lower bound or after a financial crisis. To return to Keystone, the persistence in 2011 of the liquidity trap, as well as other negative macroeconomic indicators, made it likely that elevated U.S. unemployment would persist through 2013, as it, in fact, did. Regulators therefore should have considered Keystone's macroeconomic implications in deciding the project's fate: there was ample strong evidence that, even at this late date, Keystone would have had a noticeable, positive macroeconomic effect.

Small reforms could help to promote regulatory consideration of macroeconomics at moments when law can have a rapid impact on spending. One option would be to provide regulators annual timelines of costs and benefits for given projects. At present, cost–benefit and feasibility analyses usually condense the costs and benefits of regulation into a single number. Although this simplifies decision-making, it does so by eschewing the business cycle. A timeline enables regulators to account for the business cycle by indicating when job losses, gains, and other benefits and costs of a regulation will emerge. Using this information, decision makers can figure out how to appropriately adjust the costs of approval in order to achieve stimulus when it is needed. If a project increases employment rates in the near term but has little effect on employment in the long run, as with Keystone, then it will be more attractive at the zero lower bound than its long-run "jobs created" figure indicates. Good regulatory decisions rarely are made without good information. Providing regulators with job creation timelines is a step toward good decisions.

In addition, some regulatory interventions are less subject to the problems of delay than others. Formulating entirely new rules to stimulate the economy is hard. Delaying the application of rules that impede spending until the economy is more robust or hastening the implementation periods of rules that stimulate demand so that spending is concentrated in the bust are easier, and more timely, interventions. By focusing on timelier interventions, regulators can have meaningful impacts on spending within time frames appropriate for episodes of the zero lower bound.

Thus, the time lags associated with regulatory intervention need not always impede that intervention.

Risks of Political Opportunism and Arbitrariness

When we introduce another regulatory consideration—here, macro-economics—we give the regulator another degree of freedom. Even if the regulation looks bad on grounds of, say, equity, environmental harm, or microeconomic efficiency, the regulator may approve it on macroeconomic grounds. But these grounds could just be a smokescreen to regulate according to the regulator's personal preferences. Do we really want to give regulators this sort of opportunity to abuse the law as they see fit?

There is risk in this sort of opportunism. Say the project aiming for regulatory approval presents an environmental threat so grave that it should never be allowed to proceed—no matter the business cycle. In the midst of a liquidity trap, an administration unconcerned about the environment, perhaps because it has been "captured" by polluters, could use macroeconomics as an excuse to approve a damaging project.

But we shouldn't exaggerate just how much risk is associated with the macroeconomic criterion. For one thing, the incremental impact on regulatory discretion is small. Regulators already enjoy a lot of leeway to impose their preferences. In 2017, for example, the Trump State Department approved Keystone, without regard to the business cycle. This approval reversed the State Department's rejection of the pipeline during the Obama administration. If the regulatory process already entails considerable discretion, then introducing macroeconomics into policy does not open the floodgates to discretion. The floodgates were already open.

We also need to keep in mind that the imperfections of regulatory stimulus, which may include a degree of opportunism, are not in and of themselves fatal to my proposal that legal decisions account for the business cycle. What matters is how the deficiencies compare to those of fiscal policy, the other option at the zero lower bound. I submit that, when it comes to political opportunism, the comparison favors regulation over fiscal policy passed by legislators. Unlike politicians, regulators are largely insulated from the pressures of elections, so they have less reason to abuse their discretion for political gain. Indeed, we delegate authority over monetary policy, our principal macroeconomic policy tool outside of the zero lower bound, to central banks precisely because we think that administrators are less prone than legislators to political opportunism.

If opportunism is our concern, then we should readily prefer legal expansion to the alternative of fiscal policy. And given the stakes in a liquidity trap—financial and social upheaval—a relatively small incremental increase in regulatory opportunism is a cost worth bearing.

The requirement to explain decisions plays an important role in constraining law and regulation from both opportunism and arbitrariness. A regulatory decision does not simply resolve an issue. It also explains the decision. This explanation guides future regulatory decisions and shapes private parties' expectations about government responses to their own proposals. For example, the lengthy "Basis for Decision" included in the 2017 approval of Keystone will be valuable to others proposing similar projects to regulators in the future because it explains why the State Department ultimately approved the project.[8]

If we use macroeconomic policy to shape regulatory decisions, then we complicate the explanations offered for decisions by regulators. In particular, we distort the signal that future regulators and private-sector actors receive from approval or denial. What if Keystone had been approved in 2011? Future regulators and private-sector actors might not know if the permit was approved because of the state of the business cycle or because of the underlying quality of the pipeline proposal.

Yet such complications are pretty well baked into the law already. The basis for decisions that explain what is and is not in the "national interest" are already so complex and multifaceted that adding macroeconomics to the evaluation is not blurring what used to be a clear line. To say that injecting macroeconomics will complicate regulatory explanations is like saying that a few drops of food coloring will make the ocean blue.

Expansionary legal policy uses preexisting legal discretion toward a new purpose—stimulus. If regulators and other legal officials abuse this discretion, then expansionary legal policy becomes unlawful. The goal of stimulus is no different than the many other goals of regulation—regulators can pursue it only when stimulus is consistent with the regulator's legal mandate. By comparison with central banks, who enjoy almost untrammeled discretion to pursue the macroeconomic policy they see fit, regulators' scope for expansionary legal policy appears narrow.

Indeed, macroeconomics would not unduly complicate a decision because its implications are much more focused than the issues already under consideration. When interest rates are zero, regulators should favor actions that promote spending more than they favor the same actions in ordinary economic conditions. That is simple. By comparison, evaluating a project's effects on national security demands appraisal of many more factors, and whatever determination is reached will be open to argument and interpretation. The precedents created by the current regulatory process are already much more opaque than any that business cycle considerations would introduce.

An office for law and macroeconomic policy such as OFRA (see Chapter 6) would further reduce the risk of arbitrariness and opportunism. When stimulus is needed, OFRA should both announce an estimate for the multiplier that all administrative agencies should apply and review agency decisions to make sure that they use this estimate in practice. With common standards and supervision, regulators' scope for arbitrariness and opportunism would be significantly curtailed.

Democratic Legitimacy

Expansionary legal policy suffers from limited democratic legitimacy. The regulators at the State Department who decided on Keystone (influenced by the presidents in power) were unelected.

Unlike the power of the purse, however, macroeconomic policy is not a core democratic function. Our most powerful tool of macroeconomic policy, monetary policy, is already delegated to the "agencies" we call central banks. The democratic legitimacy problem associated with expansionary legal policy cannot be the use of regulatory power for macroeconomic ends. Moreover, many regulatory bodies enjoy more democratic legitimacy than the central bank because they are less independent than the central bank. Elected officials, such as the president of the United States, choose many of the regulators and can fire the most senior of them at will. As a result, expansionary legal policy improves the democratic legitimacy of macroeconomic policy. (When democracies are not healthy, democratic responsiveness can be a vice rather than a virtue.)

Perhaps, then, the problem is that, by considering macroeconomics in making regulatory policy, the regulators acquire too much power? But asking regulators to consider macroeconomics does not arrogate new powers to the regulator. Instead, it uses power already granted to the regulator in a new way. Executive Order 13337, which defined the State Department's role, ordered that the State Department evaluate Keystone's "economic, environmental, national security, and foreign policy" effects. (Presidents issue executive orders to govern the operations of the executive branch, subject to authority granted by statute.) This executive order, which references "economic effects," gave the State Department all the authority it needed to consider macroeconomic effects.

Executive Order 13337, rather than the consideration of macroeconomics, creates the democratic legitimacy problem by giving the State Department, an unelected part of government, incredibly broad authority. In order to reduce the problem of democratic legitimacy, we should reduce the scope of the State Department's authority in general, rather than focusing on the difficulties posed by expansionary legal policy.

Moreover, the problem with regulatory power is not necessarily democratic legitimacy. Agencies like the State Department of the United States are part of the executive branch of government, which enjoys democratic legitimacy in the United States through presidential elections. Instead, the problem is more accurately described as regulatory arbitrariness caused by the open-ended executive order.

If expansionary legal policy is implemented by the legislature, then there is no concern about democratic legitimacy. For example, if a legislature complements increased infrastructure spending in response to a recession with the passage of more rapid regulatory approval procedures in order to ensure that the spending is shovel ready, then the change in regulatory procedures enjoys a degree of democratic legitimacy unusual for any aspect of regulation.

Spillovers

When a job is created as a result of expansionary legal policy in Nebraska, such as approval for Keystone, the new hire purchases additional goods and services produced locally and in other jurisdictions. As a result, the benefits of expansionary legal policy in Nebraska spill over to neighboring jurisdictions, such as Kansas. Although the benefits of expansionary legal policy are diffuse, the costs tend to be concentrated in the home area. Only regions hosting portions of Keystone face risks of oil spills, for instance.

When a federal regulator makes the decision, as in Keystone, then this asymmetric geographic distribution of costs and benefits should not hinder policy. Although the costs of expansionary legal policy are concentrated while the benefits are more diffuse, the regulator considers both the diffuse benefits and the concentrated costs equally when making policy. Although Nebraska may come out behind with respect to Keystone, it will also benefit from demand spilllovers from expansionary legal policy elsewhere.

When Nebraska regulators choose to make or avoid expansionary legal policy, by contrast, then the asymmetry of diffuse benefits and concentrated costs hinders policy. If they focus only on Nebraska, Nebraska regulators may reject Keystone at the zero lower bound even if the national benefits exceed the costs because Nebraska reaps only some of the aggregate demand benefits but bears all of the costs. Even this concern, however, should not be exaggerated. As discussed in Part I, increased aggregate demand creates many jobs at the local level in a liquidity trap, meaning that Nebraska regulators have ample incentive to engage in expansionary legal policy.

Coordination Problems

If we use regulation to stimulate the economy in liquidity traps, then we need to calibrate regulatory decisions to get the right amount of stimulus. This would be easy if there were one regulator, with a simple set of rules, making just a few decisions. But many regulators, following several rulebooks, are involved in making thousands of regulatory decisions each year. Keystone represents just one important regulatory decision among thousands. If the economy were mired in a liquidity trap, and every regulator changed policy in order to stimulate aggregate demand, the result might be excessive aggregate demand, causing inflation to rise.

The OFRA proposed in Part I addresses this weakness of expansionary legal policy. If OFRA observes some agencies putting more weight on expansionary legal policy than justified by its estimate of the "aggregate demand externalities" of spending, then OFRA should use its supervisory powers to mitigate this problem.

OFRA, like any agency, will be imperfect. Coordinating expansionary legal policy will remain more difficult than coordinating fiscal policy or monetary policy. But the difficulty of coordinating expansionary legal policy suggests an advantage for legal policy as well as a disadvantage. A system with overlapping policy instruments is not just clunkier than a one-dimensional system. The diffuse system is also more robust. If a preferred macro policy tool fails by overstimulating or understimulating, then we can use another tool to offset the failures of the first. If monetary and fiscal policy prove inadequate, the ability of law, however imperfectly coordinated, to respond to inadequate aggregate demand may prevent economic depressions and recessions that threaten the social order.

Indeed, we saw the robustness advantage of multiple macroeconomic policy tools in Part I. When fiscal policy failed to stimulate at the zero lower bound, central banks responded with unconventional monetary policy, even when the policy's constitutional legitimacy was in question. The availability of multiple policies, however imperfect, enabled a better policy response to the Great Recession than would have been available if fiscal policy, the textbook lever at the zero lower bound, had been relied upon exclusively.

The possibility of monetary offset of excess regulatory stimulus reduces the costs associated with poor coordination of expansionary regulatory policy. If lack of coordination drove regulatory policy to overstimulate the economy, the result would likely be monetary offset, with the central bank responding to inflation by raising interest rates. This would represent a net loss: regulation would grow more complicated thanks to the introduction of macroeconomics, but there would be no aggregate-demand benefit to compensate. But this would be the sole cost of overstimulating by regulation. There would be little risk of macroeconomic excess leading to inflation.

As with other institutional weaknesses of law and regulation, the problem of coordination is not so fearsome that we must forgo expansionary legal policy entirely. We have to balance the downsides of coordination problems with the potential of a novel macroeconomic policy tool and with the painful reality of inadequate aggregate demand at the zero lower bound. And it is not clear that the problem is large in the first place. Not only are we a long way from regulatory overstimulus, but the experience of the Great Recession also suggests that more is needed. Most observers believe fiscal policy provided too little. If regulators overcorrect, approving too many Keystone pipelines and causing inflation, then there will be a good argument for imposing limits on regulatory stimulus. Until then, we should be willing to experiment with liquidity-trap fixes rather than worry that they will be too effective.

When Should Law and Regulation Consider Macroeconomics?

That law and regulation affect aggregate demand is uncontroversial. But should judges and regulators actively use law to stabilize the economy? Not in ordinary economic conditions. The institutional weaknesses of law and regulation as a tool of macroeconomic policy make conventional monetary policy a better instrument of stabilization in these circumstances. Unlike legal policy, monetary policy is determined by independent experts with the power to move quickly in response to macroeconomic conditions. Therefore, there should generally be a presumption against expansionary legal policy. In the circumstances I describe here, however, the presumption may be overcome.

The Zero Lower Bound

The case for expansionary legal policy strengthens (as I've suggested throughout Chapters 8 and 9) at the zero lower bound. The value of expansionary legal policy increases at the zero lower bound while the costs decrease.

The value of stimulus rises at the zero lower bound for several reasons. Mitigating widespread unemployment, hysteresis, and the attendant risks of political upheaval justifies reliance on clunky instruments like law and regulation in a way that mitigating a short recession or stabilizing inflation does not. This becomes especially true when our default macroeconomic stimulus instrument—using monetary policy to change interest rates—becomes impotent, as at the zero lower bound. Desperate for effective stimulus tools during the Great Recession, central banks turned to unconventional monetary policy techniques that are risky, have questionable efficacy, and undermine central bank legitimacy. If central banks perceive the need for macroeconomic stimulus to be so urgent that they have pursued unconventional monetary policy nonetheless, then arguments for any alternative macro policy tools, including law, should be seriously entertained.

While the benefits of expansionary legal policy rise at the zero lower bound, the costs go down. The unusually long duration of liquidity traps, for example, mitigates the costs imposed by the slow-moving nature of legal policy. Although regulators usually should avoid accounting for macroeconomic conditions, they should do so enthusiastically at the zero lower bound. That is because liquidity traps tend to be prolonged. While most recessions are brief and soon corrected by relatively rapid recoveries, prolonged periods of economic weakness tend to follow financial crises, triggering zero interest rates. The last two episodes of zero short-term interest rates in the United States, the Great Depression and the Great Recession, lasted longer than five years. Japan is arguably the textbook case of secular stagnation, with growth anemic and interest rates stuck near zero since the 1990s. At this time scale, expansionary legal policy can effectively stimulate the economy even if it moves slowly.

In addition, liquidity traps are signaled by a relatively objective and easy-to-observe indicator—zero short-term interest rates (for example, ninety-day government bills yielding approximately zero interest). And zero short-term interest rates are also almost always associated with depressed macroeconomic conditions, as demonstrated in Figure 9.1. In the United States, three-month U.S. Treasury rates have fallen as low as 0.0 percent to 0.5 percent only twice, from 1934 to 1942 (the Great Depression) and from December 2008 to December 2015 (the Great Recession). Other than these two periods of prolonged depressed growth and low employment rates, the three-month U.S. Treasury rate has not reached zero in the last century.

We observe similar correlations between zero interest rates and anemic growth and employment in other industrialized democracies. In the United Kingdom and Japan, short-term interest rates reached 0 percent to 0.5 percent in late 2008—the nadir of the Great Recession—and remained there through 2017, reflecting chronic low growth in Japan and Brexit turmoil in the United Kingdom. In the Eurozone, interest rates on overnight bank deposits reached 0.5 percent in 2011—at the heart of the Euro crisis—fell into negative territory in 2014, and remained fractionally below zero through 2017, reflecting continued economic weakness. The rare exceptions to this rule, such as Germany and North Dakota during the Great Recession, which experienced robust growth with zero interest rates, reflect out-of-sync conditions between the jurisdiction and the currency union it is a part of, a problem I discuss shortly. If Germany had used its own currency instead of the Euro, then the Bundesbank would almost certainly have raised short-term interest rates above zero during the latter part of the Great Recession.[9]

Because of the availability of the zero lower bound as a proxy for depressed economies, regulators and judges do not need to be macroeconomic experts in order to diagnose the need for expansionary legal policy. They need only observe zero short-term interest rates.

The observability of the zero lower bound also reduces the risk that regulators and judges opportunistically and arbitrarily use expansionary legal policy. Instead of picking and choosing among macroeconomic indicators, they must demonstrate that aggregate demand is depressed by pointing to zero interest rates and explain why their judgment should increase spending. If these explanations are lacking, then arbitrary decisions will be reversed upon appeal. By cabining expansionary legal policy to well-defined periods

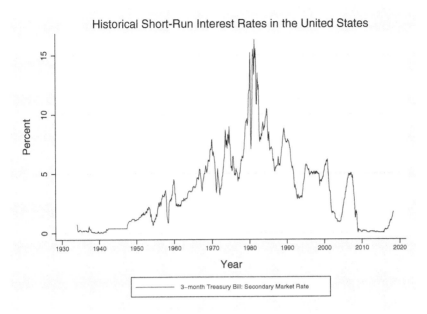

Figure 9.1 Short-run interest rates have hit the zero lower bound in the United States during only two periods: the Great Depression (1933–1942) and the Great Recession (2008–2015).

Data Source: Board of Governors of the Federal Reserve System, "3-Month Treasury Bill: Secondary Market Rate [TB3MS]," retrieved from FRED, Federal Reserve Bank of St. Louis, https://fred.stlouisfed.org/series/TB3MS.

and practices, the zero lower bound reduces the risk of arbitrariness and helps clarify the law.

Although periods of zero interest rates have been rare in the past, they have been particularly important. Moreover, the secular decline in interest rates from 1980 to the present (presented in Figure 9.1) means that episodes of the zero lower bound will likely be more common in the future than they have been in the past. Recent research estimates that zero lower bound "episodes are likely to be substantially more frequent . . . occurring nearly 40 percent of the time."[10]

Because short-term interest rates can fluctuate from day to day, a strict rule of zero interest rates to consider expansionary legal policy looks unwise. Instead, I recommend that expansionary legal policy be considered when short-term interest rates fall below 0.5 percent. But the presumption against expansionary legal policy should be strong when interest rates exceed 0.5 percent and weaker as rates hits zero or below.

After Financial Crises

In Chapter 4, I explained that the liquidity trap and secular stagnation accounts were not universally accepted. Instead, many blame the "debt supercycle" for causing prolonged recessions. When asset values go down dramatically, prolonged recessions ensue because borrowers can no longer maintain their spending by obtaining credit. With aggregate demand inadequate, production falls and unemployment rises. Lower production triggers more defaults and a further decline in asset values, and the cycle continues.

The debt supercycle and zero lower bound accounts of prolonged periods of economic weakness are not mutually exclusive. Using the zero lower bound as a trigger for expansionary legal policy will effectively respond to some financial crises because episodes of the zero lower bound often follow financial crises (as in the Great Depression and the Great Recession).

The debt supercycle and zero lower bound explanations are not equivalent, however. According to the debt supercycle theory, economies should suffer prolonged recessions after financial crises even if interest rates do not go down to zero. Advocates of the debt supercycle theory of prolonged recessions should support expansionary legal policy in the aftermath of every financial crisis, even if interest rates do not go to zero.

Although interest rates may exceed zero during a financial crisis, monetary policy loses efficacy. Even if the central bank lowers short-term interest rates during a financial crisis, rates for ordinary borrowers may not follow short-term rates downward because the primary transmitters of interest rate decreases into the economy, financial institutions, do not work effectively. Likewise, a decline in the value of collateral renders many willing borrowers ineligible to borrow at any interest rate. As a result, expansionary monetary policy cannot quickly mitigate recessions after a financial crisis. Finding other stimulus tools, such as legal policy, therefore becomes more urgent.

Like episodes of the zero lower bound, the aftermath of financial crises lingers. Reinhart and Rogoff document that, after a typical financial crisis, "unemployment rises for almost five years."[11] They also show that, even after unemployment stops rising, "growth is sometimes quite modest in the aftermath" of a recession resulting from a financial crisis. The United States, for example, actually beat expectations in this regard during the Great

Recession, with peak unemployment in 2010, but unemployment remained well above pre–Great Recession norms—indicating deficient aggregate demand—through 2015.

With recoveries delayed after financial crises, law offers a realistic stimulus instrument in their aftermath. Even though expansionary legal policy moves slowly, it can operate effectively at horizons of five years or more.

Financial crises are also relatively easy to identify—though not as easy as the zero lower bound. Objective indicators of financial crises include the failure of many financial institutions and an increase in "spreads" (differences in interest rates) between ordinary borrowers and sovereign borrowers. In order to justify expansionary legal policy in the long recessions that follow financial crises, regulators and judges should demonstrate that a financial crisis has occurred by pointing to these indicators.

Fiscal Policy Is Hamstrung

At the zero lower bound or after a financial crisis, conventional monetary policy cannot stimulate moribund economies. As we've seen, the standard macroeconomic policy prescription in such cases is expansionary fiscal policy. But expansionary fiscal policy is limited by a lack of fiscal space, deficit restrictions, and legislative gridlock.

Expansionary legal policy offers the most utility when both monetary and fiscal policy are hamstrung. As a result, law and macroeconomic efforts should be most active when fiscal policy is not responding to the zero lower bound. If fiscal policy is responding to the zero lower bound with stimulus, then law and regulation should stand back because the legislature—a more democratically legitimate instrument of government than judges and regulators—is addressing the problem of inadequate aggregate demand and excess unemployment.

In the right conditions, even the legislature may pursue expansionary legal policy. When market conditions or constitutional restrictions prevent fiscal stimulus, even an active legislature lacks tools to stimulate aggregate demand. In response, the legislature should consider legal reforms that stimulate aggregate demand. In the aftermath of many previous financial crises, for example, governments implemented large-scale debt relief laws (discussed in Chapter 11).

Policies enacted by the legislature enjoy maximum democratic legitimacy and are therefore preferable to expansionary legal policy implemented by regulators or judges. Relying on the legislature, however, also limits policymaking expertise and subjects expansionary legal policy to legislative gridlock. To mitigate these costs, legislatures routinely grant regulators and judges wide discretion over some decisions—discretion that can be used to pursue expansionary legal policy.

Where Regulators and Judges Already Exercise a Lot of Discretion

In order to minimize opportunism, respect for the rule of law and democratic legitimacy, regulators or judges should pursue expansionary legal policy when they are implementing vague legal "standards" rather than applying clear legal "rules." "The national interest"—the standard the U.S. State Department applied to Keystone—is an already vague test that enables regulators or judges to consider context. Adding macroeconomics to "the national interest" with respect to Keystone adds little risk that isn't already there. As a result, adding macroeconomic considerations to an already blurry standard neither adds much risk of opportunism nor does it arrogate extra power to unelected regulators and judges.

Modifying a rule, by contrast, makes opportunism more likely. Rules dictate how a legal actor is supposed to make decisions without reference to context. For example, a speed limit indicates that any speed over the limit is unlawful, even if the driver is driving safely. As such, a speed limit restricts police discretion and thus the opportunity for police to indulge their preferences in enforcement. (Because speed limits are not uniformly enforced, these benefits are attenuated in any case.)

If we tried to stimulate the economy by changing rigorous enforcement of speed limits to allow police to consider the business cycle effects of enforcement in addition to a driver's speed, then expansionary legal policy makes opportunism easier. With the introduction of expansionary legal policy, our ability to evaluate police action diminishes, making it easier for opportunism to go undetected. As a result, expansionary legal policy should be implemented by adjusting standards rather than adjusting rules.

Out-of-Sync Jurisdictions in a Currency Union

We have seen in Chapter 3 that stabilization options are limited in jurisdictions that are part of currency unions—such as U.S. states, Eurozone countries, and countries that maintain a currency peg. These jurisdictions do not control monetary policy, which is subordinated to the purpose of facilitating trade.

In these jurisdictions, monetary policy is controlled by a central bank for the entire currency union or by the central bank of the country that maintains the reference currency. If, say, a jurisdiction's economic cycle is attuned to the cycle of the whole currency union, then there is little cost associated with the loss of monetary policy. If, however, the jurisdiction's economy is poorly correlated with the economy of the whole currency union, then the jurisdiction may suffer for the loss of monetary control.

If the jurisdiction is suffering from a recession when the rest of the currency union's economy is thriving, then contractionary monetary policy (appropriate for the currency union as a whole) may entrench the recession and cause hysteresis and political unrest. Moreover, constitutional budget restrictions limit the ability of many jurisdictions, such as U.S. states and Eurozone countries, to pursue fiscal stabilization. To avoid a painful downturn, the jurisdiction should consider expansionary legal policy in spite of its institutional flaws. And if the jurisdiction is thriving when the rest of the currency union's economy is struggling, then the jurisdiction should consider contractionary legal policy in order to mitigate the costs of the boom.

The experience of North Dakota during the Great Recession exemplifies this sort of poor correlation, the only condition in which contractionary legal policy makes sense. In the midst of the Great Recession, the state underwent a shale oil boom, which induced labor and housing shortages, traffic congestion, environmental degradation, and sharply higher prices there.[12]

Monetary policy did not respond to the strain caused by the isolated boom, because the economy in most of the United States was stumbling, so the Fed kept rates low—at zero, in fact. North Dakota's fiscal response was also hamstrung by a combination of public need and poor design. While the state ran budget surpluses at the height of the boom, it also reduced taxes, stimulating rather than contracting aggregate demand. Thanks in part to the tax cuts, the state faced a crunching deficit after the oil price collapsed in late 2014 and early 2015.[13] North Dakota's hands were also tied in terms of government spending. Cuts would have reduced aggregate demand, but doing so would have been extremely difficult. The boom put great strain on the provision of public goods; curtailing them in the midst of the boom would have induced a lot of suffering and political backlash.

Lacking fiscal means of restraining an overheating economy during the boom, and lacking control over monetary decisions, North Dakota should have considered contractionary legal policy. For instance, the state could have imposed more exacting standards for obtaining pipeline permits during the boom. (Although the Keystone pipeline did not go through North Dakota, other pipeline proposals were put forward, including the controversial Dakota Access Pipeline.) A slower pace of pipeline construction would have reduced inflationary pressures and enabled the North Dakota labor and housing markets, as well as investment in public goods such as roads and schools, to catch up to the sudden increase in demand caused by the oil boom.

Unlike at the zero lower bound, identifying and remedying inappropriate macroeconomic policy in a currency union requires macroeconomic expertise from regulators and judges. They must know (1) whether the jurisdiction is in recession or boom, (2) whether the currency union as a whole is in recession or boom, and (3) whether macroeconomic policy is inappropriate in the jurisdiction as a result of a mismatch in business cycles. In addition, the regulator or judge needs to be confident that the macroeconomic mismatch will linger in order to justify turning to legal policy.

Because there are no simple and verifiable indicators for all of these variables, the risks of opportunistic or arbitrary law loom larger than they do at the zero lower bound. As a result, regulators and judges should engage in legal policy stabilization to respond to macroeconomic conditions in out-of-sync jurisdictions in a currency union only if macroeconomic conditions in the jurisdiction are truly dire.

I've argued for expansionary legal policy at the zero lower bound, in the aftermath of financial crises, and when a jurisdiction's economy is wildly out of sync with the economy of the rest of a currency union. But I've provided only one example of expansionary legal policy—approving the Keystone pipeline in 2011 but not in 2017. And even Keystone represents a hypothetical, rather than real, example of using law for macroeconomic ends.

In Chapter 10, I focus on two periods in which macroeconomic policy often meant law rather than fiscal or monetary policy—the New Deal of Franklin D. Roosevelt in response to the Great Depression and the price controls implemented by President Nixon in response to the "Great Inflation" of the 1970s. The New Deal was a partial success, while the price controls mostly failed. These cases show us that (1) law can be an important tool of macroeconomic policy and (2) the institutional weaknesses of law as a macroeconomic policy instrument mean that we should use law sparingly.

TEN

Law and Macroeconomics:
Lessons from History

L aw and regulation played almost no role in the macroeconomic policy response to the Great Recession. But policymakers have not always spurned law, as we'll explore in this chapter. The New Deal response to the Great Depression consisted largely of legal interventions rather than fiscal stimulus. And the U.S. "stagflation" of the 1970s was met with the full force of law. As inflation exceeded 6 percent a year, Congress authorized the Economic Stabilization Act of 1970. Using his authority under this Act, President Nixon imposed a set of wage and price controls. In both cases, macroeconomic challenges prompted legal responses.

Why have we forgotten about law as a macroeconomic policy tool? The simplest explanation is that previous legal interventions for macroeconomic purposes have not worked well. Price controls failed during the 1970s. The record of the New Deal attempts at expansionary legal policy was better. Although the Supreme Court ruled the National Recovery Administration—the centerpiece of the efforts to stimulate the U.S. economy through legal means during the Great Depression—unconstitutional, the U.S. economy dramatically rebounded shortly after Congress enacted the (mostly legal) reforms of the first "hundred days" of Franklin D. Roosevelt's presidential administration in 1933. Even the New Deal efforts at law and macroeconomics, however, did not reflect the macroeconomic "state of the art."

For the most part, I agree that price controls and central planning are like magic bullets that too often miss their targets. But I submit that we should not therefore eschew macroeconomic tools of law entirely. Legal intervention is potentially dangerous, but it can also provide a powerful remedy. The New Dealers had the right intuitions about turning to law and macroeconomics at the zero lower bound. Indeed, even their unfocused attempts at legal stimulus worked impressively from 1933 to 1937. If future law and macroeconomic interventions enjoy better grounding in macroeconomic theory and directly adjust aggregate demand in conditions when other macro tools are wanting, then we can expect law and macroeconomics to become an invaluable policy option.

The Law and Macroeconomics of the New Deal

Whereas lawmakers balked at expansionary legal policy during the Great Recession, such an approach was almost self-evident to President Franklin D. Roosevelt and other New Dealers amid the Great Depression. The signature piece of legislation passed during the first hundred days of Roosevelt's administration was the National Industrial Recovery Act (NIRA). Upon the passage of the NIRA, Roosevelt declared:

> History probably will record the National Industrial Recovery Act as the most important and far-reaching legislation ever enacted by the American Congress. It represents a supreme effort to stabilize for all time the many factors which make for the prosperity of the nation and the preservation of American standards.

NIRA inaugurated sweeping legal changes. The goal of many was to increase prices in order to facilitate spending: if people expected prices to rise in the future, then real interest rates at the zero lower bound would decrease even if nominal rates stayed at zero; with real rates lower, spending would increase. To this end, NIRA suspended antitrust laws that prevented the formation of cartels. It strengthened labor unions. And it created the National Recovery Administration, an agency charged with reducing unemployment by imposing standards of fair conduct on most employers. *Time* magazine named the Administration's chief, Hugh Johnson, "Man of the Year" in 1933.

President Roosevelt and Congress also passed other laws and regulations with important macroeconomic effects during the first hundred days. Upon taking office, FDR declared a "bank holiday," temporarily closing banks to prevent bank runs. Congress ratified FDR's declaration with the passage of the Emergency Banking Act shortly thereafter. It worked. The bank holiday effectively suspended depositors' contractual rights to their money, but this extraordinary invasion of contractual rights "ended the bank runs that had plagued the Great Depression."[1] The Emergency Banking Act also weakened the United States' adherence to the gold standard, decreasing deflationary pressures.

The Supreme Court ruled NIRA unconstitutional in *A.L.A. Schechter Poultry Corp. v. United States* because the law delegated too much congressional authority to the National Recovery Administration.[2] In addition, the Court held that the legislation violated Congress's powers under the commerce clause of the Constitution, reasoning the Court disavowed just two years later.

Even after the demise of NIRA, the United States continued to pursue law and macroeconomics. As Steven Ramirez explains, much of the New Deal legal apparatus, such as the introduction of corporate income taxation and the National Labor Relations Act of 1935 (NLRA), sought to stimulate the economy.[3] As originally conceived by President Roosevelt, the corporate income tax reached only cash rather than profits and encouraged corporations to spend rather than hoard cash.[4] The NLRA aimed to empower unions so that workers' wages would increase. This would raise inflation expectations, stimulating spending.

Many have criticized NIRA—and, to a lesser extent, the NLRA—on microeconomic grounds. In ordinary times, suspending antitrust laws reduces output, decreasing the economy's potential even as prices increase.

For many, the New Deal policies also appeared flawed from a macroeconomic perspective. Notably, most of the legal interventions did not aim to stimulate aggregate demand directly. In a 1933 open letter to President Roosevelt, John Maynard Keynes acknowledged that raising the price level through the suspension of antitrust law might indirectly stimulate aggregate demand in theory but criticized Roosevelt's economic policy for excessive reliance on this effect.[5] Instead, Keynes preferred policies that directly increased aggregate demand. He argued that increases in "governmental expenditure," not increases in the price level, were the "prime mover" of recovery. Keynes wrote of "the failure of [FDR's] administration to organize any material increase in . . . expenditure during your first six months in office."

The early New Deal thus looks like a failure on both macroeconomic and microeconomic grounds. But we should not be too hasty in condemning this early example of expansionary legal policy. In the short run, NIRA and the other legal interventions of the first hundred days dramatically increased inflation expectations and stimulated spending.[6] The U.S. economy, which shrank an incredible 30 percent from 1929 to 1933, rebounded noticeably in 1933–1936, growing by more than 10 percent per year before slumping again in late 1937. Although NIRA likely decreased economic potential over the long run, Gauti Eggertsson argues that the U.S. economy was not constrained by potential in 1933 but rather by inadequate demand. As a result, NIRA's indirect aggregate demand-enhancing effects outweighed its harm to long-term potential.

I do not disagree with those accusing New Dealers of making legal interventions that imposed considerable microeconomic harm. But this is not a reason to condemn law and macroeconomics generally. From the macro perspective, the New Deal was at least a short-term success. In spite of their flaws, New Deal laws helped U.S. output rebound. Other legal and regulatory interventions, which directly increase aggregate demand while imposing smaller microeconomic harms, should offer economies even more stimulus than NIRA did, without NIRA's long-term harms to potential output.

The Rise and Fall of Price Controls

After World War II, law continued to play a vital role in macroeconomic policy. As described in Chapter 3, the Bretton Woods system of international macroeconomics was premised on capital controls, which subordinated fundamental principles of law, such as the enforcement of contracts, to macroeconomic needs. By using law to restrict international capital flows, the Bretton Woods regime enabled countries to enjoy stable exchange rates while retaining control over monetary policy.

Bretton Woods came to an end with the "Nixon Shock" delivered on August 15, 1971. Unwilling to undertake the painful macroeconomic reforms needed to support an overvalued dollar, President Nixon suspended the United States' participation in the international currency system. But the suspension of Bretton Woods did not end the reliance on law and macroeconomics. Instead, President Nixon replaced one law and macroeconomics regime—capital controls—with another—price controls. In the same speech that suspended the Bretton Woods currency system, Nixon imposed price controls authorized by the Economic Stabilization Act of 1970. President Nixon's Executive Order 11615 sought to tame inflation by initially freezing all U.S. prices and wages for a period of ninety days. After the ninety days ended, all increases in wages and prices needed to be approved by governmental "pay boards" and "price commissions."

Wage and price controls seemed to succeed at first. Just before the imposition of price controls, inflation exceeded 4 percent a month on an annualized basis. After the price freeze, inflation quickly fell below 4 percent. In mid-1972, during the second phase of price controls, inflation dropped under 3 percent.

But by 1974, annual inflation had exploded to more than 10 percent. It remained high into the 1980s. Consumers faced shortages of gasoline, meat, and other goods and were forced to queue for them.[7]

To reduce inflation, the government finally turned to monetary, not legal, policy. Under the leadership of Chair Paul Volcker, the Fed tightened monetary policy sharply, raising short-term interest rates from roughly 11 percent in 1979 to 20 percent in 1981. Inflation in the United States plummeted from more than 13 percent annually in 1981 to slightly over 3 percent in 1983. Since then, it has never exceeded 5 percent. But taming inflation came at the high cost of successive severe recessions, with unemployment reaching its post–World War II peak in 1982.

Criticisms of Wage and Price Controls

Wage and price controls are potentially powerful tools of contractionary legal policy, at least in the short run. But price controls do not offer the only means of quelling high inflation. In addition, price controls did not prove effective over the long run. Contractionary monetary policy, and not price controls, quelled rampant inflation in the United States and elsewhere. And price controls also caused significant microeconomic harms. Thus, the failure of price controls supports the conclusion that we should consider using law for macroeconomic ends only when monetary alternatives are inaccessible. Indeed, price controls illustrate many of the institutional weaknesses of law and macroeconomics.

Lack of Expertise

Experts, who know that inflation is caused by a money supply that is expanding too quickly and aggregate demand that exceeds capacity at the current inflation level, know that price controls are not a long-term solution to inflation. But price controls offer an intuitively direct "solution" to the problem of rising prices. As a result, nonexperts engaged in law may prefer price controls to better alternatives for controlling inflation.

Inequity and Microeconomic Inefficiency

When we use law for macroeconomic purposes, we sacrifice goals of equity, justice, and microeconomic efficiency. If the sacrifice is too great, then we should refrain from using law as a macro policy lever. That was the case in the 1970s: price controls imposed excessive efficiency and equity costs.

Wage and price controls necessarily come at great cost because they degrade the capacity of the price system to do its essential task: coordinate the market economy.[8] When coordination breaks down, shortages and rationing result. These impose serious microeconomic harm. (If the price mechanism perfectly coordinated the economy, then there would be no recessions, also known as coordination failures. Thus, price is not a perfect coordination mechanism. But price works better than price controls.)

To reduce these harms, sophisticated regulators developed clever price control mechanisms that restricted average prices without undermining the price system entirely. But these mechanisms introduced complications in addition to improving incentives. In particular, complicated price control mechanisms wreaked havoc with contract terms and engendered considerable litigation.

The body formed to implement price controls in the United States in the 1970s, the Cost of Living Council, did its best to keep a lid on prices while retaining incentives for producers to produce. Although it might have placed a price ceiling on all oil produced in the United States, a simple price cap would have reduced incentives to produce additional oil. Instead, the regulator separated oil production into two categories and capped only one of them. "Old oil"—the amount produced in the previous year—was subject to a price freeze. If an oil producer produced the same amount of oil in the current year as in the previous year, then all of the producer's production for this year would be considered "old oil" and subject to a price cap. In order to create incentives to produce additional oil, however, the price of "new oil" was uncontrolled. A producer's new oil equaled the excess of this year's oil production over last year's production. Additional production was therefore rewarded with a higher price than steady production. To give even stronger incentives to increase production, each barrel of new oil enabled the producer to relabel a barrel of its old oil as new. If a producer produced one more barrel of oil than last year, then it would be allowed to sell two barrels of oil at an uncontrolled price (one barrel of new oil and one barrel of old oil relabeled as "new").

This creative pricing system aimed both to limit inflation and to stimulate oil production. By regulating the price of old oil for which producers already had the capacity to produce, the Council hoped to limit inflation. But with the price of new oil uncontrolled, firms were also incentivized to keep producing in spite of the price caps. Indeed, the ability to relabel old oil as new made producers' incentives to increase production stronger than they would have been in an economy without any price controls. If the ingenious scheme worked, producers would have every reason to increase their output, but the average price of all barrels of oil (new and old) would be lower than it would have been without price controls.

Although it looks good on paper, the scheme proved less viable than its architects hoped. In order to mitigate the harm caused by price controls, the Council needed to calculate the value of old oil for every producer and measure its new oil production, a crushing administrative task. The system also created inefficiencies and inequities, as illustrated by a contract law battle between Gulf Oil and Eastern Airlines.[9]

Before the imposition of price controls, Eastern signed a contract indexing the purchase price of Gulf oil at certain airports to an oil price measure calculated by Platt's Inc.'s OilGram. When price controls were imposed, Platt's had to revise its indexing method. Platt's decided to index according to old oil, which slanted the contract in Eastern's favor. Now the airline could buy oil from Gulf at the old oil price, making Gulf oil cheaper than oil from many other suppliers at the same airports, who were selling new oil. Instead of turning the profit it otherwise would have, Gulf wound up losing from the contract, a direct result of the price controls.

In addition to creating an unfair outcome, the contract incentivized inefficiency. Before the price controls, Eastern did not usually fill its tanks with Gulf fuel at airports subject to the contract. A full tank added weight to the airplane, reducing efficiency. But when the price controls artificially lowered the contracted price of Gulf fuel, Eastern began filling its tanks when it had access to Gulf's product. Gulf's fuel was so cheap that Eastern didn't mind wasting it. Gulf eventually took Eastern to court over the contract, and in 1975 a federal court decided that Eastern could continue to fill its airplanes with Gulf oil at the desirable price. This inefficiency and the litigation that ensued were all direct results of the price controls.

Uncertain Effects

The effects of price controls proved volatile and unpredictable. They may have been beneficial in the short run but failed to restrain inflation over the longer term. If we cannot rely on price controls to restrain inflation over the long run, then we should refrain from using them for purposes of long-run macroeconomic policy.

Political Opportunism

Like any legislative effort, price controls are subject to political calculation. Such was the case in Congress, according to William N. Walker, the general counsel of the Cost of Living Council. "Congressional Democrats had championed the Economic Stabilization Act, enacted in 1970 over Nixon's opposition," Walker wrote. "Congress assumed a conservative President like Nixon would never invoke the authority and they intended to use it to embarrass him."[10] In turn, Nixon's decision to implement the authorized controls "was aimed at deflecting Democratic criticism of his economic performance as the countdown began to the 1972 elections," Walker alleges.

The imposition of price controls was politically popular, but it harmed the economy, without restraining inflation. Price controls and other such instruments, which enable politicians to impose long-run harms in exchange for short-run benefits, should be discouraged. Indeed, price controls epitomize the high institutional costs that may be associated with using law for macroeconomic ends.

Reconsidering Wage and Price Controls: The Case of Greece

While wage and price controls proved costly and ineffective forms of contractionary legal policy, even they are worth considering if the macroeconomic alternatives are sufficiently dire. Under the right conditions (which will be rare), price controls offer a powerful tool for overcoming price rigidities that keep output below potential in depressed economies. If even the most unlikely tools of law and macroeconomics, such as price controls, occasionally have their uses, then we should never dismiss law and macroeconomic interventions absolutely. Rather, we need to compare legal solutions to macroeconomic problems with fiscal and monetary alternatives.

Greece is a signature case. The term "Great Recession" fails to convey Greece's struggles from 2009 to the present. Unemployment there peaked at a remarkable 29 percent in 2013 and remained well above 20 percent into 2018. Seven years into the Great Recession, Greek output was 26 percent smaller in real terms than at its pre-recession height. For comparison, U.S. output during the Great Depression bottomed out at 25 percent below its peak. Seven years after the onset of the Great Depression, real output in the United States had fully recovered. Greek social indicators, such as plummeting birthrates and a sharp increase in incidence of depression and suicide, testify to the human cost of Greece's economic tragedy.

Many economists blame Greece's astronomic unemployment rates on prevailing wages. Greeks who do work are paid too much in relation to overall labor productivity, and those who don't work demand too much to get back into the labor market. Since Milton Friedman's seminal analysis of this issue, the conventional macroeconomic prescription for a country in Greece's position has been currency devaluation, which would be accomplished by expansionary monetary policy.[11] By devaluing its currency, Greece would, in a single stroke, make its labor and capital more competitive, enabling it to increase exports and mitigate the depression.

However, as a member of the Eurozone, Greece does not control its own currency. It cannot devalue its currency in order to make its economy competitive with its neighbors'. Instead of devaluing its currency, Greece was forced to "internally devalue" by allowing wages and other prices to decline. A market-led process of wage declines, however, moves fitfully and painfully, leading to further reduction in output. Because the market system cannot coordinate rapid downward wage and price adjustment, inefficiencies such as sky-high unemployment also follow. As Friedman explained, "Wage rates tend to be among the less flexible prices. In consequence, . . . a policy of permitting . . . [wages] to decline is likely to produce unemployment rather than, or in addition to, wage decreases."

Greeks have borne witness to the accuracy of Friedman's prediction. Instead of lowering wages, many Greek employers chose to keep nominal wages fixed and instead cut employment. Prices and wages have since decreased, but the process has been agonizingly slow and economically painful.

Even with currency devaluation off the table, Greece need not have left macroeconomic management to market forces: there are other ways of combating the notorious downward inflexibility of wages. Expansionary legal policy was still available. And law—in particular, price controls—offered yet another alternative, an instrument for lowering real wages and prices rapidly and in a more coordinated fashion than isolated market actors could achieve. If Greece had passed a law requiring all nominal wages, prices, and domestic debts to be briefly reduced by a significant amount—say, 10 percent for three months—then real wages and prices would have adjusted as quickly as if Greece had devalued its currency. (A simpler alternative would cut wages by 10 percent, but leave other prices unregulated.) In one stroke, a regime of price controls would have made Greek labor and production more competitive relative to those of other Eurozone countries.[12]

There would have been, as one might expect, trade-offs. Any devaluation—whether through currency devaluation or legally imposed deflation—puts the financial system at risk. And devaluing via price controls adds an additional complication. Greek banks' domestic assets would lose value, but foreign liabilities wouldn't, taxing the banks' solvency. A financial meltdown would, of course, exacerbate the depression. In addition, Greek products included inputs from outside the country. The cost of these inputs would not have changed, even as the domestic revenues of those firms would lose value. Either Greek businesses would have to bear this painful shock—which might cause many to collapse—or be able to adjust their individual price deflation to reflect the foreign component of their inputs, which would make legally imposed deflation very complex. More broadly, devaluation squeezes the profits of importers who charge consumers in domestic currency but pay their suppliers in foreign currency. Finally, there is no simple way to determine what debt is domestic, and therefore subject to price controls, and what is foreign. This means that lawyers would have had to draw fine lines between what accounts are subject to price controls and what are not. To mitigate these harms, Greek price controls would have needed the cooperation of the European Central Bank and Greece's most important creditors.

But desperate times called for desperate measures. Greece was suffering an unprecedented economic cataclysm, with both supply-side (uncompetitive labor costs) and demand-side (aggregate demand short of supply capacity) dimensions. European monetary policy was stuck at the zero lower bound, limiting monetary stimulus. Greek fiscal policy also had no scope for stimulus, as national debt levels were astoundingly high. And in spite of the horrendous costs, neither Greece nor the "troika" of the IMF, ECB, and European Commission were willing to accept a Greek exit from the Eurozone, which would enable direct devaluation. (Like a legally imposed domestic deflation, "Grexit" would also require difficult determinations of what assets would remain denominated in Euros versus drachmas.)

Legally mandated deflation didn't have to be perfect. It just had to be better than internal devaluation, which proved incredibly costly. Mandated deflation would have used law to coordinate a rapid change in prices, potentially facilitating less painful adjustment to the problem of wages disproportionate to productivity. And unlike the Nixon-era price controls in the United States, which targeted inflationary symptoms rather than inflation's causes, mandated deflation in Greece would have directly addressed one of the central problems of Greek macroeconomic underperformance: the downward rigidity of prices.

Amid the worst economic crisis in modern history, a short period of legally mandated deflation, so long as it was developed cooperatively by Greece and the troika, was probably worth the accompanying risks.

As we've seen in this chapter, law and regulation plays a more prominent, if checkered, role in the history of macroeconomic policy than many appreciate. The New Deal's primary response to the Great Depression was legal, not monetary or fiscal. An extraordinary incursion into contract law (the bank holiday) facilitated the end of a series of bank runs. And even though the NIRA increased aggregate demand only indirectly (by raising inflation expectations to encourage more spending in the present), inflation expectations and spending rose rapidly after its passage, contributing to a remarkable recovery.

In the aftermath of World War II, industrialized democracies created an international macroeconomics regime with law—in the form of capital controls—at its heart. The Bretton Woods era witnessed historically unprecedented growth rates in industrialized democracies and rapid increases in international trade (facilitated by the fixed exchange rates established by Bretton Woods). Although there are many causes of this economic miracle, the success of the Bretton Woods economy proves that a macroeconomic regime that leans heavily on law is consistent with a "Golden Age of Capitalism."

Given this historical success, the choice of law—price controls—to address the primary macroeconomic ailment of the 1970s—inflation—looks less surprising. Unlike the New Deal and Bretton Woods, price controls failed as macroeconomic policy. They harmed microeconomic efficiency without controlling inflation.

Wage and price controls demonstrate the power and the peril of law and macroeconomics. By intervening in the price system, law can respond directly to the most pressing macroeconomic problems. At its best, law can coordinate macroeconomic rebalancing when other tools for such coordination, such as monetary or exchange-rate policy, prove wanting. But given the major downsides of wage and price controls, they should be used only when the macroeconomic policy toolkit is almost bare, as in Greece from 2010 to 2017.

During its long history, legal policy stabilization has been plagued by the absence of theoretical grounding. Although the NIRA and the Nixon-era price controls sought to improve macroeconomic conditions, macroeconomic theory did not guide their design. (Bretton Woods, by contrast, enjoyed expert macroeconomic input. Keynes himself was one of its chief architects.) Without theoretical guidance, neither NIRA nor price controls implemented programs whose primary effect was to adjust aggregate demand, compromising the effectiveness of each policy.

Effective law and macroeconomics requires more attention to macroeconomic theory. In Chapter 11, I develop three types of expansionary legal policy that increase aggregate demand without causing microeconomic distortions as severe as suspending antitrust law or limiting the use of price as a coordination mechanism. These policies, and others like them, offer stimulus alternatives when monetary and fiscal policy are hamstrung.

ELEVEN

Expansionary Legal Policy Options

In this chapter, I apply the lessons about law and macroeconomics developed in the previous chapters. I formulate novel legal tools that stimulate aggregate demand without requiring comprehensive legislative action or increasing government budget deficits. These tools provide options for stimulating moribund economies at the zero lower bound.

The tools I describe here—countercyclical utility-rate regulation, adjusting debtor–creditor law for the business cycle, and changing the law of remedies with the business cycle—do not exhaust the universe of expansionary legal policy options. Almost every law and regulatory policy could be modified to stimulate (or depress) aggregate demand. Instead, the tools illustrate how law and regulation can provide economically meaningful stimulus when monetary and fiscal policy are hamstrung.

One important category of expansionary legal policy that I sidestep here is interventions in the labor market. Legal interventions in the labor market, such as minimum wage laws, could have important effects on unemployment and aggregate demand. When the economy is producing below capacity, changes to labor law offer a potentially powerful tool of expansionary legal policy.

Changing labor law, however, causes two countervailing effects. Consider the effect of lowering minimum wages at the zero lower bound. Lower minimum wages cheapen low wage labor, potentially reducing unemployment and thus increasing aggregate demand. Lower minimum wages, however, also reduce the purchasing power of minimum wage workers who would be employed at any minimum wage level. Reducing the income of these cash-strapped workers reduces aggregate demand. These effects may cancel out. Indeed, we see exactly this with respect to unemployment insurance. The best empirical evidence suggests that the unemployment-increasing effects of work disincentives caused by more generous unemployment benefits offset the unemployment-decreasing effects of the increase in spending associated with higher benefits.[1] As a result, labor market interventions like unemployment insurance offer less potent stimulus tools than might be suspected. (They may be highly desirable on other grounds, however.) I therefore focus my attention on expansionary legal policy measures that stimulate the economy in a more theoretically and empirically robust manner.

Countercyclical Utility Regulatory Policy

Distributing electricity, natural gas, water, and other essentials to consumers is expensive. Much of the cost is incurred in building the distribution network itself; once installation is complete, the costs of supply go down considerably. When, say, an electricity grid is established, the marginal costs are just the cost of producing the electricity consumed. But the massive fixed costs of building the production and distribution network means there is little economic sense in multiple suppliers competing for the same consumers.

These qualities place utilities in an unusual category: "natural monopolies." Typically, laws preventing anticompetitive practices would intervene to protect consumers from monopolist utilities. After all, monopolies inefficiently reduce output and raise prices. But because it would be extraordinarily expensive to develop multiple distribution networks for the same service, governments instead allow natural monopolies to persist and regulate their prices to reduce inefficiencies. Utilities gain the security of local monopoly and steady returns on capital, and consumers gain from government oversight to prevent price gouging and efficient provision of distribution networks. When utility regulators work effectively, utilities charge prices reflecting the average costs of supply and distribution, not monopoly power.

This is, in theory, an elegant solution to what could be a vexing problem. But the current U.S. utility regulation framework process has perverse macroeconomic effects. Specifically, utility prices rise when aggregate demand is low, further reducing consumer spending and exacerbating sluggish demand.

Instead of exacerbating business cycles, utility regulators should mitigate them, adjusting utility rates with an eye on their aggregate demand effects.

Today's Utility-Rate Regulation

As it stands, utilities are regulated according to a "cost of service" framework. Utilities periodically propose rates to regulators, who then set the rates so that utility investors earn a competitive, but not excessive, return on their capital. By providing a competitive return, regulators enable the capital formation necessary to construct and maintain high fixed-cost distribution networks.

Regulators scour the market to decide what prices are acceptable and assess utilities' investment levels to ensure they are reasonable. Otherwise, utilities could raise profits by undertaking unnecessary investment to justify higher prices.

Many considerations underlie final utility pricing. For instance, the state of Connecticut prescribes that its Public Utilities Regulatory Authority account for "economy, efficiency and care for public safety and energy security" and "promote economic development within the state with consideration for energy and water conservation [and] energy efficiency." Furthermore, the law stipulates that the "level and structure of rates be sufficient, but no more than sufficient, to allow public service companies to cover their operating costs including, but not limited to, appropriate staffing levels, and capital costs, to attract needed capital and to maintain their financial integrity."[2]

This system makes for unusual pricing. Usually, when demand for a commodity falls, prices drop over the medium- to long-term. But utilities are different. When demand goes down, as in recessions, prices don't naturally follow. In fact, the opposite happens. In order to cover their costs amid lower sales, utilities may ask to raise prices. This appears to be what happened in the United States during the Great Recession and the recession of 2001. As Figure 11.1 shows, U.S. electric power output during both downturns fell, but retail prices rose sharply before stabilizing. Unregulated wholesale electricity prices, by contrast, declined dramatically between 2008 and 2010. In March–April 2010, average wholesale electricity prices in two deregulated U.S. markets (Massachusetts and California) languished more than 50 percent below their March–April 2008 levels.[3]

From the perspective of stabilizing aggregate demand, this price pattern is unfortunate. Utilities tend to be necessities; most consumers can cut down

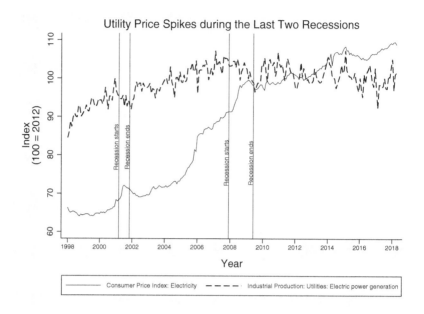

Figure 11.1 Observe the rapid increase in utility prices coinciding with the beginning of the last two recessions.

Data Source: U.S. Bureau of Labor Statistics, "Consumer Price Index—All Urban Consumers—Electricity," retrieved from Federal Reserve Bank of St. Louis, https://fred .stlouisfed.org/series/CUSR0000SEHF01; Board of Governors of the Federal Reserve System, "Industrial Production: Utilities: Electric Power Generation," retrieved from Federal Reserve Bank of St. Louis; https://fred.stlouisfed.org/series/IPG22111S.

only slightly when prices increase. Higher prices for utilities therefore act like a tax hike: just about everyone feels the pain. Utility price spikes reduce discretionary income and, thus, aggregate demand.

Business Cycle–Sensitive Utility-Rate Regulation

Utility regulators could work differently. They could account for aggregate demand when considering rate proposals. At the zero lower bound, regulators could reject rate increases. And if their quadrennial reviews of utility prices happen to occur during a liquidity trap, they could demand lower rates. After the slump is over, regulators could then allow higher rates to enable the utility to cover its cost of capital over the business cycle.[4]

Reducing utility rates at the zero lower bound raises the discretionary income of utility consumers. With less spending on utilities, consumers spend more on everything else. If utilities respond to lower rates by reducing their cash holdings, then lower rates in a liquidity trap directly stimulate the economy. Instead of cash sitting on utility balance sheets, aggregate demand increases as consumers spend much of their increased discretionary income.

While business-cycle sensitivity should raise output and employment at the zero lower bound, it doesn't affect output in ordinary times. This may seem counterintuitive, because higher utility prices impede aggregate demand in ordinary economic times. But in ordinary times, aggregate demand does not determine output. Interest rates and prices adjust to aggregate demand fluctuations, leaving output and unemployment unchanged.

If utilities respond to lower rates by reducing dividend payments at the zero lower bound, however, then we can no longer be certain that business cycle–sensitive utility regulation stimulates the economy. Utility consumers spend more at the zero lower bound, but the utility's investors earn less and spend less. Here, we have to consider the propensity of individual market participants to spend. On balance, we would expect utility customers to have a higher propensity to spend an additional dollar than utility investors. This is because utility customers often do not have access to capital markets and so cannot borrow in hard times. Their spending is therefore determined by their discretionary income. Decreases in utility rates increase discretionary income and should thus increase spending by these customers.

By contrast, utility investors, even the proverbial "widows and orphans," can more easily offset decreases in discretionary income by borrowing or by selling stock rather than reducing consumption. Dividend recipients also tend to be wealthier than the average consumer, increasing their propensity to save an additional dollar rather than spend it on essentials. Indeed, a considerable body of empirical research supports the prediction that the rich spend less of an incremental dollar than the poor.[5] In total, the consumption of utility investors should be less sensitive than the consumption of utility customers to short-run changes in discretionary income at the zero lower bound. As a result, aggregate demand should increase in response to lower utility rates at the zero lower bound.

Because the utility still earns its costs of capital over the course of the business cycle, its investment patterns should not change as a result of business cycle–sensitive regulation. Utility investment depends on long-range risk-adjusted returns, which will be unaffected by the change in regulation. Investment theory requires assets whose returns are more correlated with aggregate income to receive a higher average return. Therefore, the utility's average profits over the business cycle must increase if regulators impose business cycle–sensitive utility regulation. Higher utility profits in ordinary times need to more than offset lower profits at the zero lower bound.

Ultimately, better access to capital markets and investors' higher propensities to save suggest that the stimulus effect of lower utility prices at the zero lower bound will hold, even though utility companies and investors will, for a time, make less money.

Magnitude of Effects

For many families, utility rates matter as much as tax rates or transfer spending. In 2010, households in the second quintile (twentieth to fortieth percentiles) of the U.S. income distribution earned an average of almost $27,000 before taxes. These households spent an average of over $1,600 on electricity and natural gas alone.[6] These households paid an average of slightly over $1,000 in combined U.S. income taxes and social security taxes.[7] Their utility bills exceeded their tax bills. The discrepancy is even larger for the lowest quintile in the income distribution, who spent approximately $1,200 on electricity and natural gas in 2010 but paid only a net $194 in federal income and social security taxes.

Because lower-income and lower-wealth households have high marginal propensities to consume, "conventional wisdom" holds that stimulus programs targeted at these households have "particularly strong" effects.[8] In the United States, the Obama administration prioritized decreases in Social Security taxes as a stimulus measure over other tax reductions because low- to middle-income households pay substantial amounts of Social Security taxes. From 2008 to 2010, net income tax and Social Security payments by households in the first income quintile decreased from $357 to $194. For the second quintile of income, average combined Social Security and income tax payments decreased from $1,667 to $1,082.

These tax reductions provided an important aggregate demand stimulus because these households consumed much of the increase in discretionary income. But business cycle–sensitive utility regulation alone could provide a comparable stimulus. If retail electricity prices decreased by 7 percent between March 2008 to March 2010 instead of increasing by over 7 percent (as they did, in fact), then business cycle–sensitive electricity regulation provides roughly the same stimulus effect as tax reductions for the lowest quintile of the income distribution and almost half as much stimulus as the tax decreases for the second quintile. This one expansionary legal policy tool alone thus offers quantitatively meaningful stimulus at the zero lower bound.

Implementability

Business cycle–sensitive rate regulation complies with the utility regulators' statutory responsibilities, which broadly mirror those assessed in Connecticut: economy, efficiency, and economic development. At the zero lower bound, lower utility rates stimulate the economy, resulting in higher output and lower unemployment. This increases "efficiency" and "development." Raising utility prices outside the zero lower bound enables utility investors to cover their operating and capital costs. Indeed, the higher returns of ordinary times could more than make up for lost profits at the zero lower bound. Under this scheme, utility regulators can maintain fidelity to statutory guidelines without falling afoul of the imperative for investor returns. Because the statutory mandate to regulators is already extremely broad, including another consideration—macroeconomics—cannot be said to obfuscate a previously clear legal process.

Utility regulators enjoy several advantages over legislators when it comes to making business cycle–responsive policy. First, public utility boards are small. Connecticut's authority, for example, consists of only three people. Smaller organizations, such as utility regulators and the Fed, can respond more quickly to changing macroeconomic conditions. Second, public utility regulators tend to be experts about the economics of utility companies. Regulators also can acquire macroeconomic expertise readily through board appointments. Lawmaking bodies, by contrast, gain macroeconomic expertise only if voters elect macroeconomists. Even if no one with macroeconomic expertise is appointed to the regulatory body, professionals on public utility boards can become informed on the macroeconomic implications of utility prices much more rapidly than can the legislature. We should therefore be confident that regulators will be more likely to successfully execute a business cycle–responsive program than a legislative body operating in an ever-changing spending environment.

In the United States, state law largely governs utility rate regulation. Because some of the stimulus effects of lower utility rates spill over into other jurisdictions, state-appointed utility regulators may not champion business cycle–sensitive regulation as much as a national regulator would. Although this is a concern, state-level stimulus programs at the zero lower bound provide important within-state stimulus effects, meaning that regulators will retain substantial incentive to stimulate the economy even if they care only about the within-state effect. Moreover, business cycle–sensitive utility regulation also provides states with a rare tool for macroeconomic policy that is tailored to state, rather than national, economic conditions.

Keeping utility rates down at the zero lower bound and allowing them otherwise to rise in order to maintain profits over the business cycle also shifts risk beneficially. Under this system, utility consumers face less risk and utility investors more. This is a positive outcome because the latter almost certainly have a higher capacity to bear risk. By shifting risk in this way, consumer spending becomes less sensitive to the business cycle, stimulating aggregate demand at the zero lower bound.

While business cycle–sensitive utility regulation offers an empirically important and institutionally realistic option for expansionary legal policy at the zero lower bound, it doesn't come without costs. Such sensitivity adds complexity to the regulatory process. Instead of aiming for a competitive annual rate of return, regulators must seek out rates over the business cycle—a more involved process. This is especially tough because utilities must be allowed a higher average rate of return to compensate for a new undesirable pattern of returns (lower when incomes are down, higher when incomes are up).

But we should not exaggerate the burdens of added complexity. Even today, regulators set utility prices in a complicated environment. As a result, utilities do not, in fact, always earn their cost of capital on an annual basis. But utilities still manage to operate. Moreover, incentive problems (we don't want utilities to expand their capital stock ad infinitum while earning a constant rate of return) and green-energy priorities (we want to encourage the use of environmentally friendly sources of power) mean that utility regulators already must consider many factors when deciding on rates. Asking sophisticated regulators to consider one additional factor—the business cycle—seems a small price to pay for a useful new macroeconomic policy tool.

The Law of Debtors and Creditors

If our goal is to use law to stimulate aggregate demand at the zero lower bound, then it is important to understand why aggregate demand falls in the first place. The sources of a crash in demand point to potential remedies. And a significant source, according to some scholars, is debt. The question for our purposes is how law can be used to modify demand-killing debts.

How Debt Affects Aggregate Demand

Atif Mian and Amir Sufi emphasize the role of mortgage and household debt in causing the Great Recession.[9] They show that the drop in housing values caused precipitous spending declines among borrowers, reducing aggregate demand.

Their basic insight is that debt amplifies the effects of changing home prices on spending and output, so that total consumption declines as a result of the decrease in home values. To see why, let's say we live in a world of savers, who tend to accumulate wealth rather than spend it, and borrowers, who have a high propensity to spend whatever they have. Although the real world is more complicated, this simplification adequately captures the overall economic balance sheet, with lending on one side and borrowing on the other.

Without debt, changes in asset value affect spenders and savers evenly. If housing values go down by 10 percent and nobody owes any debt, then everyone's housing assets shrink by 10 percent. Borrowers and savers reduce spending accordingly. Because borrowers have a higher marginal propensity to spend than savers, they are likely to reduce their consumption by more than savers even though the value of their asset has changed by the same amount.

With debt, however, changes in housing values affect savers and spenders asymmetrically. Suppose a saver lends $80,000 to a borrower to buy a home worth $100,000. The saver's wealth is the value of the loan—$80,000. The borrower's housing wealth is the excess of the house's value over the debt obligation, or $20,000 = $100,000 − $80,000. The $80,000 debt must be paid off in full before the borrower can enjoy any equity. With debt, a 10 percent decline in home values, from $100,000 to $90,000, leaves the value of the saver's assets unchanged. Because the saver enjoys a debt claim to the first $80,000 in house value, the reduction in housing values from $100,000 to $90,000 has no affect. The borrower's wealth, by contrast, falls by half as a result of the 10 percent decline in housing values, from $20,000 = $100,000 − $80,000 to $10,000 = $100,000 − $90,000. Even though housing values have fallen by only 10 percent, the borrower's wealth has fallen by more than the saver because the borrower bears the entire risk of changes in housing values above $80,000.

With debt, the value of the borrower's assets becomes very sensitive to changes in the value of assets overall while the value of the saver's assets becomes relatively stable. Because the borrower has a higher marginal propensity to consume out of wealth than the saver in any case, debt makes the economy more sensitive to changes in asset values. Changes in asset values primarily affect the balance sheets of the people who are most likely to increase or decrease spending in response. As a result, total spending fluctuates more in response to changes in asset values with debt than without.

In general, Mian and Sufi argue, when housing values go down in an economy where debt levels are high, spending declines precipitously because borrowers lose a great deal of wealth. This reduces their spending directly. These losses also limit borrowers' access to credit, reducing their spending further and amplifying the debt supercycle. The resulting shortage of aggregate demand may cause a recession or depression, as in the United States during the Great Recession, according to Mian and Sufi's findings. Spending on durable goods such as cars fell most in areas with the highest levels of mortgage indebtedness and in areas with the greatest decline in housing values.[10]

If debt throttles aggregate demand, then there is a straightforward solution to deep recessions caused by inadequate demand: debt forgiveness.

The distribution of wealth—and therefore spending capacity—between debtors and creditors is largely determined by bankruptcy law. If bankruptcy law and court rulings favor debtors, then spending will be higher than if the law favors creditors, who have lower propensity to spend. In ordinary economic conditions, pro-debtor law would shift the pattern of aggregate demand but would not increase output by much because changes in aggregate demand primarily cause changes in interest rates rather than changes in output. At the zero lower bound, however, pro-debtor bankruptcy laws do not just reshuffle aggregate demand; they increase it.

Mian, Sufi, and coauthor Francesco Trebbi have looked into the evidence.[11] U.S. states offer valuable test cases because they differ in their foreclosure laws. In some states, foreclosure sales must take place through the judicial system and are subject to extensive and costly review. Other states handle foreclosure proceedings outside the judicial system. Mian, Sufi, and Trebbi find that this variation has a large effect: in states that make foreclosure more difficult, foreclosures happen much less frequently—about half as often as in the other states.[12] The authors also find that, during the Great Recession, increased foreclosure sales caused substantial declines in home prices and spending as proxied by auto sales. The claim that the law of debtors and creditors affects spending is thus more than theoretical. It has sound empirical footing.

In light of this research, Mian and Sufi argue that reducing borrowers' debt obligations can mitigate demand slumps. They favor widespread debt forgiveness and recommend legislative changes in bankruptcy law to enable it during recessions.[13] The idea is that eliminating or reducing repayment obligations puts money in the hands of borrowers—people with high propensities to spend.

If this approach strikes the reader as novel, that is only because many governments have forgotten how to forgive. State action to reduce debt and thus induce debtors to spend is a tried-and-true response to demand crises. During the Great Depression, for example, the U.S. federal and state governments passed many laws improving borrowers' access to credit or restricting creditors' rights to repayment. Congress established the Federal Housing Administration, which guaranteed mortgage loans, enabling borrowers to access private credit markets that would otherwise have been closed to them. Congress also created the Home Owners Loan Corporation, which lent money at low interest rates to homeowners who could not meet their mortgage obligations, effectively paying off portions of the homeowners' debt by reducing their interest burden.

Some states were more assertive, restructuring loan contracts themselves to favor borrowers over creditors. Famously, Minnesota passed a law temporarily limiting banks' rights to foreclose on homes, even if their owners were in default on their mortgages. Bankers sued, arguing that the law violated the contracts clause of the U.S. Constitution, but the Supreme Court sided with Minnesota. The justices ruled, "If state power exists to give temporary relief from the enforcement of contracts in the presence of disasters due to physical causes such as fire, flood or earthquake, that power cannot be said to be nonexistent when the urgent public need demanding such relief is produced by other and economic causes."[14]

Mian and Sufi propose that policies such as these could have substantially mitigated the effects of the Great Recession. But their proposals are politically unrealistic. The recommended policies demand action from the same legislatures that failed to deliver fiscal stimulus during the Great Recession and from the same administrators who were unable to spend the tens of billions allocated for debt forgiveness by TARP. Debt forgiveness is a good idea when unemployment is high and interest rates are at or near zero, but we cannot expect legislatures to simply take up the cause or administrators to understand it without more sustained focus on law and macroeconomics.

But all is not lost. Although comprehensive intervention into credit markets requires legislative action, legislatures have already vested considerable discretion over bankruptcy law to courts and regulators. Although courts cannot overturn settled bankruptcy law, they make many decisions on the margins of existing law. At the zero lower bound, a pro-debtor tendency among judges in marginal cases can provide significant stimulus without requiring legislative approval.

The Role of Bankruptcy Law

Bankruptcy law provides debtors with a "fresh start" and solves a collective action problem among creditors. When a debtor is insolvent, each creditor has an incentive to seize the debtor's assets in order to secure repayment before the other creditors. But if every creditor rushes to seize critical assets (such as the debtor's car or factory), then the debtor's earning capacity suffers. To maximize the debtor's earning capacity and the return to creditors as a whole, bankruptcy law imposes a collective decision-making procedure for restructuring the debt of insolvent debtors. Instead of pursuing repayment individually, each creditor and the debtor resolve their disputes collectively through bankruptcy.

In the United States, an insolvent debtor follows one of three bankruptcy "chapters" (Chapters 7, 11, and 13). Most personal debtors file for Chapter 7 bankruptcy, which benefits debtors by discharging debts entirely. Chapter 7 seizes and sells the debtor's assets (subject to some "exemptions") to repay creditors. The U.S. bankruptcy code instructs judges to dismiss Chapter 7 filings in the case of "abuse" and instructs judges to presume abuse if a debtor's income exceeds a specified percentage of debts and expenses. The code vests bankruptcy judges with the discretion to allow a Chapter 7 filing to continue in spite of income over the threshold if the debtor shows "special circumstances that justify additional expenses."

If an insolvent personal debtor is ineligible for Chapter 7 or hopes to retain some assets, then the debtor typically files for Chapter 13 bankruptcy. Chapter 13 allows the individual debtor to keep some assets but requires the debtor to make ongoing payments to existing creditors rather than discharging obligations completely. To confirm a Chapter 13 plan, the bankruptcy judge must determine that the plan is "feasible" and has been offered "in good faith." Needless to say, judges enjoy discretion in making these determinations.

While insolvent personal debtors choose between Chapter 7 and 13 bankruptcy, insolvent business debtors choose between liquidation under Chapter 7 and reorganization under Chapter 11 of the bankruptcy code.[15] Many businesses that first file for Chapter 11 reorganization subsequently convert their bankruptcy filing to a Chapter 7 liquidation. Indeed, creditors can compel a debtor to convert a Chapter 11 reorganization into a Chapter 7 liquidation if the creditors demonstrate that conversion is "in the best interests of creditors."[16] Bankruptcy judges exercise considerable discretion in applying the "best interest of the creditors" test.

Student Loan Forgiveness

In the United States, the federal government funds or guarantees most student loans—and there are a lot of student loans. In 2015–2016, federal loans or guarantees accounted for 90 percent of $107 billion in student borrowing.[17] More than $1.2 trillion in student loans were outstanding as of 2015,[18] the vast majority either disbursed directly by the federal government or guaranteed by it.

With this expansive government role, widespread forgiveness of student debt held or guaranteed by the government offers an excellent means of stimulating aggregate demand without intervening in private credit markets. In a sense, this is fiscal policy because when the government writes off a loan or makes good on a guarantee, its debt rises. Unlike conventional fiscal policy, however, student loan forgiveness occurs through the legal system, making that forgiveness a form of expansionary legal policy.

Bankruptcy law treats student loans differently than other loans. Unlike most debt, student debt is not generally dischargeable in bankruptcy.[19] But judges still exercise considerable discretion over student loan discharge. If a judge rules that repayment of student loans causes "undue hardship,"[20] then the student loans become dischargeable. "Undue hardship" provides a vague standard recognized as leaving much to the judgment of the court.[21] Judges have no qualms exercising this discretion either. Rafael Pardo's research shows that

> Legally irrelevant factors unrelated to the merits of a debtor's claim for relief (e.g., the level of experience of the debtor's attorney and the identity of the judge assigned to the debtor's case) influence the extent to which a debtor obtains a discharge of her student loans. Importantly, such factors appear to have a stronger effect than the handful of legally relevant factors associated with discharge outcomes.[22]

Although they haven't so far, bankruptcy judges could, in theory, use this discretion to account for the macroeconomic environment. They should. When short-term interest rates are zero and employment rates are low, judges should be more inclined to find undue hardship and discharge student debt than they would in ordinary economic times.

A variable undue hardship standard that adjusts to the business cycle offers two advantages over a nonadjustable standard. First, in a depressed economy, well-paying jobs are scarce, making it more likely that repayment of student debt constitutes an undue hardship. Attention to the wider economy just gives the debtor her due, recognizing that, in the midst of recession, it really is harder to pay off loans. Second, student loan forgiveness promotes aggregate demand and output at the zero lower bound.

In addition to expansionary legal policy, student loan forgiveness could also become a target of expansionary fiscal policy by administrative agencies (see Chapter 7). Presently, when a bankruptcy filer seeks discharge of student debt, a private nonprofit corporation under contract with the U.S. Department of Education pursues repayment, if necessary by litigation. The company, Educational Credit Management Corporation (ECMC), has only one goal: to minimize government losses on loans. According to a *New York Times* report, it pursues that end with such singular focus that it has attempted to collect even from severely ill debtors and debtors caring for others with costly medical bills.[23]

The Department of Education can and should change ECMC's behavior by allowing public policy considerations to inform recovery strategies. If a debtor seeks discharge of student loans during a liquidity trap with high unemployment, then the department could presumptively accept discharge in bankruptcy rather than challenge it. At the very least, contracts with ECMC should allow the department to provide policy guidance on ECMC's bankruptcy litigation strategies—guidance that should attend to the business cycle.

Because there are $1.2 trillion in student loans outstanding, business cycle–sensitive discharge policy—implemented by either the judiciary or by the Department of Education—could have an empirically important stimulus effect. If even 5 percent of student debt were discharged at the zero lower bound, cash-strapped individuals would gain $60 billion to spend precisely when stimulus is most needed to raise output and lower unemployment.

Personal Bankruptcy Forgiveness

As significant as student debt forgiveness might be, much more stimulus can be achieved through changes to private credit markets. Bankruptcy judges exercise authority over the loans of all debtors who file for bankruptcy, confirming or rejecting Chapter 7 and Chapter 13 personal bankruptcy plans. (Personal debtors rarely file under Chapter 11.)

Chapter 13 plan confirmation standards such as "feasibility" and "good faith" are difficult to apply. Judges vary in their beliefs about the good faith of debtors and the merits of their bankruptcy plans, with significant effects on outcomes. Research indicates that a bankruptcy judge in the 95th percentile for confirmation likelihood (a pro-debtor judge) approves over 50 percent of Chapter 13 plans. A judge in the 5th percentile approves less than 40 percent of plans.[24] Applying the same rules, bankruptcy judges come to different outcomes.

There thus exists considerable discretion with respect to Chapter 13 bankruptcy. Bankruptcy judges could use this leeway to account for the business cycle. At the zero lower bound, they could all behave like pro-debtor judges, raising aggregate demand by confirming more Chapter 13 plans and forgiving more debt. This would give borrowers—again, people with high marginal propensities to consume—more resources. Because debtors filed for relief for almost $200 billion in debt in the United States in 2010,[25] a 10 percentage-point increase in Chapter 13 confirmation rates would provide substantial stimulus without exceeding the range of discretion currently exercised by bankruptcy judges.

Liquidation versus Reorganization in Business Bankruptcy

Bankruptcy judges also exercise discretion in determining whether requests by creditors to convert a Chapter 11 business reorganization into a Chapter 7 liquidation is in "the best interests of creditors." (Businesses rarely file under Chapter 13). Recent research indicates that Chapter 11 filing with a randomly assigned judge who is in the 95th percentile for converting a reorganization into a liquidation has a 55 percent chance of being converted into a liquidation.[26] An otherwise identical Chapter 11 filing with a bankruptcy judge in the 5th percentile has only a 25 percent chance of conversion into a Chapter 7 liquidation. Business bankruptcy judges apply the same standards to produce different outcomes, exercising considerable discretion.

Zach Liscow suggests that bankruptcy judges use this discretion to favor the creation or preservation of jobs during recessions.[27] The idea here is that reducing returns to the creditors of a bankrupt firm—that is, allowing the firm to reorganize and continue rather than liquidate—may enable that firm to keep more employees on staff. If the reorganized firm and its employees have a higher propensity to spend than the investors whose return is reduced, then rulings against creditors and in favor of reorganization raise aggregate demand. And at the zero lower bound, increases in aggregate demand translate into increases in output.

In the United States, tens of thousands of businesses file for bankruptcy every year.[28] Although most of these are small, in 2015 almost a hundred were publicly traded companies. If keeping jobs via reorganization has the positive effects on aggregate demand that Liscow hypothesizes, then business bankruptcy rulings offer another important mechanism for the application of expansionary legal policy.

Implementation

Unlike most of the expansionary legal policy discussed in this part, judges, and not regulators, implement changes in emphasis in the law of debtors and creditors. Judges are not macroeconomic policy experts, so we should not rely on them to fine-tune business cycles. Moreover, judge-made legal stimulus cannot be coordinated and supervised by a law and macroeconomics oversight body such as OFRA. For these reasons, expansionary legal policy implemented by judges should be subject to tighter restrictions than expansionary legal policy implemented by regulators.

To ensure that judges implement expansionary legal policy without exceeding their legitimate discretion over bankruptcy law, appeals courts should not consider the state of the business cycle when reviewing a bankruptcy judge's attempt at expansionary legal policy. Instead, they should reverse a bankruptcy judge's pro-debtor decision when that decision violates the preexisting law. Only when an appeals court would affirm a pro-debtor ruling in ordinary circumstances should the appeals court affirm a pro-debtor ruling made for the purpose of stimulating the economy.

Even with this restriction, we should be wary of expansionary legal policy implemented by judges. For the most part, judges should avoid expansionary legal policy. But bankruptcy judges occupy a central place in resolving the debt crises that are the proximate cause of most prolonged downturns. As a result, bankruptcy judges are uniquely well placed to implement expansionary legal policy. Moreover, judges do not need great acumen to know when debt burdens are unusually high and interest rates are close to or at zero. We should feel confident trusting bankruptcy judges to undertake expansionary legal policy in those conditions.

If debt is more likely to be discharged or invalidated at the zero lower bound, then should we not be wary about opportunistic debtors filing bankruptcy or challenging debts during downturns? Indeed, judges would have to be alert to such abuses. But there is good reason to suspect the risks here are more theoretical than real. Filing bankruptcy entails significant social and financial costs, even if one is successful. So great are these costs that most of those who would benefit financially from bankruptcy do not file.[29] As long as statutes do not change, these incentives will hold even if judges are more apt to side with debtors. Moreover, debtors cannot file for bankruptcy repeatedly, restricting the most opportunistic from exploiting time-varying bankruptcy rules.

A more pressing concern is that easy debt discharge during liquidity traps will spook creditors at precisely the moment when the economy needs more lending. Creditors will not lend money during liquidity traps if they fear that it will be quickly discharged. Lenient discharge standards therefore should be limited to debts incurred before the economy hit the zero lower bound. Judges should be less inclined to use their discretion to discharge credit agreements formed during a liquidity trap.

Expansionary Policy through the Law of Remedies

In addition to deciding who wins and who loses a legal dispute, courts fashion remedies. Remedies vindicate the legal rights of the winning party. In fashioning remedies, courts exercise enormous discretion, as we will see below. And different remedies have disparate effects on aggregate demand. "Injunctive" remedies, which require or proscribe actions, sometimes promote aggregate demand (when spending is required) and sometimes stifle it (when spending is forbidden or delayed). In fashioning remedies, which are famously subject to considerable judicial discretion, courts should promote aggregate demand at the zero lower bound.

Two Kinds of Remedies

When a court decides that a plaintiff's rights have been violated, it can respond with two basic classes of remedies: liability-rule protection and property-rule protection. If the liability rule is applied, the defendant pays damages. If the court favors property-rule protection, the defendant is ordered to cease whatever behavior has caused the suit. Almost every legal right can be protected by either a property rule or a liability rule.

Say a developer intends to build a block of apartments. The neighbors worry that noise from the building will be a nuisance and that the structure will block the view from their homes, hurting the existing homes' market value. Faced with imminent construction, the neighbors sue to halt the developer. The court first has to decide if the developer has the right to build or the neighbors have the right to be free of the nuisances associated with the development. If the court sides with the neighbors, then it must further decide how it will remedy this right. Under property-rule protection, the court issues an injunction restricting construction. The developer cannot build unless it finds a way to comply with relevant nuisance rules or else the neighbors agree to waive their right, probably in exchange for a settlement. Alternatively, the court might favor liability-rule protection for the neighbors, estimating the reduction in the neighbors' home values and compensating them for this reduction in value. In this case, construction could continue, but the developer must pay damages to the neighbors.

The relative advantages of property and liability rules are the subject of a foundational debate in law and economics. Much has been written about the microeconomic efficiency of each kind of remedy in various contexts. What has rarely been considered are the macroeconomic ramifications of each kind of remedy.

Macroeconomic Effects of the Choice of Remedies

When courts use property rules to stop economic activity, they reduce spending, or at least delay it. In ordinary economic conditions, this effect of property rules is irrelevant. The workers who would have contributed to the now-barred activity find other employment. At the zero lower bound, however, injunctive remedies can have serious direct costs because workers taken off a project won't find other jobs. If the neighbors successfully halt the proposed development in a liquidity trap, the construction workers tasked with building it won't have another job to turn to.

My argument has been that, at the zero lower bound and amid high unemployment, courts should favor the rule that promotes spending. When it comes to lawsuits, this usually means favoring the liability rule, which enables a project to move forward as long as the entities responsible for it can pay damages.

Preferring damages over injunctions in construction disputes offers the possibility of meaningful stimulus. At the start of the Great Recession, construction spending in the United States exceeded $1 trillion annually. If 5 percent of this construction is subject to injunction, then a shift to damages at the zero lower bound could enable $50 billion in spending. Plaintiffs' rights retain liability rule protection, limiting the scope for inefficient projects to go forward.

The same logic applies to the law of preliminary injunctions, which temporarily prohibit activities subject to ongoing litigations. In some cases, a party to a suit may plan to take action before a verdict is reached. The opposing party, usually the plaintiff, may ask for a preliminary injunction to preserve the status quo until the legal issue can be resolved. For example, it may take a while to determine whether the developer has the right to build or the neighbors have the right to be free of nuisances. The law of preliminary injunctions determines what happens while that right is being litigated: Can construction move forward, or must it wait?

Courts grant preliminary injunctions when they determine: first, the plaintiff has a substantial likelihood of success on the merits; second, the plaintiff faces a substantial risk of irreparable damage if the injunction is not granted; third, the balance of the harms weighs in the favor of the party seeking the preliminary injunction; and, finally, injunction serves the public interest.

Law and macroeconomics suggests that courts should be less inclined to grant preliminary injunctions during liquidity traps. Doing so halts spending, reduces aggregate demand, and raises unemployment. The forgone output is multiplied significantly. Granting the injunction during a time of robust growth, by contrast, has much smaller effects on nonparties. During a liquidity trap, the balance of the harms weighs less in favor of the party seeking the injunction, and the public interest is less well served by an injunction. Again, liability-rule protection would be more beneficial, enabling the stimulus that the property rule prevents.

There are, however, some cases in which property rule remedies promote spending. Consider the seminal 1921 contract-law case *Jacob and Youngs v. Kent,* heard by the New York Court of Appeals. The case concerned an alleged breach by a developer, Jacob and Youngs, who contracted to build a house for a wealthy landowner, George E. Kent. The contract required Jacob and Youngs to install in the house a particular brand of piping—Reading Pipe. However, the developer used other brands identical in quality. When Kent found out, he withheld payment. Jacob and Youngs sought to recoup what it thought it was owed.

Both sides agreed that the developer breached the contract. The dispute was, in part, over remedies. The developer argued that "substantial performance" had been provided, so that the remedy should be nominal monetary damages. Kent argued that performance was defective, and the remedy should provide property-rule protection, possibly including an injunction requiring the builder to knock down the newly constructed home and reconstruct it with Reading brand pipe. Justice Benjamin Cardozo, writing for the majority of New York's high court, ruled in favor of the developer. In essence, the court favored liability-rule protection of Kent's right to Reading brand pipe and assessed the monetary damages at zero. Traditional law and economics scholars, as well as academics writing from other perspectives, continue to dispute the appropriate remedy in *Jacob and Youngs.*[30]

With respect to macroeconomic outcomes, the effects of the ruling are more clear-cut. An injunction requiring the developer to spend to knock down and rebuild the house would have raised aggregate demand. Awarding Kent money damages, by contrast, left spending flat. Money damages shift wealth around, but not necessarily spending. At the zero lower bound, therefore, a court concerned with macroeconomics facing a *Jacob and Youngs*–like case should prefer the injunctive remedy. In such cases, courts are effectively in a position to follow Keynes's suggestion that, in depressions, we should pay people to dig holes and fill them up. Keynes was being facetious, but in the circumstances we are concerned with—high unemployment at the zero lower bound—there is merit to the idea.

Implementation

Judges are generally ill suited for expansionary legal policy. As a result, judges should generally steer clear of attempting to stimulate the economy. In the case of some remedies, however, existing legal standards call for the consideration of macroeconomic factors. In these cases, judges need to consider remedies in order to fulfill their legal obligation.

In articulating the standard for issuing a "preliminary injunction," the U.S. Supreme Court explained that "courts must balance the competing claims [by plaintiff and defendant] of injury and must consider the effect on each party of the granting or withholding of the requested relief. In exercising their sound discretion, courts of equity should pay particular regard for the public consequences in employing the extraordinary remedy of injunction."[31]

If courts ignore the effects of an injunction on aggregate demand, then they fail to consider the "public consequences" of the injunctions that they issue. Injunctions often delay spending. And this delay has public consequences, as injunctions against spending cause third parties economic harm at the zero lower bound while injunctions that favor spending benefit third parties. Moreover, these harms are "irreparable"—another important consideration for preliminary injunctions. Spending after the merits have been resolved, when the multiplier may well be lower, does not redress the harms third parties suffered because of the original injunction. As a result, courts need to consider macroeconomic effects when issuing preliminary injunctions.

Many different actors in the legal system can help to ensure that remedial decisions are appropriate to macroeconomic conditions. Courts should promote aggregate demand during liquidity traps by favoring damage remedies instead of injunctions against economic activity. Although judges are unlikely to be macroeconomic experts, they should be able to identify periods of zero short-term interest rates. In addition to judges, government plaintiffs, such as zoning boards suing developers, can tailor their remedial requests to the state of the business cycle by requesting damages, rather than injunctions of economic activity, at the zero lower bound. (If a plaintiff does not request an injunction, then the court is unlikely to grant one.) By doing so, government plaintiffs can protect their interests through damages without standing in the way of much-needed spending.

As in other cases we have examined, relying on business cycle–varying remedies to stimulate the economy raises the risk of opportunism. Developers whose projects will be forestalled by property-rule injunctions in ordinary times may commence projects at the zero lower bound in hopes of profiting from the increased likelihood that the project will be allowed to move forward in the face of potential lawsuits. If the project is a harmful one, then its construction at the zero lower bound constitutes inefficient behavior prompted by legal variation over the business cycle.

Judges, exercising their "sound discretion," should be wary of such opportunism and make efforts to thwart it. But, in practice, opportunism may not pose great risk. Importantly, varying remedies over time does not alter legal rights. If a developer's project violates neighbors' rights, then the developer will have to pay damages equal to the harm caused by the project. Unless the developer expects the court to underestimate the value of the harm, the developer will not have incentive to push through an inefficient project at the zero lower bound. In addition, holding back spending until liquidity traps are present may in fact be efficient behavior worth encouraging. Incentivizing spending during liquidity traps fosters private stimulus at precisely the time it is most needed.

In this chapter, I developed three examples of expansionary legal policy—utility rate regulation, bankruptcy law, and the law of remedies—to illustrate the tool's potential. Each policy offers the potential for meaningful stimulus worth billions of dollars—and none of the interventions require legislative approval. Instead, they direct preexisting regulatory or judicial discretion toward a new policy end—macroeconomic stimulus.

Law pervades economic life. As a result, the three examples developed here only scratch the surface of expansionary legal policy. If every judge and regulator worked through the macroeconomic implications of their actions and chose the option that stimulated aggregate demand in close cases at the zero lower bound, then expansionary legal policy could end or mitigate prolonged periods of economic weakness, even if monetary and fiscal policy were hamstrung. There would be collateral damage—judges and regulators are flawed policymakers, with respect to macroeconomics and everything else—but the potential gains are well worth pursuing.

Conclusion: Five Lessons
of Law and Macroeconomics

W e should not be surprised that central banks dominated the making of macroeconomic policy during the Great Recession. While other institutions charged with macroeconomic policy, such as legislatures, balance macroeconomic stability with numerous other goals, central banks focus primarily on macroeconomic stability. Unlike legislatures, central banks also enjoy the services of macroeconomic policy experts. Finally, central banks make decisions rapidly. Because of these advantages, jurisdictions naturally preferred central banks' macroeconomic policies to the alternatives.

Relying on Central Banks to Address All Macroeconomic Ills Threatens Their Legitimacy

This dependence on central banks never came free. The structure that produces central banks' focus, expertise, and agility also limits their democratic legitimacy. But this cost seemed bearable. Although the institution of central banks proved controversial for much of modern history, polities in nearly every industrialized democracy gradually accepted central-bank control over monetary policy and short-term interest rates after World War II. So long as fiscal policy remained the province of the legislature, central-bank control over monetary policy was acceptable. Indeed, so noncontroversial was central banking that many democracies imposed constraints on the primary alternative—fiscal policy—through deficit restrictions.

This consensus crumbled during the Great Recession. At the zero lower bound, conventional monetary policy proved impotent; interest rates could go no lower. With fiscal policy neutered by deficit restrictions, legislative inertia, and debt fears, equally hamstrung central banks were left facing a cataclysmic recession on their own. In response, they adopted aggressive unconventional monetary policy, creating money on an unprecedented scale to buy assets they had formerly shunned.

The pursuit of unconventional monetary policy was a reasonable response to fraught macroeconomic conditions. It probably prevented the Great Recession from being even worse. But unconventional monetary policy didn't work that well. The Great Recession and its aftermath lingered for most of a decade. Political orders frayed in almost every industrialized democracy. Unconventional monetary policy may also have fueled asset price bubbles whose eventual bursting could cause yet more damage. Even if unconventional monetary policy prevented worse outcomes, such as the hasty demise of the European monetary union, we cannot rely exclusively on unconventional monetary policy to mitigate future recessions. More aggressive forms of unconventional monetary policy, such as helicopter money, might work better. But they would suffer even more egregiously from a lack of democratic legitimacy.

Indeed, unconventional monetary policy already threatens central bank legitimacy. The ECB's Outright Monetary Transactions program, which may have saved the Eurozone from collapse, placed the ECB in a newly prominent role in policymaking, creating legal tension that effectively forced an amendment of the Maastricht Treaty. The ECB's actions also proved politically costly. They fed into a narrative of an undemocratic elitist European project. Many commentators attribute the rise of the populist Alternative für Deutschland party in Germany to anger over the ECB's unconventional policies. Similarly, the Federal Reserve's use of its balance sheet to rescue Bear Stearns, AIG, and other financial institutions helped fuel the rise of populist movements such as the Tea Party and Occupy Wall Street. These movements and their political heirs (including President Trump in the United States) not only reject central banks' use of unconventional monetary policy but also question central banks' long-established control over short-term interest rates. We have good reason to worry that future unconventional monetary policies will trigger backlash that threatens even traditional areas of central bank authority.

If central banks cannot survive the next episode of the zero lower bound by pushing boundaries ever further, then what to do? Doing nothing should not be an option—the populism that thrived in the wake of the Great Recession (and the Great Depression before it) endangered too many cherished institutions of the Western political order, not just central banks. In the remainder of this conclusion, I present principles for a robust law and macroeconomics policy alternative.

We Have Many Stimulus Options at the Zero Lower Bound

At present, expansionary fiscal policy offers the textbook cure for depressed aggregate demand at the zero lower bound. But the Great Recession demonstrated the perils of relying on discretionary fiscal stimulus. Constitutional deficit restrictions, fears about unsustainable debt burdens, and political frictions combined to keep fiscal stimulus well below the levels recommended by macroeconomists at institutions such as the IMF and most central banks.

The failure of discretionary fiscal stimulus exhausted the menu of conventional policy responses to the zero lower bound. As a result, public policy, with the exception of unconventional monetary policy, did not respond decisively to the prolonged economic tragedy of the Great Recession.

Expansionary fiscal policy offers a less attractive response to deep recessions under the debt-supercycle theory of prolonged recessions. If a depressed economy is held back by a lack of spending caused by excess debt, then increasing spending by issuing yet more debt is highly risky. We need alternatives that do not raise our cumulative indebtedness.

If there is only one lesson that I hope future policymakers take from this book, it is that this apathetic policy response was unwarranted. Almost every law, regulation, or other form of public policy affects aggregate demand. If monetary and fiscal policy prove incapable of stimulus, we should turn to our other tools of public policy.

Indeed, the historical response to macroeconomic problems leaned on law heavily. The New Deal relied primarily—and successfully—on law and regulation, rather than government spending or tax cuts, to raise inflation expectations and spending. The post–World War II global economic order subordinated laws governing capital investments to the macroeconomic goal of promoting stable exchange rates.

The use of law to solve macroeconomic problems didn't always succeed. Price controls, which used law and regulation rather than monetary policy to subdue inflation, failed. But the failure of some attempts at law and macroeconomics does not justify doing nothing at the zero lower bound. Instead, policymakers need to search for expansionary legal policy options that are more likely to achieve their desired macroeconomic end. The proposals developed in this book—ranging from "nudges" such as altering income tax–withholding rules, to radical interventions such as price controls—just begin to explore the universe of law and macroeconomics policy options.

Different policies respond to different constraints on fiscal stimulus. If debt limitations constrain expansionary fiscal policy, then legislatures should pursue private-sector stimulus, adjusting law and regulation to encourage the private sector to spend more. And if political gridlock prevents effective expansionary fiscal policy, then regulators and judges should consider using the policy discretion they already enjoy to promote spending in addition to their other goals.

At the Zero Lower Bound, All Policymakers Should Consider Stimulating Aggregate Demand

Expanding the goals of law and regulation to include macroeconomic stability adds complexity. Policymakers prefer to limit the number of problems they solve with one legal instrument. It is hard enough to know how to pursue a single aim, such as justice. As a result, regulators, administrators, judges, and other policymakers usually "stick to their knitting," emphasizing a limited set of goals. And while legislatures address multiple goals, they often delegate important tasks to more focused experts.

But this approach fails at the zero lower bound. The expert entity charged with macroeconomic stability—the central bank—loses traction. If everyone continues with business-as-usual and ignores macroeconomics, recessions linger, with potentially catastrophic economic and political consequences. To mitigate a recession at the zero lower bound, everybody—from legislatures to judges—needs to consider the effects of their decisions on spending in addition to other factors.

We should not exaggerate the complications associated with this new perspective. As it stands, policymakers rarely focus exclusively on one goal. Utility regulators, for example, already consider rates of return on investment, public safety, energy security, economic development, and energy and water conservation when setting rates. At worst, countercyclical utility regulatory policy adds some complication to an already-complex decision; it doesn't render a previously clear-cut policy calculus obscure. What is true for utility regulation will also be true of many other regulatory and legal decisions.

We Need an Institution That Focuses on Law and Macroeconomics

By itself, asking policymakers to expand their horizons offers an inadequate response to recessions at the zero lower bound. Even if policymakers seem to understand the case for expansionary policy, they will likely forget over time. Outside the zero lower bound, they will return to other goals. When the next episode of the zero lower bound arrives, they will be hesitant to consider stimulus and again insist that the central bank come to the rescue.

Macroeconomic concerns need an institutional home, to ensure that they receive the attention they deserve. This might be the Office of Fiscal and Regulatory Affairs I've advocated, or some other law and macroeconomics czar. OFRA would make certain that expansionary legal and fiscal policy by administrative agencies follows expert economic advice and is applied consistently across different substantive areas of law and regulation.

The perspective offered by OFRA, like that offered by central banks, can also inform judicial decision-making in the rare cases when judges should consider expansionary legal policy. In addition to using zero short-term interest rates as a trigger for macroeconomic considerations, judges can also observe OFRA and central bank suggestions. If both OFRA and the central bank indicate that aggregate demand is inadequate, then judges should have more confidence in taking decisions that promote aggregate demand.

We Should Apply Law and Macroeconomics Perspectives When the Economy Is Robust as Well as When It Is Ailing

Outside the zero lower bound, OFRA should have less policy input. But the office would still perform an invaluable function. Bad macroeconomic policy at the zero lower bound often follows less from bad motives than from inattention to macroeconomics in ordinary times.

Examples unfortunately abound. When Congress repeatedly instituted new varieties of tax expenditures, it did not intend pro-cyclical fiscal policy.

After all, tax expenditures offer a valuable fiscal policy tool, enabling government to channel private spending rather than spend directly. An inadvertent by-product of tax expenditures, however, is that government subsidies track private spending. If private spending falls, effective government spending through tax expenditures follows, exacerbating the fall in aggregate demand and prolonging a recession. Likewise, experience-rated government insurance programs and cost-plus utility regulation were never intended to destabilize the economy. But the logic of these programs often means that rates go up when the economy struggles, further dampening aggregate demand.

To prevent the passage of similarly destabilizing laws in the future, OFRA should evaluate proposed legislation and regulation from a macroeconomic perspective. If a proposed rule is likely to destabilize the economy by raising government revenue or lowering government spending during recessions, then OFRA should highlight this cost

Law is staggeringly powerful, affecting almost every decision. It is puzzling, then, that we no longer consider the macroeconomic effects of important legal tools such as tax expenditures or try to address macroeconomic problems with legal interventions. An institutional home for law and macroeconomics would help change this inadequate status quo—an urgent priority now that central banks no longer enjoy the power to single-handedly keep the macroeconomy stable.

Appendix

The restaurant analogy usefully illustrates some of the basic concerns of macro-economics, but of course it doesn't capture all of the key relationships. To enable interested lawyers to "speak the language" of macroeconomics and facilitate the link between law and the macroeconomic research frontier, I therefore develop law and macroeconomics in terms of the IS-LM (Investment / Savings—Liquidity / Money) model, first developed by Hicks. Unlike the basic IS-LM model I emphasize here, most academic research in macroeconomics uses New Keynesian dynamic stochastic general equilibrium (DSGE) variants of the IS-LM model.[1]

The IS-LM model constitutes the simplest useful formal macroeconomic model and forms the starting point for modern Keynesian economics. The IS-LM model describes macroeconomic fluctuations in the context of two interlocking markets—goods and money. Goods benefit people and governments directly. Money facilitates the purchase of goods. People hold savings in the form of bonds from borrowers, which yield interest, or money, which doesn't. The IS curve maps equilibrium points in the goods market (where the cumulative demand for goods—and services—equals production), and the LM curve maps equilibrium points in the money market (where demand for money equals its supply). (A third market, the market for bonds, which fund investment, will be in equilibrium if the markets for goods and money are in equilibrium.) Interest rates and economic output (of goods and services) adjust to bring both the goods and money markets into equilibrium, meaning that the output of goods must equal the demand for goods, and the supply of money must equal the demand for money.

Chapter 1

Together, the IS and LM curves determine equilibrium in the macroeconomy, which occurs when the two curves intersect, meaning that the markets for both goods and money are in equilibrium.[2] These equilibria are partially determined by the interest rate, which plays two key roles.[3] (For now, I assume that prices are fixed, meaning that the nominal rate of interest equals the real rate.) First, the interest rate equilibrates the market for goods, so that private and public spending equals actual production of those goods.[4] This is the investment-saving, or IS, curve. Second, the interest rate equilibrates the money market so that the demand for money (for example, cash and checking accounts) equals the supply of money—the amount of cash in the economy. (Unlike money, bonds offer interest, which induces people to hold savings in the form of bonds rather than more liquid money.) This is the liquidity-money, or LM, curve.[5]

The interest rate—a single variable—cannot equilibrate two different markets alone. Instead, interest rates and output move jointly to equilibrate the two markets.[6] Reflecting this joint determination of output and interest rate, the IS and the LM equations are mapped onto a grid (Figure A.1), with the x-axis measuring national income and/or economic output Y and the y-axis representing the interest rate i.

The IS curve (IS_1 in Figure A.1) displays the set of output and interest-rate combinations at which demand for goods (spending) equals output of goods. Every point on the IS curve thus represents an equilibrium point in the goods market. At lower interest rates, demand for goods is higher because people want to invest more. In order for the goods market to be in equilibrium, output must be correspondingly higher. The IS curve is therefore downward sloping; lower interest rates correspond to higher levels of output.[7]

Expressed as an equation, the IS curve becomes

$$Y = C(Y - T) + I(i) + G \qquad \text{(IS)},$$

where Y is output; $C(Y - T)$ is the amount of consumption (as a function of income and taxation, T; $I(i)$ is investment as a function of the interest rate, i; and G is government spending.

The LM curve represents the set of output and interest-rate levels at which the demand for money equals the supply of money (equilibrium in the market for money). As output rises, people demand more cash to facilitate more transactions. But the supply of cash is fixed by the central bank and the banking system. To keep the demand and supply of cash in equilibrium when demand for cash is high, we need a higher interest rate, which decreases the demand for cash (relative to the demand for bonds). The LM curve is therefore upward sloping. Expressed as an equation, the LM curve is denoted as

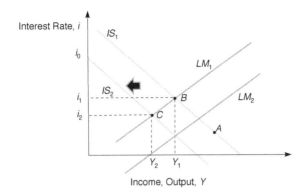

Figure A.1 Point A is an equilibrium point for the goods market but not for the money market. Money demand exceeds supply. Interest rates increase and output declines until the economy hits point B, where both the goods and money markets are in equilibrium. Output equals Y_1 at point B and interest rates equal i_1. Decreases in demand for goods at any interest rate can shift the IS curve inward (from IS_1 to IS_2). This moves the economy's equilibrium point from point B to C, with lower output ($Y_2 < Y_1$) and lower interest rates ($i_2 < i_1$).

$$\left(\frac{M}{P}\right) = L(i, Y) \tag{LM},$$

where $\left(\frac{M}{P}\right)$ (the real money supply) is the nominal money supply, M, divided by the price level, P; and $L(i, Y)$ is demand for real money balances as a function of the interest rate and output.

The economy is in equilibrium when IS = LM. When this condition does not hold, output and the interest rate adjust accordingly.

Fluctuations in the IS-LM Model

Say the economy starts out with a combination of output and interest rates at which the goods market is in equilibrium but the demand for money exceeds the supply of money, represented as point A in Figure A.1 (point A is on the IS_1 curve but off the LM_1 curve). Because demand for money exceeds supply at point A, the interest rate has to rise, output has to fall, or both, reducing demand for cash so that it equals supply. In order to reach equilibrium in both the IS and LM markets, output needs to decrease and interest rates need to rise along the IS curve until we reach the unique output and interest rate combination at point B (with output of Y_1 and an interest rate of i_1). Point B, where the IS_1 and LM_1 curves intersect, is an equilibrium point for both the goods and money markets.

The IS-LM model offers a theory of fluctuations. If there is a negative shock to demand—for example, bad weather reduces consumption (reducing consumption C), or animal spirits diminish investment (reducing I)—then aggregate demand decreases for every interest rate. This corresponds to a leftward or inward shift in the IS curve from IS_1 to IS_2. While the economy used to be in equilibrium at point B, with actual output Y_1 equal to potential output, output now exceeds spending. A combination of output and interest rates (for example, at point B and all other points on IS_1) that once constituted equilibrium in the goods market now implies that output exceeds desired spending. Reduced output and interest rates will bring the goods and money markets back into equilibrium at point C, where the IS_1 and LM_2 curves intersect (with output of Y_2 and an interest rate of i_2).

The initial decrease in aggregate demand from IS_1 to IS_2—the horizontal distance between the two IS curves, $IS_1(i_1) - IS_2(i_1)$—does not translate into a one-for-one reduction in output (from Y_1 to Y_2). Instead, some of the reduction in aggregate demand is offset by a reduction in interest rates, which in turn stimulates demand for investment. A reduction in the interest rate therefore offsets some of the effects of an initial decrease in output demand.

Potential Output, Inflation, and the Long-Run Effects of Demand Shocks

The IS-LM model assumes prices are fixed, while output levels and interest rates adjust to changes in spending. The assumption of fixed prices gives a reasonable approximation of short-run economic behavior, but it is not realistic over long periods of time. If the economy's potential output, determined by exogenous factors such as the size of the labor force, the capital stock, and the economy's technological sophistication, is given by Y_1, then a shift in the IS curve from IS_1 to IS_2, moving the economy from point B to C, moves output to Y_2, well below its potential. This creates an output gap equal to $Y_1 - Y_2$.

Over the long run, the spare capacity implied by the output gap puts downward pressure on prices. As prices decrease, demand for cash holdings decreases, as a given amount of cash facilitates more transactions. This shifts equilibrium in the money market. The LM curve moves from LM_1 to LM_2—at any output level, we need a lower interest rate to balance the (reduced) demand for cash with supply. In turn, the shift in the LM curve reduces interest rates. With interest rates lower, output increases. Prices continue decreasing and output continues increasing until output returns to its potential level Y_1, and we are at long-run (stable price) equilibrium as well as short-run equilibrium.

In the long run, flexible prices thus enable the economy to respond to shocks to aggregate demand and bring output back to potential. In the short run, however, the IS-LM model assumes prices are fixed, so output does not return to capacity.

Modern macroeconomics focuses on the relationship between inflation and output relative to potential instead of the relationship between prices and output relative to potential. In addition to being a function of output relative to potential, inflation is also a function of inflation expectations. The Phillips curve represents this relationship as follows:

$$\pi = b(Y - Y_{POT}) + \pi^e \qquad \text{(PC)},$$

where π is inflation, b is the sensitivity of inflation to output above or below potential, Y_{POT} is potential output, and π^e is expected inflation.

Chapter 2

In the IS-LM model depicted in Figure A.1, the goods and money markets begin in equilibrium at point B, where $IS_1 = LM_1$. If, regardless of the interest rate, demand for spending falls due to a loss of confidence—for example, $C(Y-T)$ or $I(i)$ in equation (IS) decrease—then B is no longer an equilibrium point in the goods market. Instead, output exceeds demand. Inventories accumulate and output decreases. The negative shock to demand shifts the IS curve from IS_1 to IS_2. The new equilibrium level of output for both the goods and money markets is now at point C. At C, output has decreased from Y_1 to Y_2, even though potential output is Y_1.

In response to this decrease, the government could increase its own demand for goods by, for instance, passing an infrastructure-spending law, raising G in equation (IS) by an amount equal to the decrease in $C(Y-T)$ or $I(i)$. This new source of demand would once again shift the equilibrium in the goods market. Assuming perfect information and policy success, the increase in G returns the IS curve to IS_1 after a short period at IS_2. Equilibrium is restored at point B, and output returns to potential (Y_1).

According to Hicks, the LM curve should be steep when interest rates are substantially greater than zero, because people need to hold a certain amount of money to facilitate consumption and investment but otherwise prefer to keep savings in the form of bonds. A steep LM curve in Figure A.2 implies that shifts in the IS curve from IS_1 to IS_2 primarily change interest rates rather than output. (The difference in Y between point A and point B is much smaller than the difference in i.) Thus, fiscal stimulus largely raises interest rates in ordinary times, as government spending "crowds out" private investment.

Chapter 3

The LM curve represents equilibrium points in the money market—where demand for money equals its supply. The central bank influences the supply of money, M. By increasing the supply of money, the central bank shifts the LM curve rightward or outward (from LM_1 to LM_2) in Figure A.2. At any given point on the old LM curve (LM_1), such as point A, the increase in money supply means that there is now more money available than would be demanded at that interest rate and output level. Point A (and any other point on LM_1) no longer represents an equilibrium in the money market. Instead, output has to be higher (bringing more demand for money to facilitate more transactions) in order to bring the supply and demand for money back into balance.

The central bank does not enjoy perfect control over the money supply. Instead, the central bank controls base money. The monetary base includes currency and private bank reserves held with the central bank. In addition to the monetary base, the money supply is determined by the "money multiplier," which involves the financial system.

The central bank controls base money but not the money multiplier. The money multiplier depends upon capital requirements, reserve requirements, and bank confidence. Banks will lend more out of each additional dollar in deposits when capital and reserve requirements are lower and when banks are more confident. The central bank therefore does not enjoy perfect control over the money supply. So long as the money multiplier remains constant, an increase in base money will shift the LM curve outward from LM_1 to LM_2, as described above. But other factors, such as reserve requirements, also shift the LM curve.

Law, Macroeconomics, and the LM Curve

Financial regulation plays an important role in determining the LM curve. Any law or regulation that affects the tendency of a financial institution to lend more or less money out of an additional dollar of deposits shifts the LM curve.

Financial regulation comprises the most well-developed existing area of law and macroeconomics. Unfortunately, most legal literature on financial regulation does not explicitly model financial regulation's role in shifting the LM curve, making it harder to link the financial regulation literature to macroeconomics more generally.

Monetary Stabilization Policy

The central bank uses its control over the money supply to stabilize inflation and keep output equal to potential. Suppose that the economy represented in Figure A.2 starts at an equilibrium at point A, with output of Y_1 and an interest

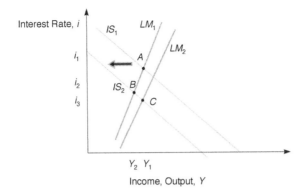

Figure A.2 At point A, the economy is in equilibrium with output of Y_1 (equal to potential output) and an interest rate of i_1 well above zero. A demand shock hits the economy, decreasing demand for goods at any interest rate. The IS curve shifts from IS_1 to IS_2. The new equilibrium in the economy, point B, has output of Y_2 and an interest rate of i_2. Because the LM curve is steeply sloped, output shifts relatively little in response to the decrease in aggregate demand from IS_1 to IS_2 (Y_1 is only slightly higher than Y_2), while interest rates decline a lot (i_1 is much greater than i_2). With output (slightly) below potential, the central bank increases the money supply, shifting the LM curve from LM_1 to LM_2. Economic equilibrium moves to point C, with output of output of Y_1 and an interest rate of i_3.

rate of i_1. A decrease in demand then shifts the IS curve inward from IS_1 to IS_2. In order for both the goods and money markets to be in equilibrium, the economy must shift to point B. Output goes down to Y_2 and the interest rate declines to i_2.

If potential output equals Y_1, then the negative shift in demand moves output below potential to Y_2. By the Phillips curve, inflation declines. Over enough time, prices continue to decline until output returns to potential. The central bank also uses monetary policy to hasten the economy's return to potential and to keep inflation stable. By increasing the supply of base money (conducting expansionary monetary policy), the central bank shifts the LM curve from LM_1 to LM_2. The increase in money supply causes interest rates to fall and output to increase. The economy's new equilibrium is point C, with output of Y_1 and an interest rate of i_3. Expansionary monetary policy stabilizes the economy after a fall in demand and brings output back to its potential.

Evidence for the Efficacy of Monetary Policy

A great deal of evidence indicates that changes in the money supply affect output as predicted by the theoretical arguments described here. Although joint causality problems—monetary policy responds to changes in output in addition to causing changes in output—make it difficult to provide precise estimates for the efficacy of monetary policy, a wide variety of econometric methods indicate that when central banks tighten monetary policy, output declines and interest rates rise.[8]

Chapter 4

In the IS-LM model, a collapse in demand—usually a dramatic reduction in $C(Y - T)$ or $I(i)$ induced by a financial crisis or some other event, such as political uncertainty—is represented by a significant inward shift in the IS curve. (The debt supercycle theory is much more precise about how a financial crisis reduces aggregate demand.) With the collapse in spending, the demand and supply of goods are no longer in equilibrium on the old IS curve (point A on IS_1 in Figure A.3). Instead, demand for goods falls short of supply. Inventories accumulate, leading to reductions in supply of goods (output) and layoffs. With enough of a reduction in supply of goods, the demand for goods will once again be equal to the supply of goods at the given interest rate. In the new IS curve (IS_2), the equilibrium level of output is much lower for any given interest rate than it was before the crisis struck.

After the inward shift in the IS curve caused by the collapse in demand for goods and services, equilibrium in the economy moves along the LM_1 curve from point A to point B. Output (Y_2) is now far below potential ($Y_1 > Y_2$).

The zero lower bound on interest rates implies that the pronounced decline in demand decreased output more than it otherwise would have. That is because when interest rates are at or below zero, many people refuse to invest. Instead, they hold money; it pays a higher return than a zero-interest bond and is more liquid. This "liquidity trap" helped to turn a financial crisis into a near decade-long period of economic stagnation and underemployment.

In IS-LM terms, the LM curve is horizontal at an interest rate of zero (see Figure A.3). The money market can be in equilibrium at a zero interest rate with many different output levels. Additions to the money supply at the zero lower bound do not affect output. Instead, changes to the money supply just mean more money sitting "under the mattress."

If the zero lower bound were not triggered by the decrease in the IS curve from IS_1 to IS_2, then the decrease in economic output (to Y_2) away from potential output (Y_1) would not have been as dramatic. Because the LM curve is horizontal at the zero lower bound, output is much more sensitive to a decrease in demand than it is when interest rates are above zero. In a liquidity trap, decreases in demand for goods translate one for one into decreases in output, without any mitigating effect from a change in interest rate. Once the IS curve has shifted so far inward that it intersects with the horizontal component of the LM curve (at IS_2), any further changes to the IS curve (for example, to IS_2) cause large shifts in output.

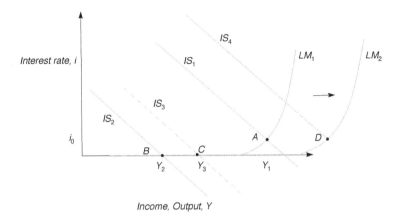

Income, Output, Y

Figure A.3 At point A, the economy is in equilibrium with output of Y_1 (equal to potential output) and an interest rate of i_0 well above zero. A significant demand shock hits the economy, dramatically decreasing demand for goods at any interest rate. The IS curve shifts from IS_1 to IS_2. The new equilibrium in the economy, point B, has output of Y_2 and an interest rate of zero. Because the zero lower bound on interest rates has been reached, with a horizontal LM curve, output decreases dramatically in response to the downturn in demand (Y_2 is much lower than Y_1), while interest rates decline relatively little (from i_0 to 0). Expanding the money supply, shifting the LM curve outward from LM_1 to LM_2 does not stimulate the economy at point B because of the zero lower bound. Equilibrium stays at point B in spite of the monetary expansion, implying a liquidity trap. Expansionary fiscal policy, by contrast, which shifts the IS curve from IS_2 to IS_3, stimulates a considerable increase in output from Y_2 to Y_3.

The liquidity trap is an important source of friction, impeding macroeconomic adjustment. When negative shocks to the economy are large, the primary macroeconomic-adjustment mechanisms—interest rates and price levels—are especially unlikely to bring the economy back to its potential. Output can remain well below capacity for an extended period of time, as it did in the Great Recession. With natural adjustment mechanisms less effective, policy interventions become even more essential.

Chapter 5

The Failure of Conventional Monetary Policy

In a liquidity trap, such as point B in Figure A.3, output lags below potential. Inflation also falls, according to equation (PC). A central bank charged with keeping inflation stable or output near potential thus wants to stimulate the economy.

When the LM curve is not horizontal, expansionary monetary policy shifts the LM curve outward: the interest rate associated with any given output level goes down. In turn, spending goes up. At interest rates of zero, however, the (horizontal) LM curve cannot shift outward, indicating that traditional monetary expansion cannot stimulate a depressed economy.

In Figure A.3, an increase in the money supply shifts the LM curve from LM_1 to LM_2. If the economy is in equilibrium at point B, however, the increase in the money supply does not change the economy's equilibrium, which remains at B. Near point B, increases in the money supply cannot shift the LM curve outward because of the zero lower bound. The curves LM_1 and LM_2 differ only when interest rates are above zero. The economy is thus trapped at point B, and expansionary monetary policy cannot stimulate it.

Unconventional Monetary Policy

To this point, this appendix has ignored the difference between real interest rates, r, and nominal interest rates, i, focusing on nominal rates exclusively by generally assuming that prices are fixed, meaning that there is no inflation.

When inflation exceeds zero, the difference between real and nominal interest rates becomes more important. Only nominal interest rates are affected by the zero lower bound. Real interest rates, which equal the nominal rate minus inflation, $r = i - \pi$, represent the inflation-adjusted returns of bonds. In making savings and investment decisions, real rates should determine economic behavior and not nominal rates. (More accurately, expected real rates, $r^e = i - \pi^e$, determine savings and investment behavior. Actual real interest rates can only be calculated once inflation is realized, which occurs after savings and investment decisions have already been made.) Expected real interest rates are not formally affected by the zero lower bound. Although nominal rates cannot be (much) below zero, expected real interest rates can be well below zero if nominal rates equal zero and expected inflation is well above zero.

Unconventional monetary policy primarily seeks to lower real interest rates by raising inflation expectations rather than lowering nominal interest rates.[9] In addition, unconventional monetary reduces the term premium associated with long-dated assets. Unlike conventional monetary policy, unconventional monetary policy should not be impaired by the zero lower bound on interest rates. So long as the central bank can raise inflation expectations sufficiently, unconventional monetary policy should succeed in stimulating a moribund economy.

Unfortunately, research and experience demonstrate that raising inflation expectations is harder for a central bank than it sounds. In order to raise inflation expectations, central banks need to pursue monetary expansion and rising prices not only in the depths of a recession but also afterward.[10] Economic actors may rationally suspect that central banks, who generally abhor inflation, will have a hard time pursuing inflationary policy after the recession has ended. As a result, even large monetary expansions may prove unsuccessful in raising inflation expectations. The experience of the Great Recession, in which inflation expectations remained anchored in spite of massive increases in central bank balance sheets, suggests that this obstacle to effective unconventional monetary policy is a significant one.

Fiscal Policy at the Zero Lower Bound in the IS-LM Model (Chapters 5–7)

At the zero lower bound, the LM curve is horizontal. An increase in demand therefore increases output, without any mitigation by changes in interest rates or from contractionary monetary policy. If demand is deficient (IS_2 in Figure A.3), then using expansionary fiscal policy, which increases G or raises $C(Y - T)$ by lowering T, shifts the IS curve from IS_2 to IS_3 and moves the economy's equilibrium from point B (with output of Y_2) to point C (with output of Y_3). At both points, the interest rate remains zero, but output is much higher at C (after fiscal stimulus) than at B (without stimulus).

When the economy's output is well below capacity, an increase in demand does not crowd out investment and drive up the interest rate. Instead, a demand increase brings the economy closer to equilibrium, partially relieving the demand shortage without making capital scarce. Expansionary fiscal policy is thus much more effective at the zero lower bound than it is when the LM curve has a steeper slope.

Central banks targeting inflation or output welcome expansionary fiscal policy at the zero lower bound because it brings output closer to potential and reduces deflationary pressures.

Chapters 8–11

In the conventional IS and LM curves, governments use their control over G, T, and M in equations (IS) and (LM) to keep output Y near potential and inflation π near its target. Many other government policies, however, also affect output and interest rate in the IS-LM model. As Chapter 8 highlights, for example, the State Department's decision about the Keystone pipeline affects investment demand.

To reflect the role of law and regulation in aggregate demand, rewrite equation IS as follows:

$$Y = C(Y - T, \mathbf{l}) + I(i, \mathbf{l}) + G \tag{IS},$$

where l represents law and regulation along many dimensions. As emphasized in Chapter 8, investment spending, $I(i,l)$ is a function of the State Department's stance with respect to Keystone, a component of l. In Chapter 11, I emphasize the role of regulatory decisions on utility rates and bankruptcy law, two more components of l, in determining total consumption spending, $C(Y - T,l)$.

Like G, T, and M, l is chosen by government agents, including regulators, judges, and administrators. Regulators, judges, and administrators can use their control of l to shift the IS curve and stabilize the economy. When they use law to stabilize the economy, they are engaging in expansionary or contractionary legal policy.

The effects of expansionary or contractionary legal policy in shifting the IS curve are analogous to fiscal policy. Fiscal policy shifts the IS curve by moving G or T, while legal policy shifts the IS curve by adjusting l. When interest rates are well above zero and the LM curve has a steep slope (as in Figure A.2), then legally induced shifts in IS have a large effect on interest rates and a relatively small effect on output, Y. At the zero lower bound, however, shifts in IS due to legal policy have a large effect on output. If fiscal policy cannot shift the IS curve from IS_2 to IS_3 in Figure A.3 because the government cannot find creditors, then expansionary legal policy of the type described here can do the job instead by shifting legal policy levers such as utility regulation, bankruptcy law, and the law of remedies.

Notes

Introduction

1. Financial Crisis Inquiry Commission, *The Financial Crisis Inquiry Report: Final Report of the National Commission on the Causes of the Financial and Economic Crisis in the United States* (Washington, DC: U.S. Government Printing Office, January 2011), 354.
2. "The Low-Rate World," *Economist,* September 24, 2016, https://www.economist.com/news/leaders/21707533-central-banks-have-been-doing-their-best-pep-up-demand-now-they-need-help-low-rate-world.
3. I adopted this question from the title and abstract of a 2016 Brookings Institution conference. See "Are We Ready for the Next Recession?," Brookings Institution, March 21, 2016, https://www.brookings.edu/events/are-we-ready-for-the-next-recession.
4. See Ben S. Bernanke, "What Tools Does the Fed Have Left? Part 3: Helicopter Money," Brookings Institution, April 11, 2016, https://www.brookings.edu/blog/ben-bernanke/2016/04/11/what-tools-does-the-fed-have-left-part-3-helicopter-money/. Chair Draghi called helicopter money "a very interesting concept" in 2016. See "Introductory Statement to the Press Conference (with Q&A)," European Central Bank, March 10, 2016, https://www.ecb.europa.eu/press/pressconf/2016/html/is160310.en.html.
5. For example, the IMF urged the Eurozone to "build a central fiscal capacity." See "Euro Area: IMF Staff Concluding Statement of the 2017 Article IV Mission," International Monetary Fund, June 15, 2017, https://www.imf.org/en/News/Articles/2017/06/15/ms061517-euro-area-staff-concluding-statement-of-the-2017-article-iv-mission.

6. U.S. Energy Information Administration, "Electricity Data Browser: Revenue from Retail Sales of Electricity, Annual," http://www.eia.gov /electricity/data/browser/#/topic/6?agg=0,1&geo=vvvvvvvvvvvvvo&endsec =vg&freq=A&start=2001&end=2015&ctype=linechart&ltype=pin&rtype =s&pin=&rse=0&maptype=0.

7. Most of my examples come from the United States for the simple reason that I know U.S. law and economic policy best. But many of the principles I establish here can be applied in any jurisdiction, and I discuss a variety of other contexts as well, such as policy in the Eurozone.

8. Michael Kiley and John Roberts, "Monetary Policy in a Low Interest Rate World," *Brookings Papers on Economic Activity* (BPEA Conference Drafts, March 23–24, 2017), https://www.brookings.edu/wp-content/uploads/2017 /03/5_kileyroberts.pdf.

9. See Figure 13.1 in Carmen Reinhart and Kenneth Rogoff, *This Time Is Different: Eight Centuries of Financial Folly* (Princeton, NJ: Princeton University Press, 2009), 205.

10. Hauthi Kingi and Kyle Rozema, "The Effect of Tax Expenditures on Automatic Stabilizers: Methods and Evidence," *Journal of Empirical Legal Studies* 14, no. 3 (2017): 548–568.

11. Mohamed El Arian, *The Only Game in Town: Central Banks, Instability, and Avoiding the Next Collapse* (New York: Random House, 2017).

12. For a detailed explanation of how populism thrived in the wake of the financial crisis of 2008 and the Great Recession, see Adam Tooze, *Crashed: How a Decade of Financial Crises Changed the World* (New York: Viking Press, 2018).

13. For an important recent exploration of the risks associated with excessive central bank power, see Paul Tucker, *Unelected Power* (Princeton NJ: Princeton University Press, 2018).

14. "Interview with President Obama," *New York Times,* July 27, 2013, http://www.nytimes.com/2013/07/28/us/politics/interview-with-president -obama.html.

15. Kiley and Roberts, "Monetary Policy in a Low Interest Rate World."

16. For related suggestions, see Laurence Kotlikoff, cited in "Are Wage and Price Controls a Solution for Greece," *Marginal Revolution*, February 19, 2010, https://marginalrevolution.com/marginalrevolution/2010/02/is-this-a -solution-for-greece.html; Emmanuel Farhi, Gita Gopinath, and Oleg Itskhoki, "Fiscal Devaluation," *Review of Economic Studies* 81, no. 2 (2014): 725–760.

17. Atif Mian and Amir Sufi, *House of Debt: How They (and You) Caused the Great Recession, and How We Can Prevent It from Happening Again* (Chicago: University of Chicago Press, 2014).

18. See Will Dobbie and Jae Song, "Debt Relief and Debtor Outcomes: Measuring the Effects of Consumer Bankruptcy Protection," *American Economic Review* 105, no. 3 (2015): 1272–1311.

1. Macroeconomics outside of a Liquidity Trap

1. John Maynard Keynes, *The General Theory of Employment, Interest and Money* (London: Macmillan, 1936), 161–162.
2. See Hyman Minsky, *Stabilizing an Unstable Economy* (New York: McGraw-Hill Professional 2008); Atif Mian and Amir Sufi, *House of Debt: How They (and You) Caused the Great Recession, and How We Can Prevent It from Happening Again* (Chicago: University of Chicago Press, 2014); John Geneakopolous, "The Leverage Cycle," in *NBER Macroeconomics Annual 2009*, ed. Daron Acemoglu, Kenneth Rogoff, and Michael Woodford (Chicago: National Bureau of Economic Research, 2010), 1–65.
3. The ratio of the debt to the value of collateral is called the leverage ratio. The fluctuation of this leverage ratio through business cycles is called leverage cycles. For more details on leverage cycles, see Geneakopolous, "The Leverage Cycle"; Mian and Sufi, *House of Debt*.
4. In an economy with only one good—meals—the effects of a change in price differ from our usual intuitions. In an ordinary economy with many goods, price decreases for one good make that good cheaper in comparison with other goods. Consumers switch from other goods to the first good and demand for the first good increases. In the restaurant economy, however, this substitution effect does not occur. If the price of meals goes down, then there is no substitution from other goods toward meals because meals are the only good. Instead, price changes function like changes in the money supply or interest rates. If prices go down today but will go back up tomorrow, then buying meals today becomes relatively cheap in terms of meals tomorrow, just like a low (or even negative) interest rate makes meals cheap today relative to tomorrow. Falling price levels also raise the real money supply (the nominal value of currency divided by the price level). A given nominal amount of currency facilitates more transactions when prices are lower.
5. This assumes that the money supply is constant.
6. For a description of the stickiness of first-year associate salaries, see David Goldman, "Big Time Lawyers Get First Pay Raise in Nearly a Decade," *CNN*, June 7, 2016, http://money.cnn.com/2016/06/07/news/companies /lawyers-pay/index.html.

7. See Truman Bewley, *Why Wages Don't Fall during a Recession* (Cambridge, MA: Harvard University Press, 2002).

2. Law and Fiscal Policy When Interest Rates Are Well above Zero

1. For a textbook discussion of automatic stabilizers, see N. Gregory Mankiw, *Principles of Economics*, 7th ed. (Nashville: South-Western College Publishers, 2014), 292–294, 446–448.

2. If prices for property were perfectly correlated with income and property tax rates remained constant in the face of changes in property valuations, then property taxes would also function as automatic stabilizers. But housing prices are not perfectly correlated with income. See Joshua Aizenman, Yothin Jinjarak, and Huanhuan Zheng, "Real Estate Valuations and Economic Growth: The Cost of Housing Cycles," *VoxEU*, October 24, 2016, http://voxeu.org/article/housing-cycles-real-estate-valuations-and -economic-growth.

3. How can the government finance these purchases? By borrowing (in fiscal policy). Government bonds are the ultimate safe asset. Thus, savers who are reluctant to put their money into unstable financial institutions will lend to the government. During financial crises, the "spread" between interest rates on government bonds and the interest rates available from financial institutions becomes much wider than it is under normal circumstances. Before the financial crisis, from January 2004 to March 2007, the spread between ninety-day commercial paper from financial institutions and ninety-day U.S. treasury bonds averaged 0.18 percent and never exceeded 0.48 percent. In October 2008 (during the financial crisis), the spread between ninety-day commercial paper and ninety-day treasuries widened to 3.24 percent—more than six times the widest spread from the pre– financial crisis era and twenty times the average spread. See Board of Governors of the Federal Reserve System, Data Download Program—H.15 Selected Interest Rates (daily), https://www.federalreserve.gov /datadownload/Choose.aspx?rel=H15.

4. See National Conference of State Legislators, "State Balanced Budget Requirements," http://www.ncsl.org/research/fiscal-policy/state-balanced -budget-requirements.aspx.

5. See Balanced Budget Amendment Task Force, *2017 Campaign Report,* http://bba4usa.org/report.

6. Consolidated Version of the Treaty on the Functioning of the European Union, art. 126, September 5, 2008, 2008 O.J. (C 115) 99.

7. See Council Regulation (EC) No. 1467/97, 1997 O.J. (L 209) 6–11, summarized at "The Corrective Arm: The Excessive Deficit Procedure,"

EUR-Lex, February 22, 2016, http://eur-lex.europa.eu/legal-content/EN
/TXT/?uri=uriserv:l25020#amendingact.

8. See, e.g., Paul Krugman, "Fifty Herbert Hoovers," *New York Times*,
December 28, 2008.

9. Alan Auerbach and Yuriy Gorodnichenko, "Output Spillovers from Fiscal
Policy," *American Economic Review* 103, no. 3 (2013): 141–146.

10. Gabriel Chodorow-Reich, "Geographic Cross-Sectional Fiscal Spending
Multipliers: What Have We Learned?," NBER Working Paper 23577
(July 2017); Emi Nakamura and Jon Steinsson, "Fiscal Stimulus in a
Monetary Union: Evidence from U.S. Regions," *American Economic
Review* 104, no. 3 (2014): 753; Daniel Shoag, "Using State Pension Shocks
to Estimate Fiscal Multipliers since the Great Recession," *American
Economic Review* 103, no. 3 (2013): 121–124; Gabriel Chodorow-Reich,
Laura Feiveson, Zachary Liscow, and William Gui Woolston, "Does State
Fiscal Relief during Recessions Increase Employment? Evidence from the
American Recovery and Reinvestment Act," *American Economic Journal:
Economic Policy* 4, no. 3 (2012): 118.

11. See Eric M. Leeper, Nora Traum, and Todd B. Walker, "Clearing up the
Fiscal Multiplier Morass," *American Economic Review* 107, no. 8 (2017):
2409–2454. This article helps explain the disparity in multiplier estimates
by observing that much of the disparity is a result of differing assumptions
about behavioral responses to government taxation practices. When the
authors use a Bayesian empirical approach that places less weight on
assumptions relative to data, they find a multiplier of 1.4.

12. See "Policy Lags," *Economist's View*, December 5, 2008, http://
economistsview.typepad.com/economistsview/2008/12/policy-lags.html.

13. John B. Taylor, "Reassessing Discretionary Fiscal Policy," *Journal of
Economic Perspectives* 14, no. 3 (2000): 21–36.

14. See William N. Eskridge Jr., "Vetogates, Chevron, Preemption," *Notre
Dame Law Review* 83 (2008): 1441.

15. See United States Government Accountability Office, "GAO-10-383:
Recovery Act—Project Selection and Starts Are Influenced by Certain
Federal Requirements and Other Factors," February 18, 2010.

16. United States Government Accountability Office, "GAO-12-195: Recovery
Act—Progress and Challenges in Spending Weatherization Funds,"
December 16, 2011, 22.

17. Richard A. Musgrave, *The Theory of Public Finance: A Study in Public
Economy* (New York: McGraw-Hill, 1959).

18. James Buchanan and Richard Wagner, *The Collected Works of James M.
Buchanan*, vol. 8, *Democracy in Deficit: The Political Legacy of John
Keynes* (Indianapolis: Liberty Fund, 2000), 7, explain that "The application
of the Keynesian precepts within a working political democracy, however,

would often require politicians to undertake actions that would reduce their prospects for survival. Should we then be surprised that the Keynesian democratic political institutions will produce policy responses contrary to those that would be forthcoming from some idealized application of the norms in the absence of political feedback?" Note, however, that, as Allan Drazen has concluded, "there is much less hard evidence than both theoretical models and the conventional wisdom about the prevalence of 'election-year economics' would suggest. . . . There is significant disagreement about whether there is opportunistic manipulation [of the economy] that can be observed in the macro data." Allan Drazen, "The Political Business Cycle after 25 Years," in *NBER Macroeconomics Annual 2000*, ed. Ben Bernanke and Kenneth Rogoff (Chicago: National Bureau of Economics Research, 2000), 75–117.

19. Vitor Gaspar, "Fiscal Policy for the Twenty-First Century," in *Progress and Confusion: The State of Macroeconomic Policy*, ed. Olivier Blanchard, Raghuram Rajan, Kenneth Rogoff, and Lawrence Summers (Cambridge, MA: MIT Press, 2016), 165–177.

20. J. Bradford DeLong and Lawrence Summers, "Fiscal Policy in a Depressed Economy," in *Brookings Papers on Economic Activity: Spring 2012*, ed. David Romer and Justin Wolfers (Washington, DC: Brookings Institution, 2012), 233–297.

21. For example, the U.S. Congress considered proposing a balanced budget amendment at the federal level in 1997 and in 2011. See Richard Kogan, "Constitutional Balanced Budget Amendment Poses Serious Risks," Center on Budget and Policy Priorities, March 16, 2018, https://www.cbpp.org /research/constitutional-balanced-budget-amendment-poses-serious-risks. Germany passed a constitutional balanced budget rule, the Schuldenbremse, in 2009. See Basic Law for the Federal Republic of Germany, art. 109 (3).

22. See Olivier Blanchard, "Contours of Macroeconomic Policy in the Future," *IMFBlog*, April 2, 2015, http://blog-imfdirect.imf.org/2015/04/02/contours -of-macroeconomic-policy-in-the-future/. For recent articles that attempt to better understand and improve the automatic stabilizing properties of fiscal policy, see Alisdair McKay and Ricardo Reis, "The Role of Automatic Stabilizers in the U.S. Business Cycle," *Econometrica* 84 (2016): 141–194; Pascal Michaillat and Emmanuel Saez, "The Optimal Use of Government Purchases for Macroeconomic Stabilization," NBER Working Paper No. 21322 (July 2015).

23. An important exception to this avoidance of macroeconomics within tax is Jeff Strnad, "Some Macroeconomic Interactions with Tax Base Choice," *SMU Law Review* 56 (2003): 171–199. Strnad's article, however, alternates

between classical and Keynesian macroeconomic approaches. As a result, it does not focus on automatic stabilizers or destabilizers.

24. Congressional Budget and Impoundment Control Act of 1974, 2 U.S.C. § 622(3) (2006).

25. Staff of Joint Committee on Taxation, "JCX-15-11: Background Information on Tax Expenditure Analysis and Historical Survey of Tax Expenditure Estimates," Joint Committee on Taxation, Congress of the United States, March 9, 2011, 2, http://www.jct.gov/publications.html?func=startdown&id =3740.

26. "Policy Basics: Federal Tax Expenditures," Center on Policy and Budget Priorities, April 9, 2018, http://www.cbpp.org/cms/index.cfm?fa=view&id =4055.

27. See table II.29 in Organisation for Economic Co-operation and Development, *Tax Expenditures in OECD Countries* (Paris: Organisation for Economic Co-operation and Development, 2012), 224.

28. Ibid.; European Commission, "Tax Expenditures in Direct Taxation in EU Member States," Occasional Papers 207 (December 2014), 9, http://ec .europa.eu/economy_finance/publications/occasional_paper/2014/pdf /ocp207_en.pdf.

29. If individual demand for health care changes with the business cycle, then government spending on health care may respond to the business cycle. Interestingly, there is some evidence that mortality is weakly pro-cyclical (people die at higher rates in booms than in recessions). See Christopher J. Ruhm, "Are Recessions Good for Your Health?," *Quarterly Journal of Economics* 115, no. 2 (2000): 617. At the same time, individuals have more time to consume health care during recessions. The total impact of these factors on health care demand over the business cycle is indeterminate.

30. See Office of Management and Budget, *Fiscal Year 2014: Analytical Perspectives—Budget of the U.S. Government* (Washington, DC: United States Government Publishing Office, 2013), 308, https://www.gpo.gov /fdsys/pkg/BUDGET-2014-PER/pdf/BUDGET-2014-PER.pdf.

31. This discussion builds on some of my earlier work. See Yair Listokin, "Stabilizing the Economy through the Income Tax Code," *Tax Notes* 123 (2009): 1575; Yair Listokin, "Equity, Efficiency, and Stability: The Importance of Macroeconomics for Evaluating Income Tax Policy," *Yale Journal on Regulation* 29 (2012): 45. For a related argument, see Brian Galle and Jonathan Klick, "Recessions and the Social Safety Net: The Alternative Minimum Tax as a Counter-Cyclical Fiscal Stabilizer," *Stanford Law Review* 63 (2010): 187.

32. See Tax Expenditure Data, data available from author. This data set records the final estimate provided by the Office of Management and Budget for

the value of the tax expenditure in a particular year. The final estimate is likely to be the most accurate because it involves no projections and relies entirely on past events. Data for the value of a tax expenditure in fiscal year 2007, for example, are therefore collected from the 2009 Office of Management and Budget report. See, e.g., Office of Management and Budget, *Fiscal Year 2009: Analytical Perspectives—Budget of the U.S. Government* (Washington, DC: United States Government Publishing Office, 2008). The data should be treated with some degree of skepticism, since they aggregate a myriad of factors, such as changes in marginal tax rates and program eligibility as well as business cycle effects.

33. Between 2004 and 2006, the cost of the exclusion rose more than 20 percent. The 2007–2009 increase in the cost of the exclusion was below 10 percent, with health care costs increasing throughout the period. See Office of Management and Budget, *Fiscal Year 2009.*

34. See, e.g., Ann C. Foster And Craig J. Kreisler, Bureau of Labor Statistics, *Health Care Spending of U.S. Consumers, by Age: 1998, 2003, and 2008 (2010),* at *https://www.bls.gov/cex/anthology11/csxanth4.pdf* (2010), http://www.bls.gov/opub/focus/volume1_number8/cex_1_8.htm (last updated August 2010).

35. Hautahi Kingi and Kyle Rozema, "The Effect of Tax Expenditures on Automatic Stabilizers: Methods and Evidence," *Journal of Empirical Studies* 14, no. 3 (2017): 548–568. To arrive at the 23 percent figure, I extrapolated from the Kingi and Rozema results. If $132.3 billion (the sum of $75.3 billion and $57 billion) of tax expenditures reduce the automatic stabilizing properties by 2.03 percent, then the total of $1.5 trillion of tax expenditures should reduce the automatic stabilizing properties of the income tax code by 23 percent. $2.03\% / \$132.3 = x / \$1500$. This rough extrapolation assumes that additional tax expenditures reduce the stabilizing properties in proportion to their value.

36. Some of this analysis was first developed in Yair Listokin, "The Republican Plan to Make the Next Recession Even Worse," *Tax Notes,* December 11, 2017.

37. See table 1, "Selected Financial Data on Businesses," in Internal Revenue Service, "SOI Tax Stats—Integrated Business Data," https://www.irs.gov/statistics/soi-tax-stats-integrated-business-data.

38. See table 2.1, "Receipts by Source: 1934–2022," in Office of Management and Budget, "Historical Tables," https://www.whitehouse.gov/omb/budget/Historicals.

39. See United States Congress Joint Committee on Taxation, "Estimated Budget Effects of the Revenue Provisions Contained in the Conference Agreement for H.R. 1, The American Recovery and Reinvestment Tax Act of 2009," February 12, 2009, http://www.jct.gov/x-19-09.pdf.

40. The dramatic reduction in the corporate income tax rate is the most destabilizing feature of the Tax Cuts and Jobs Act, but it is not the only one. The reduction in tax rates on unincorporated business income, which, like corporate income, is highly business-cycle sensitive, has a similarly destabilizing effect on the economy. Even an important tax *increase* associated with the TCJA—the elimination of "net operating loss carrybacks"— weakened the income tax's automatic stabilizing properties. The availability of loss "carrybacks" to previous years ensured that U.S. corporate income tax revenues plunged in proportion to corporate income during the Great Recession. Carrybacks enabled corporations who made annual losses in 2009 to get a tax refund—that is, a check from the U.S. government—if they paid income taxes in 2007 or 2008. (A 2009 expansion of the carryback regime further increased refunds associated with carrybacks, but this temporary provision constituted discretionary, rather than automatic, fiscal policy.) Because the corporate tax refunds arrived in 2009, the carryback structure stimulated the economy by providing cash to corporations exactly when they needed it most. Without the carrybacks, corporations would have needed to wait until future years in order to claim the tax benefit associated with having made losses in 2009.

41. In an important article, David Super analyzes a wide variety of federal state budget interactions for unexpected linkages. See David A. Super, "Rethinking Fiscal Federalism," *Harvard Law Review* 118 (2005): 2544–2652. Although he does not describe the automatic destabilizer that I find here, he does identify many other unintended consequences of this system of federal support for state government.

42. See Kaiser Family Foundation, *Federal and State Share of Medicaid Spending*, https://www.kff.org/medicaid/state-indicator/federalstate-share -of-spending/?currentTimeframe=0&sortModel=%7B%22colId%22:%22L ocation%22,%22sort%22:%22asc%22%7D.

43. Congressional Budget Office, *Federal Grants to State and Local Governments* (2013), https://www.cbo.gov/sites/default/files/113th-congress-2013 -2014/reports/03-05-13federalgrantsonecol.pdf.

44. Medicaid and CHIP Payment and Access Commission, "Medicaid's Share of State Budgets," https://www.macpac.gov/subtopic/medicaids-share-of -state-budgets/.

45. See Phil Oliff, Jon Shure, and Nicholas Johnson, "Federal Fiscal Relief Is Working as Intended," Center for Budget and Policy Priorities, June 29, 2009, https://www.cbpp.org/research/federal-fiscal-relief-is-working-as -intended.

46. This discussion assumes that some busts are inevitable but that booms and busts don't carry information about long-run risks, which are constant (after

adjusting for the business cycle). If a recession gives information about the future (e.g., a bust today makes future busts more likely), then an increase in insurance rates is more defensible, even though it destabilizes the economy.

47. 12 USC 1711(f)(4)).

48. See figure included in Financial Services Committee, "HUD IG: Department's Eight Year Delay Impacts FHA Fund by $15 Billion," September 17, 2013, https://financialservices.house.gov/blog/?postid=349961.

49. See Keith Jurow, "FHA Insured Mortgages: A Disaster in the Making," *Business Insider*, August 9, 2010, http://www.businessinsider.com/fha -insured-mortgages-a-disaster-2010-8; Financial Services Committee, "HUD IG: Department's Eight Year Delay Impacts FHA Fund by $15 Billion."

50. For an empirical analysis of the destabilizing effects of Florida's unemployment insurance system, see Andrew C. Johnston, "Unemployment Insurance Taxes and Labor Demand: Quasi-Experimental Evidence from Administrative Data" (July 2017), http://conference.nber.org/confer//2017 /SI2017/PE/Johnston.pdf.

51. See Eric Lipton, "F.D.I.C. Increases Fees to Insure Bank Deposits," *New York Times*, February 27, 2009, http://www.nytimes.com/2009/02/28 /business/28banks.html.

3. Law and Monetary Policy When Interest Rates Are Well above Zero

1. See N. Gregory Mankiw, *Principles of Economics*, 7th ed. (Nashville: South-Western College Publishers, 2014), 550.

2. Lawrence J. Christiano, Martin Eichenbaum, and Charles L. Evans, "Monetary Policy Shocks: What Have We Learned and to What End?" in *Handbook of Macroeconomics*, vol. 1A, ed. John B. Taylor and Michael Woodford (Philadelphia: Elsevier, 1999), 65–148. In a more recent review of the empirical literature, Ramey supports this finding but observes that true "shocks" to monetary policy have become very rare. See Valerie Ramey, "Macroeconomic Shocks and Their Propagation," in *Handbook of Macroeconomics*, vol. 2, ed. John B. Taylor and Harold Uhlig (Philadelphia: Elsevier, 2016), 71–162.

3. This analysis was composed before the publication of Paul Tucker's comprehensive 2018 monograph, which develops a theory of legitimate delegation of power to central banks. See Paul Tucker, *Unelected Power*

(Princeton, NJ: Princeton University Press, 2018). Another important recent contribution on this topic is Phillip A. Wallach, *To the Edge: Legality, Legitimacy, and the Responses to the 2008 Financial Crisis* (Washington: Brookings Institution Press, 2015).

4. The Federal Reserve Act, 12 U.S.C. §§ 221–522, December 23, 1913.

5. Treaty on European Union (Consolidated Version), Treaty of Maastricht, art. 127, February 7, 1992, O.J. (C 325/5).

6. Consolidated Version of the Treaty on the Functioning of the European Union, art. 130, September 5, 2008, O.J. (C 115) 99.

7. The theory of optimal currency areas examines the tradeoffs between larger and smaller currency unions. See Robert A. Mundell, "A Theory of Optimum Currency Areas," *American Economic Review* 51, no. 4 (1961): 657–665.

8. During the "free banking" era in the United States (1837–1864), states, and not the federal government or a national bank, regulated the issue of currency.

9. The Bretton Woods Conference of July 1944 negotiated the Bretton Woods agreements, which established a regime of pegged foreign exchange rates to facilitate global trade and investment.

10. See Atish R. Ghosh and Mahvash S. Qureshi, "What's in a Name? That Which We Call Capital Controls," International Monetary Fund, February 2016, https://www.imf.org/external/pubs/ft/wp/2016/wp1625.pdf, 17. My discussion here parallels that of the IMF's working paper, which was developed independently.

11. Ibid.

12. J. Bradford DeLong and Lawrence H. Summers, "Fiscal Policy in a Depressed Economy," *Brookings Papers on Economic Activity: Spring 2012,* ed. David H. Romer and Justin Wolfers (Washington, DC: Brookings Institution, 2012), 233–274.

13. See Jonathan L. Willis and Guangye Cao, "Has the U.S. Economy Become Less Interest Rate Sensitive?," *Economic Review* 100, no. 2 (2015): 6, https://www.kansascityfed.org/~/media/files/publicat/econrev/econrevarchive/2015/2q15willis.pdf.

14. Ibid.

15. Permit Extension Act of 2008, N.J.S.A. 40:55D-136.1–136.6, http://www.nj.gov/dep/landuse/pea.html.

16. For a discussion of the economic effects of zoning laws on U.S. housing prices from the 1970s to the present, see Edward Glaeser, "Reforming Land Use Regulations," Brookings Institution, April 24, 2017, https://www.brookings.edu/research/reforming-land-use-regulations/.

17. See Scott Sumner, "Why the Fiscal Multiplier Is Roughly Zero," Mercatus Center, George Mason University, September 11, 2013, https://www .mercatus.org/publication/why-fiscal-multiplier-roughly-zero-0.

18. Jason Furman, chair of the U.S. Council of Economic Advisers during the Obama administration, summarized the old consensus as follows: "Discretionary fiscal policy is dominated by monetary policy as a stabilisation tool because of lags in the application, impact, and removal of discretionary fiscal stimulus." See Jason Furman, "The New View of Fiscal Policy and Its Application," *VoxEU*, November 2, 2016, http://voxeu.org/article/new-view -fiscal-policy-and-its-application.

19. "The Wars of Independence: How to Preserve the Benefits of Central Bank Autonomy," *Economist*, April 27, 2017, http://www.economist.com/news /leaders/21721380-twenty-years-after-bank-england-was-given -independence-powers-central-banks-are.

20. See Tucker, *Unelected Power*.

21. See Jeff Black, Craig Torres, and Jeanette Rodrigues, "Populism Is Shaking the Edifice of Central Bank Independence," *Bloomberg*, February 27, 2017, https://www.bloomberg.com/news/articles/2017-02-27/age-of-populism -shakes-pedestal-of-central-bank-independence.

22. See Federal Reserve Transparency Act of 2017, 115th Cong., Senate. 16, https://www.congress.gov/bill/115th-congress/senate-bill/16. See also United States House of Representatives Financial Services Committee, "Federal Reserve Reform: The Fed Oversight Reform and Modernization Act (FORM Act), H.R. 3189," https://financialservices.house.gov/issueshome /issue/?IssueID=100094.

23. See Stefan Wagstyl and Claire Jones, "Germany Blames Mario Draghi for Rise of Rightwing AfD Party," *Financial Times,* April 10, 2016.

24. See Simon Osborne, "ECB Backlash: Anger as Fifth of German Firms Face Negative Interest Rates," *Express,* August 10, 2017, http://www.express.co .uk/news/world/839565/ECB-European-Central-Bank-Germany-negative -interest-rates-eurozone-economic-powerhouse.

25. United States House of Representatives Financial Services Committee, "Federal Reserve Reform: The Fed Oversight Reform and Modernization Act (FORM Act), H.R. 3189."

4. The Painful Costs of Prolonged Recessions: Evidence and Theory

1. See Lawrence Summers, "The Age of Secular Stagnation: What It Is and What To Do about It," *Foreign Affairs,* February 15, 2016, https://www

.foreignaffairs.com/articles/united-states/2016-02-15/age-secular
-stagnation.

2. See David Luttrell, Tyler Atkinson, and Harvey Rosenblum, "Assessing the Costs and Consequences of the 2007–09 Financial Crisis and Its Aftermath," *Economic Letter* 8, no. 7 (September 2013), http://www.dallasfed .org/research/eclett/2013/el1307.cfm. This is a 2013 estimate from the Dallas Federal Reserve Bank's Research Department. The $30 trillion figure represents almost two years of lost output. The wide range comes from uncertainty about the ultimate length of the recession and likelihood of catchup growth. The wide range is also caused by uncertainty about "hysteresis."

3. See Peter S. Goodman, "Europe's Economy, after 8-Year Detour, Is Fitfully Back on Track," *New York Times*, April 29, 2016, https://www .nytimes.com/2016/04/30/business/international/eurozone-economy-q1 .html?_r=0.

4. For a survey of the research on sources of hysteresis in unemployment flows, see Michael W. L. Elsby, Ryan Michaels, and David Ratner, "The Beveridge Curve: A Survey," *Journal of Economic Literature* 53, no. 3 (2015): 571–630.

5. Summers, "Age of Secular Stagnation."

6. Manuel Funke, Moritz Schularick, and Christoph Trebesch, "Going to Extremes: Politics after Financial Crises, 1870–2014," *European Economic Review* 88 (2016): 227–260.

7. The theory of the liquidity trap was first developed during the Great Depression by John Hicks to reconcile Keynesian and classical macroeconomics. Hicks theorized that, in ordinary times, economies were prone only to temporary recessions, in accord with the classical view of the business cycle. When interest rates hit the zero lower bound, however, Hicks argued that the Keynesian view, in which prolonged recessions or depressions are caused by stagnant aggregate demand, becomes more relevant. Since the 1990s, Paul Krugman has developed a modern version of Hicks's liquidity trap. See Paul Krugman, "This Age of Hicks," *New York Times*, July 22, 2011, https://krugman.blogs.nytimes.com/2011/07/22/this-age-of-hicks/.

8. For the most part, no impassable barrier bars interest rates from falling below zero—at least in the private sector. Indeed, we saw slightly negative interest rates (below zero, but above −1.0 percent) in many countries during the Great Recession—without cash hoarding. But these episodes are the exception that proves the rule. If interest rates of −0.4 percent are a newsworthy "act of desperation," then the zero lower bound on interest rates is an important constraint. See Jana Randow and Simon Kennedy,

"Negative Interest Rates," *Bloomberg,* March 21, 2017, https://www
.bloomberg.com/quicktake/negative-interest-rates; Matthew Rognlie, "What
Lower Bound? Monetary Policy with Negative Interest Rates," http://
mattrognlie.com/negative_rates.pdf.

Law may restrict the Federal Reserve from paying negative interest rates.
See Josh Zumbrun, "Four Legal Questions the Fed Would Face If It
Decided to Go Negative," *Wall Street Journal,* February 10, 2016, https://
blogs.wsj.com/economics/2016/02/10/four-legal-questions-the-fed-would
-face-if-it-decided-to-go-negative/. Yet again, we see the intimate connection between monetary policy and law. I am skeptical of these legal qualms,
which pale in comparison to the legal uncertainty of the ECB's Outright
Monetary Transactions program (discussed in Chapter 5).

9. Kenneth Rogoff calls the zero lower bound the "curse of cash." He recom-
mends that, if cash's zero rate of return constrains interest rates, then one
response is to abolish cash and similar instruments in favor of alternatives
that yield less than zero. The suggestion is intriguing; its radicalism speaks
to the depth of macroeconomists' worries about liquidity traps. See
Kenneth S. Rogoff, *The Curse of Cash: How Large-Denomination Bills Aid
Crime and Tax Evasion and Constrain Monetary Policy* (Princeton, NJ:
Princeton University Press, 2016).

10. For a counterargument that negative interest rates are both achievable and
constitute "conventional monetary policy, see Miles Kimball, "Negative
Interest Rate Policy as Conventional Monetary Policy," *National Institute
Economic Review* 234, no. 1 (2015): R5–R14.

11. The theory of secular stagnation was developed during the Great Depression by Alvin Hansen. See Alvin H. Hansen, "Economic Progress and
Declining Population Growth," *American Economic Review* 29, no. 1
(March 1939): 1–15. In the aftermath of the Great Recession, Larry
Summers has advocated a modern version. See, e.g., Lawrence H. Summers, "The Age of Secular Stagnation," *Foreign Affairs,* March/April 2016,
https://www.foreignaffairs.com/articles/united-states/2016-02-15/age
-secular-stagnation.

12. See Michael T. Kiley and John M. Roberts, "Monetary Policy in a Low
Interest Rate World," *Brookings Papers on Economic Activity,* March 23,
2017.

13. For an explanation of the debt supercycle theory of the Great Recession,
see Kenneth S. Rogoff, "Debt Supercycle—Not Secular Stagnation," in
Progress and Confusion: The State of Macroeconomic Policy, ed. Olivier
Blanchard, Raghuram Rajan, Kenneth Rogoff, and Lawrence Summers
(Cambridge, MA: MIT Press, 2016), 19–28.

14. Officially, the Great Recession began in December 2007. At this time, financial markets were jittery—subprime mortgages were beginning to default—but not in crisis. The Financial Crisis of 2008 transformed what many guessed would be an ordinary recession into the worst global downturn since the Great Depression.

5. Law, Monetary Policy, and Fiscal Policy in a Liquidity Trap

1. Olivier Blanchard, Giovanni Dell'Ariccia, and Paolo Mauro, "Rethinking Macroeconomic Policy," International Monetary Fund, February 12, 2010, https://www.imf.org/external/pubs/ft/spn/2010/spn1003.pdf; Ben S. Bernanke, "The Zero Lower Bound on Interest Rates: How Should the Fed Respond?," Brookings Institution, April 13, 2017, https://www.brookings.edu/blog/ben -bernanke/2017/04/13/the-zero-lower-bound-on-interest-rates-how-should -the-fed-respond/; Stephen G. Cecchetti and Kermit L Schoenholtz, "The Case for a Higher Inflation Target Gets Stronger," *Money, Banking and Financial Markets,* April 3, 2017, http://www.moneyandbanking.com /commentary/2017/4/2/the-case-for-a-higher-inflation-target-gets-stronger.
2. See Neil Irwin, "Of Kiwis and Currencies: How a 2% Inflation Target Became Global Economic Gospel," *New York Times,* December 19, 2014, https://www.nytimes.com/2014/12/21/upshot/of-kiwis-and-currencies-how-a -2-inflation-target-became-global-economic-gospel.html.
3. See Bank of Canada, "Inflation Control Target," http://www.bankofcanada .ca/rates/indicators/key-variables/inflation-control-target/.
4. It is very difficult for long-term interest rates to fall to zero, even when short-term rates are zero. When interest rates are zero, they cannot go lower. Locking money up for a long term at a rate that cannot go lower but might go higher is unattractive for investors. Put another way, short-term investments have "option" value for savers. If interest rates subsequently go up, then holders of short-term savings vehicles can take advantage of the higher rates. Savers in long-term assets cannot take advantage of the uptick in rates. In order to induce savers to hold long-term assets, long-term assets must offer some interest rate premium over short-term rates. If short-term rates are zero, long-term rates need to be above zero.
5. For example, the Bank of England's quantitative easing program brought the value of its assets to over 24 percent of GDP, a figure never before reached in the Bank's more-than-three-hundred-year history. Previous peaks in Bank of England asset holdings included the Napoleonic Wars and the immediate aftermath of World War II. In both of these extraordinary

cases, the Bank's assets never reached 20 percent of GDP, well short of their Great Recession peak. See Bank of England Balance Sheet—Total Assets in the United Kingdom, https://fred.stlouisfed.org/series /BOEBSTAUKA.

6. Paul Krugman, "Second-Best Macroeconomics," *New York Times,* July 28, 2015, https://krugman.blogs.nytimes.com/2015/07/28/second-best -macroeconomics/. For a thorough discussion of the exclusivity of monetary policy as a response to the Great Recession, see Mohamed El Arian, *The Only Game in Town: Central Banks, Instability, and Avoiding the Next Collapse* (New York: Random House, 2017).

7. In the quantity theory of money, the real value of output multiplied by the price level (nominal GDP) equals the amount of money in the economy multiplied by money's velocity (how often the money gets used): $MV = PY$. The value of the money supply rose by a factor of five, but the value of nominal GDP (the price level multiplied by output) did not change much. This implies that the velocity of money decreased. At the zero lower bound, people hold money as an asset rather than using it to facilitate transactions.

8. R. A., "The Economist Explains: What Is Quantitative Easing?," *Economist,* March 9, 2015, http://www.economist.com/blogs/economist-explains/2015 /03/economist-explains-5.

9. "Speech by Mario Draghi, President of the European Central Bank at the Global Investment Conference in London," European Central Bank, July 26, 2012, https://www.ecb.europa.eu/press/key/date/2012/html /sp120726.en.html.

10. Ben S. Bernanke, "What Tools Does the Fed Have Left? Part 1: Negative Interest Rates," Brookings Institution, March 18, 2016, https://www .brookings.edu/blog/ben-bernanke/2016/03/18/what-tools-does-the-fed -have-left-part-1-negative-interest-rates/.

11. See Kenneth S. Rogoff, *The Curse of Cash: How Large-Denomination Bills Aid Crime and Tax Evasion and Constrain Monetary Policy* (Princeton, NJ: Princeton University Press, 2017).

12. Ben S. Bernanke, "What Tools Does the Fed Have Left? Part 3: Helicopter Money," Brookings Institution, April 11, 2016, https://www.brookings.edu /blog/ben-bernanke/2016/04/11/what-tools-does-the-fed-have-left-part-3 -helicopter-money/.

13. Ibid.

14. See European Central Bank, "Compliance of Outright Monetary Transactions with the Prohibition of Monetary Financing," October 2012, https://www.ecb.europa.eu/pub/pdf/other/mb201210_focus01.en.pdf.

15. Clemens Fuest, president of the Centre for European Economic Research, quoted in Stephanie Bodoni, "Draghi Get EU Top Court's Backing for 2012

OMT Plan," *Bloomberg,* June 16, 2015, http://www.bloomberg.com/news /articles/2015-06-16/draghi-gets-eu-top-court-s-backing-for-2012-bond -buying-plan.

16. BVerfG, "Order of the Second Senate of 14 January 2014–2 BvR 2728/13," January 14, 2014, http://www.bverfg.de/e/rs20140114_2bvr272813en.html [hereinafter cited as 2 BvR 2728/13].

17. See Court of Justice of the European Union, "The OMT Programme Announced by the ECB in September 2012 Is Compatible with EU Law," June 16, 2015, http://curia.europa.eu/jcms/upload/docs/application/pdf/2015 -06/cp150070en.pdf.

18. As the ECJ's press release describes it, ECB "monetary policy decisions in fact depend, to a great extent, on the transmission of the 'impulses' which the [ECB] sends out across the money market to the various sectors of the economy. Consequently, if the monetary policy transmission mechanism is disrupted, that is likely to render the [ECB's] decisions ineffective in a part of the euro area." Ibid.

19. See 2 BvR 2728/13, paras. 71–72.

20. Judgment of June 16, 2005, Gauweiler, C-62/14, EU:C:2015:400, para. 103, http://curia.europa.eu/juris/document/document.jsf;jsessionid=9ea7d2dc30d d19f21764461846cfb192a20f48b71d6f.e34KaxiLc3qMb40Rch0SaxuQaxf0 ?text=&docid=165057&pageIndex=0&doclang=en&mode=lst&dir=&occ =first&part=1&cid=660213.

21. In amending the constitutional arrangement in this way, the ECB and ECJ followed a long tradition of responding to crisis by modifying a constitutional order without recourse to a formal amendment. For a discussion of such "constitutional moments", see, e.g., Bruce Ackerman, *We the People,* vol. 1, *Foundations* (Cambridge, MA: Belknap Press, 1991). Note that a "constitutional moment" in the European Union is hard to define because of the difficulty of popular ratification and legitimation via democratic election.

22. See "How to Address the EU's Democratic Deficit," *Economist,* March 23, 2017, https://www.economist.com/news/special-report/21719196-institutions -need-reform-how-address-eus-democratic-deficit.

23. Òscar Jordà, Moritz Schularick, and Alan M. Taylor, "Financial Crises, Credit Booms, and External Imbalances: 140 Years of Lessons," *IMF Economic Review* 59, no. 2 (2011): 340–378; Carmen M. Reinhart and Kenneth S. Rogoff, "The Aftermath of Financial Crises," *American Economic Review* 99, no. 2 (2009): 466–472.

24. Gabriel Chodorow-Reich, "Geographic Cross-Sectional Fiscal Spending Multipliers: What Have We Learned," NBER Working Paper No. 23577 (July 2017), https://scholar.harvard.edu/chodorow-reich/publications /geographic-cross-sectional-fiscal-multiplierswhat-have-we-learned.

25. See box 1.1 in International Monetary Fund, *World Economic Outlook: Coping with High Debt and Sluggish Growth* (Washington, DC: International Monetary Fund, October 2012), http://www.imf.org/external/pubs/ft/weo/2012/02/pdf/text.pdf.

26. Ibid.

27. Ibid. Furthermore, some recent empirical estimates of multipliers during periods of slack demand are 1.5 or more over three years. Alan J. Auerbach and Yuriy Gorodnichenko, "Measuring the Output Responses to Fiscal Policy," *American Economic Journal: Economic Policy* 4, no. 2 (2012): 1, 11, 19. See also Alan J. Auerbach and Yuriy Gorodnichenko, "Fiscal Multipliers in Recession and Expansion," in *Fiscal Policy after the Financial Crisis*, ed. Alberto Alesina and Francesco Giavazzi (Chicago: University of Chicago Press, 2013), 63–98. Other sources suggest that the multiplier is well above one during periods of slack. See, e.g., International Monetary Fund, *Fiscal Monitor: Balancing Fiscal Policy Risks* (Washington, DC : International Monetary Fund, April 2012), http://www.imf.org/external/pubs/ft/fm/2012/01/pdf/fm1201.pdf; Nicoletta Batini, Giovanni Callegari, and Giovanni Melina, "Successful Austerity in the United States, Europe, and Japan," International Monetary Fund Working Paper 12/190 (July 2012), 23–25; Michael Woodford, "Simple Analytics of the Government Expenditure Multiplier," *American Economic Journals: Macroeconomics* 3, no. 1 (2011): 1, 33. See also Emi Nakamura and Jon Steinsson, "Fiscal Stimulus in a Monetary Union: Evidence from U.S. Regions," *American Economic Review* 104, no. 3 (2014): 753–792, who show that a $1 increase in government spending in one U.S. state relative to a neighbor is associated with a $1.50 increase in that state's output. They observe that this estimate is higher than the average estimate of fiscal multipliers and attribute the difference to the fact that, when government spending goes up in one state relative to another, monetary policy does not change. Similarly, monetary policy does not change in response to fiscal policy in a liquidity trap. However, another article suggested the multiplier to be 0.7 to 0.9 over two to four years, and the authors argue that empirical evidence does not show that multipliers are higher in recessions. See Valerie A. Ramey and Sarah Zubairy, "Government Spending Multipliers in Good Times and in Bad: Evidence from U.S. Historical Data," *Journal of Political Economy* 126, no. 2 (2018), table 1.

28. Nicoletta Batini, Luc Eyraud, and Anke Weber, "A Simple Method to Compute Fiscal Multipliers," International Monetary Fund Working Paper 14/93 (June 2014), https://www.imf.org/external/pubs/ft/wp/2014/wp1493.pdf; "Successful Austerity in the United States, Europe and Japan," International Monetary Fund Working Paper 12/190, (2012); Anja Baum,

Marcos Poplawski-Ribeiro, and Anke Weber, "Fiscal Multipliers and the State of the Economy," International Monetary Fund Working Paper 12/286 (December 2012), https://www.imf.org/en/Publications/WP/Issues /2016/12/31/Fiscal-Multipliers-and-the-State-of-the-Economy-40146; Matthew Canzoneri, Fabrice Collard, Harris Dellas, and Behzad Diba, "Fiscal Multipliers in Recessions," *Economic Journal* 126, no. 590 (February 2016), 75–108; Pablo Hernández de Cos and Enrique Moral-Benito, "Fiscal Multipliers in Turbulent Times: The Case of Spain," Banco de Espana Working Paper No. 1309 (June 2013); Michael T. Owyang, Valerie A. Ramey, and Sarah Zubairy, "Are Government Spending Multipliers Greater during Periods of Slack? Evidence from 20th Century Historical Data," *American Economic Review* 103, no. 3 (May 2013), 129–134.

29. J. Bradford DeLong and Lawrence H. Summers, "Fiscal Policy in a Depressed Economy," in *Brookings Papers on Economic Activity: Spring 2012*, ed. David H. Romer and Justin Wolfers (Washington, DC: Brookings Institution, 2012), 233–274.

30. See "Economic Stimulus (Revisited)," IGM Forum, University of Chicago Booth School of Business, July 29, 2014, http://www.igmchicago.org/surveys /economic-stimulus-revisited.

31. Martin Feldstein, "The Future of Fiscal Policy," in *Progress and Confusion: The State of Macroeconomic Policy*, ed. Oliver J. Blanchard, Raghuram G. Rajan, Kenneth S. Rogoff, and Lawrence H. Summers (Cambridge, MA: MIT Press, 2016), 181.

32. See International Monetary Fund, *Fiscal Monitor: Now Is the Time: Fiscal Policies for Sustainable Growth* (Washington DC: International Monetary Fund, April 2015), http://www.imf.org/external/pubs/ft/fm/2015/01/pdf /fm1501.pdf.

33. European Central Bank, "Hearing of the Committee on Economic and Monetary Affairs of the European Parliament: Introductory Statement of Mario Draghi, President of the ECB, at the ECON Committee of the European Parliament, Brussels, 28 November 2016," November 28, 2016, https://www.ecb.europa.eu/press/key/date/2016/html/sp161128_1.en.html.

34. Ben S. Bernanke, "The Federal Reserve: Looking Back, Looking Forward," Board of Governors of the Federal Reserve System, January 3, 2014, https://www.federalreserve.gov/newsevents/speech/bernanke20140103a.htm.

35. Jason Furman, "The New View of Fiscal Policy and Its Application," *VoxEU*, October 5, 2016, https://voxeu.org/article/new-view-fiscal-policy -and-its-application.

36. See Eswar Prasad and Isaac Sorkin, "Assessing the G-20 Stimulus Package: A Deeper Look," Brookings Institution, March 5, 2009, http://www .brookings.edu/research/articles/2009/03/g20-stimulus-prasad.

37. See Jennifer Pietras, "European Affairs: Austerity Measures in the EU: A Country by Country Table," European Institute, https://www .europeaninstitute.org/index.php/112-european-affairs/special-g-20-issue -on-financial-reform/1180-austerity-measures-in-the-eu.

38. Bernanke, "The Federal Reserve: Looking Back, Looking Forward."

39. See Jonathan D. Ostry, Prakash Loungani, and Davide Furceri, "Neoliberalism: Oversold?," *IMF Finance & Development* 53, no. 2 (June 2016), http://www.imf.org/external/pubs/ft/fandd/2016/06/pdf/ostry.pdf.

40. For the European Commission's description of the Stability and Growth Pact, see https://ec.europa.eu/info/business-economy-euro/economic-and -fiscal-policy-coordination/eu-economic-governance-monitoring-prevention -correction/stability-and-growth-pact_en.

41. Marco Buti, "What Future for a Rules Based Fiscal Policy?," in Blanchard, Rajan, Rogoff, and Summers, *Progress and Confusion,* 184.

42. See figure 1.2, panel 4, "Fiscal Space," in International Monetary Fund, *Fiscal Monitor: Now Is the Time,* 7.

43. See Carmen M. Reinhart and Kenneth S. Rogoff, "Growth in a Time of Debt," *American Economic Review* 100, no. 2 (May 2010): 573–578.

44. See Thomas Herndon, Michael Ash, and Robert Pollin, "Does High Public Debt Consistently Stifle Economic Growth? A Critique of Reinhart and Rogoff," *Cambridge Journal of Economics* 38, no. 2 (March 2014): 257–279.

45. International Monetary Fund, *World Economic Outlook, October 2012: Coping with High Debt and Sluggish Growth* (Washington, DC: International Monetary Fund, October 2012), https://www.imf.org/en/Publications /WEO/Issues/2016/12/31/World-Economic-Outlook-October-2012-Coping -with-High-Debt-and-Sluggish-Growth-25845.

46. For treatments of unconventional fiscal policy, see Martin Feldstein, "A Role for Discretionary Fiscal Policy in a Low Interest Rate Environment," NBER Working Paper No. 9203 (September 2002); Gauti B. Eggertsson, "What Fiscal Policy Is Effective at Zero Interest Rates?," Federal Reserve Bank of New York, November 2009, https://www.newyorkfed.org /medialibrary/media/research/staff_reports/sr402.pdf; Isabel Correia, Emmanuel Farhi, Juan Pablo Nicolini, and Pedro Teles, "Unconventional Fiscal Policy at the Zero Bound," *American Economic Review* 103, no. 4 (June 2013): 1172–1211.

6. Institutional Reform of Fiscal Policy

1. See, e.g., James M. Poterba, "Balanced Budget Rules and Fiscal Policy: Evidence from the States," *National Tax Journal* 48 (1995): 329–336;

Daniel Shoag, "The Impact of Government Spending Shocks: Evidence on the Multiplier from State Pension Plan Returns," Job Market Paper (2015).

2. Poterba, "Balanced Budget Rules."

3. European Union, "Budget," April 11, 2018, http://europa.eu/pol/financ /index_en.htm.

4. European Commission, "Where Does the Money Come From?," February 15, 2017, http://ec.europa.eu/budget/explained/budg_system /financing/fin_en.cfm.

5. See Treaty on the Functioning of the European Union, article 126.1.

6. See Jost Angerer, "Stability and Growth Pact—An Overview of the Rules," European Parliament, December 18, 2015, http://www.europarl.europa.eu /RegData/etudes/note/join/2014/528745/IPOL-ECON_NT(2014)528745 _EN.pdf.

7. For instance, in 2003, the European Council voted not to apply the punitive measures to Germany and France, which had experienced rising levels of government debt. James K. Jackson, *Limiting Central Government Budget Deficits: International Experiences,* CRS Report No. R41122 (Washington, DC: Congressional Research Service, 2011), 17–18. Due to this shortcoming of the rules-based approach, in 2005, the EU members adopted a number of changes to this enforcement regime where they moved from a rules-based approach to a principle-based approach to give more discretion in enforcing the corrective mechanisms. This gave a wide berth for member states to exceed 3 percent of GDP in government deficit in certain circumstances and made the enforcement mild even in the case of excessive debt. Ibid.

8. See Gilles Mourre, George-Marian Isbasoiu, Dario Paternoster, and Matteo Salto, "The Cyclically-Adjusted Budget Balance Used in the EU Fiscal Framework: An Update," European Commission Directorate-General for Economic and Financial Affairs Economic Paper No. 478 (March 2013), http://ec.europa.eu/economy_finance/publications/economic _paper/2013/pdf/ecp478_en.pdf.

9. Eurostat, "General Government Deficit (–) and Surplus (+)—Annual Data," http://ec.europa.eu/eurostat/tgm/table.do?tab=table&plugin=1&language =en&pcode=teina200.

10. See, e.g., Paul Krugman, "Much Too Responsible," *New York Times,* January 22, 2015, http://www.nytimes.com/2015/01/23/opinion/paul -krugman-much-too-responsible.html.

11. International Monetary Fund, "Structural Fiscal Balances," http://www.imf .org/external/np/fad/strfiscbal.

12. The Census Bureau reported that home construction costs fell almost 12 percent between 2007 and 2010. United States Census Bureau,

"Constant Quality (Laspeyres) Price Index of New Single-Family Houses under Construction," http://www.census.gov/construction/nrs/pdf/price_uc .pdf.

13. Martin Shubik, "A Proposal for a Federal Employment Reserve Authority," Levy Institute Policy Note 2009/5 (April 2009), http://www.levyinstitute .org/publications/a-proposal-for-a-federal-employment-reserve-authority.

14. See, e.g., Mathias Dolls, Clemens Fuest, and Andreas Peichl, "Automatic Stabilizers and Economic Crisis: U.S. vs. Europe," *Journal of Public Economics* 96 (2012): 279–294.

15. A number of scholars have made suggestions along these lines. David Kamin, "In Good Times and Bad: Designing Legislation That Responds to Fiscal Uncertainty," Brookings Institution, December 15, 2014, http://www .brookings.edu/research/in-good-times-and-bad-designing-legislation-that -responds-to-fiscal-uncertainty; Alisdair McKay and Ricardo Reis, "Optimal Automatic Stabilizers," October 2017, http://people.bu.edu/amckay/pdfs /OptStab.pdf. Pascal Michaillat and Emmanuel Saez, "The Optimal Use of Government Purchases for Stabilization," National Bureau of Economic Research Working Paper No. 21322 (2015), discuss how optimal spending on public goods varies with the business cycle.

16. 20 C.F.R. § 615.12.

17. For a recent example, see James R. Hines Jr. and Kyle D. Logue, "Delegating Tax," *Michigan Law Review* 114 (2015): 235–274. For a history of proposals for administrative discretion over fiscal policy stabilization, see Orsola Costantini, "The Cyclically Adjusted Budget: History and Exegesis of a Fateful Estimate," Institute for New Economic Thinking Working Paper No. 24 (October 2015), http://www.ineteconomics.org/uploads/papers /WP24-Costantini.pdf.

18. Xavier Debrun, Tidiane Kinda, Teresa Curristine, Luc Eyraud, Jason Harris, and Johann Seiwald, "The Functions and Impact of Fiscal Councils," International Monetary Fund Policy Paper (July 16, 2013), http://www .imf.org/external/np/pp/eng/2013/071613.pdf.

19. U.S. Constitution, art. I, sec. 7, cl. 1; art. I, sec. 9, cl. 7.

20. Paperwork Reduction Act of 1980, Pub. L. No. 96-511.

21. Council on Wage and Price Stability Act of 1974, Pub. L. No. 93-387.

22. See Gerald R. Ford, Exec. Order No. 11,821, "Inflation Impact Statements," 39 Federal Register 41501 (November 29, 1974).

23. Ibid., secs. 2a and 2b.

24. See Thomas D. Hopkins, Benjamin Miller, and Laura Stanley, "The Legacy of the Council on Wage and Price Stability," Research Paper / Study, Mercatus Center, George Mason University (August 26, 2014), http://www .mercatus.org/publication/legacy-council-wage-and-price-stability.

25. Dan Slater, "Barack Obama: The U.S.'s 44th President (and 25th Lawyer-President!)," *Wall Street Journal Law Blog*, November 5, 2008, https://blogs.wsj.com/law/2008/11/05/barack-obama-the-uss-44th-president-and-24th-lawyer-president/; "There Was a Lawyer, an Engineer and a Politician," *Economist*, April 16, 2009, http://www.economist.com/node/13496638.

7. Expansionary Fiscal Policy by Administrative Agencies

1. See Internal Revenue Service, "Offer in Compromise," February 6, 2018, http://www.irs.gov/individuals/offer-in-compromise-1.

2. See John A. Koskinen, Alain A. Dubois, Barry W. Johnson, Darien B. Jacobson, and Wayne K. Kei, *Internal Revenue Service Data Book, 2015* (Washington, DC: Internal Revenue Service, 2015), http://www.irs.gov/pub/irs-soi/15databk.pdf.

3. See U.S. Department of the Treasury, Internal Revenue Service, *Employer's Supplemental Tax Guide (Supplement to Pub. 15, Employer's Tax Guide)*, February 21, 2018, http://www.irs.gov/pub/irs-pdf/p15a.pdf.

4. See Internal Revenue Service, "2016 Filing Season Statistics," http://www.irs.gov/newsroom/filing-season-statistics-for-the-week-ending-december-30-2016.

5. See Barry Schwartz, "On the Economic Stimulus Package: The 'Packaging' Counts," *Psychology Today*, February 1, 2009, http://www.psychologytoday.com/us/blog/the-choices-worth-having/200902/the-economic-stimulus-package-the-packaging-counts. But see Claudia R. Sahm, Matthew D. Shapiro, and Joel Slemrod, "Check in the Mail or More in the Paycheck: Does the Effectiveness of Fiscal Stimulus Depend on How It Is Delivered?," *American Economic Journal: Economic Policy* 4 (2012): 216–250 (finding the opposite effect).

6. Compare 26 C.F.R. § 31.3402(b)-1 with 26 CFR § 31.3402(c)-1.

7. For a description of this change in withholding, see Matthew D. Shapiro and Joel Slemrod, "Consumer Response to the Timing of Income: Evidence from a Change in Tax Withholding," *American Economic Review* 85 (1995): 274–283.

8. See "Revisiting Notice 2008–83," Jones Day, December 2008, http://www.jonesday.com/revisiting-notice-2008-83-12-19-2008.

9. See Rich Delmar, "Inquiry Regarding IRS Notice 2008–83" (official memorandum, Washington, DC: Department of the Treasury, 2009), http://www.treasury.gov/about/organizational-structure/ig/Documents/Inquiry%20Regarding%20IRS%20Notice%202008-83.pdf.

10. See U.S. Department of the Treasury, "Daily TARP Update (Figures as of 02/09/2011)," February 9, 2011, http://www.treasury.gov/initiatives/financial -stability/reports/Documents/Daily_Tarp_Update_02.09.2011.pdf (under "Treasury Housing Programs under TARP"); Office of the Special Inspector General for the Troubled Asset Relief Program (SIGTARP), *Quarterly Report to Congress, April 29, 2015* (Washington, DC: Office of the Special Inspector General for the Troubled Asset Relief Program, 2015), http://www.sigtarp.gov/Quarterly%20Reports/April_29_2015 _Quarterly_Report_to_Congress.pdf, table 4.1.

11. See U.S. Department of the Treasury, "Monthly TARP Update for 02/01/2017," February 1, 2017, http://www.treasury.gov/initiatives/financial -stability/reports/Documents/Monthly_TARP_Update%20-%2002.01.2017 .pdf (under "Treasury Housing Programs under TARP," note that, after much of the money went unspent, the amount appropriated for housing programs decreased from $46 billion to $37 billion); SIGTARP, *Quarterly Report to Congress,* 149.

12. See, e.g., Clara Benson, "TARP Funds for Housing Relief 90 Percent Unspent, Auditor Says," Bloomberg, July 25, 2012, http://www.bloomberg .com/news/articles/2012-07-25/tarp-funds-for-housing-relief-90-percent -unspent-auditor-says; "Three Years Later, 90 Percent of TARP Housing Relief Remains Unspent," ThinkProgress, July 25, 2012, http:// thinkprogress.org/three-years-later-90-percent-of-tarp-housing-relief -remains-unspent-497bbe66eb8e#.1t41pdf1l.

13. Letter from Edward J. DeMarco, Acting Director of the Federal Housing Finance Agency, to Elijah E. Cummings, Ranking Member of the Committee on Oversight and Government Reform, January 20, 2012, http://www.fhfa.gov/Media/PublicAffairs/Documents/Letter-To-Congress -Principal-Forgiveness_12312.pdf.

14. Neil Barofsky, *Bailout: An Inside Account of How Washington Abandoned Main Street While Rescuing Wall Street* (New York: Free Press, 2012), 133–134.

15. Sheila Bair, *Bull by the Horns: Fighting to Save Main Street from Wall Street and Wall Street from Itself* (New York: Simon and Schuster, 2012).

16. See Janet Currie, "The Take up of Social Benefits," National Bureau of Economic Research Working Paper No. 10488 (May 2004), http://www .nber.org/papers/w10488.pdf.

17. Casey Mulligan, *The Redistribution Recession* (New York: Oxford University Press, 2012). See also Robert Barro, "The Folly of Subsidizing Unemployment," *Wall Street Journal*, August 30, 2010.

18. See Gabriel Chodorow-Reich, John Coglianese, and Loukas Karabarbouni, "The Limited Macroeconomic Effects of Unemployment Benefit Exten-

sions" (2018), http://scholar.harvard.edu/chodorow-reich/publications
/limited-macroeconomic-effects-unemployment-benefit-extensions; John
Coglianese, "Do Unemployment Insurance Extensions Reduce Employment?" (November 30, 2015), http://scholar.harvard.edu/files/coglianese
/files/coglianese_2015_ui_extensions.pdf. These papers use unemployment
forecast errors that inadvertently made unemployment more generous in
some areas than others as a "natural experiment" for the effect of more
generous unemployment benefits.

19. For an example of IRS discretion in action, observe that audit rates are
higher in the United States in Democratic administrations than in Republican administrations. See Sutirtha Bagchi, "The Political Economy of Tax
Enforcement: A Look at the IRS from 1978–2010" (March 12, 2015),
http://ssrn.com/abstract=2091796.

20. See Interagency Working Group on Social Cost of Carbon, United States
Government, "Technical Support Document: Social Cost of Carbon for
Regulatory Impact Analysis under Executive Order 12866," February 2010,
http://obamawhitehouse.archives.gov/sites/default/files/omb/inforeg/for
-agencies/Social-Cost-of-Carbon-for-RIA.pdf.

8. Expansionary Legal Policy: The Case of the Keystone Pipeline

1. Juliet Eilperin, "Trump Administration Proposes Rule to Relax Carbon
Limits on Power Plants," *Washington Post*, August 21, 2018, https://www
.washingtonpost.com/national/health-science/trump-administration
-proposes-rule-to-relax-carbon-limits-on-power-plants/2018/08/21
/b46b0a8a-a543-11e8-a656-43eefab5daf_story.html?utm_term=
.f172bc2410d8.

2. Coral Davenport, "Keystone Pipeline Pros, Cons and Steps to a Final
Decision," *New York Times*, November 18, 2014, http://www.nytimes.com
/2014/11/19/us/politics/what-does-the-proposed-keystone-xl-pipeline-entail
.html.

3. House Energy and Commerce Committee, "Keystone XL Opposition Turns
to Beetle in the Effort to Block the $7 Billion Project, Its Thousands of
Jobs, and Energy Security," March 6, 2013, http://energycommerce.house
.gov/content/keystone-xl.

4. Davenport, "Keystone Pipeline Pros, Cons."

5. Carol Davenport, "President Rejects Keystone Pipeline, Invoking Climate,"
New York Times, November 7, 2015, A1.

6. See Memorandum from President Donald J. Trump to the Secretary of
State and the Secretary of the Army, "Presidential Memorandum Regarding

Construction of the Keystone XL Pipeline," January 24, 2017, White House, http://www.whitehouse.gov/the-press-office/2017/01/24/presidential -memorandum-regarding-construction-keystone-xl-pipeline.

7. See Clifford Krauss, "U.S., in Reversal, Issues Permit for Keystone Oil Pipeline," *New York Times*, March 24, 2017, http://www.nytimes.com/2017 /03/24/business/energy-environment/keystone-oil-pipeline.html.

8. See "Keystone XL Pipeline Political Timeline," Ballotpedia, http:// ballotpedia.org/Keystone_XL_Pipeline_political_timeline.

9. Davenport, "Keystone Pipeline Pros, Cons."

10. Cost–benefit analysis is not always so rigorous. In some cases, costs are estimated by forgone production rather than forgone surplus. Forgone production is a poor but easily estimated proxy for the costs of, for example, a logging restriction. It fails to account for the fact that consumers, workers, and investors can substitute other goods or jobs to replace what has been restricted by a regulation.

11. For a careful discussion of the moral and practical advantages and disad-vantages of conventional cost–benefit analysis, see Amartya Sen, "The Discipline of Cost–Benefit Analysis," *Journal of Legal Studies* 29 (2000): 931–952. Although it is important to consider these dimensions of projects up for approval, conventional cost–benefit analysis also ignores a great deal. Conventional cost–benefit analysis omits deontological considerations, such as how we can put a price on the degradation of a unique and fragile ecosystem.

12. In theory, cost–benefit analysis always compares the jobs created by the project with the jobs that the workers would have had otherwise and includes the difference between these two numbers as a benefit. See Anthony E. Boardman, David Greenberg, Aidan Vining, and David Weimer, *Cost–Benefit Analysis: Concepts and Practice* (New York: Pearson Press, 2011), 99–106. In practice, however, this requires knowing worker's wages in alternative employment, a very difficult quantity to estimate. As a result, this adjustment is usually ignored.

13. Jonathan Masur and Eric Posner offer a powerful critique of this flawed assumption. See Jonathan S. Masur and Eric A. Posner, "Regulation, Unemployment, and Cost–Benefit Analysis," *Virginia Law Review* 98 (2012): 579–634.

14. United States Department of State, Bureau of Oceans and International Environmental and Scientific Affairs, *Executive Summary: Final Environ-mental Impact Statement for the Proposed Keystone XL Project ES-22*, August 26, 2011, http://keystonepipeline-xl.state.gov/documents /organization/182010.pdf.

15. See Congressional Budget Office, "Estimated Impact of the American Recovery and Reinvestment Act on Employment and Economic Output from April 2012 through June 2012," August 2012, http://www.cbo.gov/sites /default/files/112th-congress-2011-2012/reports/arraone-col00.pdf. (The 750,000 jobs estimate is derived from the midpoint of the Congressional Budget Office's low estimate of 200,000 additional jobs and its high estimate of 1.3 million additional jobs.)

16. Farhi and Werning present a model in which government purchases have aggregate demand externalities. Emmanuel Farhi and Ivan Werning, "A Theory of Macroprudential Policies in the Presence of Nominal Rigidities," *Econometrica* 84 (2016): 1645–1704.

17. See Robert H. Haveman and Scott Farrow, "Labor Expenditures and Benefit–Cost Accounting in Times of Unemployment," *Journal of Benefit– Cost Analysis* 2 (2011): 1–9. For a critical literature review on adjusting cost–benefit analysis for employment and other macroeconomic effects, see Timothy J. Bartik, "Including Jobs in Benefit–Cost Analysis," *Annual Review of Resource Economics* 4 (2012): 55–73.

18. Robert H. Haveman and David L. Weimer, "Public Policy Induced Changes in Employment: Valuation Issues for Benefit–Cost Analysis," *Journal of Benefit-Cost Analysis* 6 (2015): 112–153 (table 4, p. 147).

19. Specifically, the "IMPLAN" (IMpact Analysis for PLANing) input-output model described in appendix O of the Keystone Final Supplemental Environmental Impact Analysis does not appear to include any parameters that vary with the business cycle. United States Department of State, Bureau of Oceans and International Environmental and Scientific Affairs, *Executive Summary: Final Environmental Impact Statement for the Proposed Keystone XL Project ES-22*, August 26, 2011, http:// keystonepipeline-xl.state.gov/documents/organization/182010.pdf.

20. Michael Greenstone has shown that, over the long run (twenty years or more), additional regulatory burdens decrease employment levels in targeted industries. Michael Greenstone, "The Impacts of Environmental Regulations on Industrial Activity: Evidence from the 1970 and 1977 Clean Air Act Amendments and the Census of Manufactures," *Journal of Political Economy* 110 (2002): 1175–1219. Denial of Keystone construction imposes a higher regulatory burden on pipeline construction. In the long run, denial of Keystone means fewer jobs in the construction industry. Over the long run, however, we should not expect a decline in employment in the construction industry to result in lower overall economy-wide employment. Instead, the workers not employed in construction should, over time, find employment in another industry. Thus, the Greenstone study must be applied to the

Keystone decision with significant caveats. Over the short run, however, job losses in construction may not be offset by additional jobs in another industry. And the difficulty of finding alternative jobs was particularly acute during the Great Recession, when job openings were scarce.

21. For a review of this literature, see Gabriel Chodorow-Reich, "Geographic Cross-Sectional Fiscal Spending Multipliers: What Have We Learned?," Natural Bureau of Economic Research Working Paper No. 23577 (July 2017), http://scholar.harvard.edu/chodorow-reich/publications /geographic-cross-sectional-fiscal-multiplierswhat-have-we-learned.

22. See Lawrence J. Christiano, "A Reexamination of the Theory of Automatic Stabilizers," *Carnegie-Rochester Conference Series on Public Policy* 20 (1984): 147–206.

23. United States Department of State, Bureau of Oceans and International Environmental and Scientific Affairs, *Executive Summary: Final Environmental Impact Statement for the Proposed Keystone XL Project ES-22,* August 26, 2011, http://keystonepipeline-xl.state.gov/documents /organization/182010.pdf.

24. United States Environmental Protection Agency, *Regulatory Impact Analysis for Mercury and Air Toxics Standards,* December 2011, http://www3.epa.gov/ttnecas1/regdata/RIAs/matsriafinal.pdf.

9. The Costs of Expansionary Legal Policy

1. We ultimately need to make a single decision, accounting for all factors, so even if we don't compare them in a cost–benefit analysis, we have to compare them in some other way.

2. Cost–benefit analysis cannot claim to identify what is efficient under the more exacting standards of Pareto efficiency, which requires that everyone be made better off by a decision in order for it to be "efficient."

3. Gauti Eggertsson, "Was the New Deal Contractionary?," *American Economic Review* 102 (2012): 524–555.

4. James Buchanan and Richard Wagner, *Democracy in Deficit: The Political Legacy of Lord Keynes,* section 6.12 (New York: Academic Press, 1977).

5. United States Department of State, Bureau of Oceans and International Environmental and Scientific Affairs, *Executive Summary: Final Environmental Impact Statement for the Proposed Keystone XL Project ES-22,* August 26, 2011, http://keystonepipeline-xl.state.gov/documents /organization/182010.pdf.

6. For example, the National Center for Environmental Economics, a research office of the EPA, describes a "research strategy" that omits macroeco-

nomics. See https://www.epa.gov/environmental-economics/environmental-economics-research-strategy. For an argument that the environment and macroeconomics are tightly linked, see Douglas Kysar, "Sustainability, Distribution, and the Macroeconomic Analysis of Law," *Boston College Law Review* 42 (2001): 1.

7. United States Department of State, *Executive Summary.*

8. See United States Department of State, "Record of Decision and National Interest Determination: TransCanada Keystone Pipeline, L.P. Application for Presidential Permit, Keystone XL Pipeline," March 23, 2017, http://keystonepipeline-xl.state.gov/documents/organization/269323.pdf.

9. See Fernando Nechio, "Monetary Policy When One Size Does Not Fit All," Federal Reserve Bank of San Francisco, June 13, 2011, http://www.frbsf.org/economic-research/publications/economic-letter/2011/june/monetary-policy-europe.

10. Michael T. Kiley and John M. Roberts, "Monetary Policy in a Low Interest Rate World," Brookings Papers on Economic Activity (March 2017), http://www.brookings.edu/wp-content/uploads/2017/03/5_kileyroberts.pdf.

11. Cameron M. Reinhart and Kenneth S. Rogoff, *This Time Is Different: Eight Centuries of Financial Folly* (Princeton, NJ: Princeton University Press, 2009), 227 and figure 14.3.

12. See William Caraher and Kyle Conway, *The Bakken Goes Boom: Oil and the Changing Geographies of Western North Dakota* (Grand Forks: Digital Press at the University of North Dakota, 2016).

13. See "North Dakota Faces Devastating Budget Shortfall Amid Oil Slump," *Cavalier County Republican,* February 6, 2016, http://www.cavaliercountyextra.com/2016/02/06/north-dakota-faces-devastating-the-2015-north-dakota-state-legislature-probably-wishes-they-could-take-back-those-congratulatory-handshakes-they-exchanged-following-the-completion-of-a-budget-for-the.

10. Law and Macroeconomics: Lessons from History

1. William L. Silber, "Why Did FDR's Bank Holiday Succeed?," *Federal Reserve Bank of New York Economic Policy Review,* July 2009, 19–30.

2. Schechter Poultry Corp. v. United States, 295 U.S. 495 (1935).

3. Steven A. Ramirez, "The Law and Macroeconomics of the New Deal at 70," *Maryland Law Review* 62 (2003): 515–572.

4. See Steven A. Bank, "Corporate Managers, Agency Costs, and the Rise of Double Taxation," *William & Mary Law Review* 44 (2002): 167–261.

5. See John Maynard Keynes, "An Open Letter to Franklin D. Roosevelt," *New York Times,* December 31, 1933, http://la.utexas.edu/users/hcleaver /368/368KeynesOpenLetFDRtable.pdf.

6. FDR's "hundred days" included so many reforms that it is impossible to disentangle the causal effect of the different measures. As a group, the reforms worked, and, at the time, the NIRA was considered the most important of them all.

7. Charles H. Whiteman, "A New Investigation of the Impact of Wage and Price Controls," *Federal Reserve Bank of Minneapolis Quarterly Review,* (Spring 1978), 2–8.

8. See, for example, Friedrich Hayek, "The Use of Knowledge in Society," *American Economic Review* 35 (1945): 528.

9. Eastern Airlines Inc., v. Gulf Oil Corp., 415 F.Supp. 429 (S.D. Fla. 1975).

10. See William N. Walker, "Forty Years after the Freeze," *Nixon's Wage and Price Freeze,* http://nixonswageandpricefreeze.files.wordpress.com/2011/07 /forty-years-after-the-freeze.pdf.

11. See Milton Friedman, "The Case for Flexible Exchange Rates," in *Essays in Positive Economics,* ed. Milton Friedman (Chicago: University of Chicago Press: 1953): 157–203.

12. See Tyler Cowen, "Are Wage and Price Controls a Solution for Greece?," *Marginal Revolution* February 19, 2010, https://marginalrevolution.com /marginalrevolution/2010/02/is-this-a-solution-for-greece.html (citing Larry Kotlikoff and linking to a currently unavailable page), . Farhi and colleagues show that a combination of an increase in import taxes and an increase in export subsidies can also replicate a currency devaluation. See Emmanuel Farhi, Gita Gopinath, and Oleg Itskhoki, "Fiscal Devaluations," *Review of Economic Studies* 81 (2014): 725–760. Note, however, that EU single-market rules would prevent Greece from "pursuing this policy with respect to its EU counterparts."

11. Expansionary Legal Policy Options

1. See John Coglianese, "Do Unemployment Insurance Extensions Reduce Employment?," https://scholar.harvard.edu/files/coglianese/files/coglianese _2015_ui_extensions.pdf; Gabriel Chodorow-Reich, John Coglianese, and Loukas Karabarbounis, "The Limited Macroeconomic Effects of Unem-ployment Benefit Extensions," https://scholar.harvard.edu/files/chodorow -reich/files/ui_macro.pdf.

2. Conn. Gen. Stat. § 16–19e (2014).

3. See U.S. Energy Information Administration, Wholesale Electricity and Natural Gas Market Data, https://www.eia.gov/electricity/wholesale/(Palo Verde Hub [CA] and Mass Hub).

4. I assume that utility investment is unchanged by the macroeconomically sensitive regulatory regime. But if long-run returns are the same for the utility, then investment should remain the same. (Financing constraints should be relatively minor for a regulated monopoly.)

5. For a recent discussion of how the marginal propensity to consume varies with income and wealth, see, e.g., Christopher D. Carroll, Jiri Slacalek, and Kiichi Tokuoka, "The Distribution of Wealth and the Marginal Propensity to Consume," European Central Bank Working Paper No. 1655 (March 2014), https://www.ecb.europa.eu/pub/pdf/scpwps/ecbwp1655.pdf, summarizing a series of studies that find "that the annual marginal propensity to consume out of one-time income shocks . . . is substantially larger for low-wealth than for high-wealth households." For an important early article in the literature, see Stephen P. Zeldes, "Consumption and Liquidity Constraints: An Empirical Investigation," *Journal of Political Economy* 97 (1989): 305–346.

6. For data from the Consumer Expenditure Survey, see U.S. Department of Labor, Bureau of Labor Statistics, Consumer Expenditure Survey, https://www.bls.gov/cex/(specific calculations available from the author). The average U.S. household also spent about $500 on water and sewer services; see Trey Talley, "How Much Do Households Pay for Utilities, Fuels, and Public Services?," http://efc.web.unc.edu/2016/10/07/households-utilities-fuels-public-services/.

7. Consumer Expenditure Survey, https://www.bls.gov/cex/(CES survey data on federal income taxes, and Social Security payments, data also available from author upon request). The Consumer Expenditure Survey lumps Social Security payments with other pension contributions. Thus, the figures provided here overstate Social Security contributions. In the first and second quintiles of the income distribution, however, pension contributions should be small, as evidenced by the low value of retirement assets for people in these categories.

8. See Carroll, Slacalek, Kiichi Tokuoka, "Distribution of Wealth and the Marginal Propensity to Consume," 10.

9. See Atif Mian and Amir Sufi, *House of Debt: How They (and You) Caused the Great Recession, and How We Can Prevent It from Happening Again* (Chicago: University of Chicago Press, 2015).

10. Mian and Sufi recognize that consumption and declines in housing values can be endogenous. They argue, however, that housing markets where

construction is sensitive to price are much less prone to changes in housing value than housing markets where supply is relatively fixed. Instead of relating changes in consumption directly to changes in housing values, they use housing market supply as an instrument for declines in housing market values. See Atif Mian, Kamalesh Rao, and Amir Sufi, "Household Balance Sheets, Consumption, and the Economic Slump," *Quarterly Journal of Economics* 128 (2013): 1687–1726.

11. See Atif Mian, Amir Sufi, and Francesco Trebbi, "Foreclosures, House Prices, and the Real Economy," *Journal of Finance* 70 (2015): 2587–2634.

12. If costly foreclosure procedures make default more likely, then this incentive effect should raise foreclosures. But overall foreclosures decline in spite of this effect.

13. Mian and Sufi, *House of Debt.*

14. Home Building & Loan Assn. v. Blaisdell, 290 U.S. 398, 399–400 (1934).

15. To file for Chapter 13, a debtor's debts must fall below a cap (11 U.S.C. 109[e]). While most individuals who file for bankruptcy have debts below this cap, large business enterprises are invariably ineligible for Chapter 13 and therefore file for Chapter 11. Some individuals choose to file under Chapter 11.

16. 11 U.S.C. 1112(b)(1).

17. See CollegeBoard, *Trends in Student Aid 2016* (Trends in Higher Education Series), https://trends.collegeboard.org/sites/default/files/2016-trends -student-aid.pdf, figure 5.

18. See Nicholas Rayfield, "National Student Loan Debt Reaches a Bonkers $1.2 Trillion," *USA Today College,* April 2015, https://www.usatoday.com /story/college/2015/04/08/national-student-loan-debt-reaches-a-bonkers-12 -trillion/37401867/

19. See 11 U.S.C. 523(a)(8).

20. Ibid.

21. See 144 A.L.R. Fed. 1, citing In re Singleton, 1994 Bankr LEXIS 2164 (Bankr. N.D. Ala. 1994).

22. See Rafael I. Pardo, "The Undue Hardship Thicket: On Access to Justice, Procedural Noncompliance, and Pollutive Litigation in Bankruptcy," *Florida Law Review* 66 (2014): 2101–2178.

23. See Natalie Kitroeff, "Loan Monitor Is Accused of Ruthless Tactics on Student Debt," *New York Times,* January 1, 2014, https://www.nytimes.com /2014/01/02/us/loan-monitor-is-accused-of-ruthless-tactics-on-student-debt .html.

24. See Will Dobbie and Jae Song, "Debt Relief and Debtor Outcomes: Measuring the Effects of Consumer Bankruptcy Protection," *American Economic Review* 105 (2015): 1272–1311.

25. See Administrative Office of the United States Courts, "Report of Statistics Required by the Bankruptcy Abuse Prevention and Consumer Protection Act of 2005" (2010) (Table 1D), http://www.uscourts.gov/sites/default/files /2010bapcpa.pdf.

26. See Shai Bernstein, Emanuele Colonnelli, Xavier Giroud, and Benjamin Iverson, "Bankruptcy Spillovers," National Bureau of Economic Research Working Paper No. 23162 (2017).

27. See Zachary Liscow, "Counter-Cyclical Bankruptcy Law: An Efficiency Argument for Employment-Preserving Bankruptcy Rules," *Columbia Law Review* 116 (2016): 1461.

28. Administrative Office of the United States Courts, "Annual Business and Non-business Filings by Year (1980–2017)", https://s3.amazonaws.com/abi -org/Newsroom/Bankruptcy_Statistics/Total-Business-Consumer1980 -Present.pdf.

29. See Michelle J. White, "Why Don't More Households File for Bank-ruptcy?," *Journal of Law, Economics, & Organization* 14, no. 2 (1998): 205–231.

30. The debate among traditional law and economics scholars concern fairness, microeconomic efficiency, waste, and so on, without any macro-economic consideration. For more information on this debate, see Richard A. Posner, *Economic Analysis of Law* (Boston: Little, Brown, 1973), 88–89; Robert Birmingham, "Breach of Contract, Damage Mea-sures, and Economic Efficiency," *Rutgers Law Review* 24 (1970): 24; Richard R. W. Brooks, "The Efficient Performance Hypothesis," *Yale Law Journal* 116 (2006): 568; Anthony T. Kronman, "Specific Performance," *University of Chicago Law Review* 45 (1979): 351; Alan Schwartz, "The Case for Specific Performance," *Yale Law Journal* 89 (1979): 271; Alan Schwartz and Robert E. Scott, "Market Damages and the Economic Waste Fallacy, *Columbia Law Review* 108 (2008): 1610.

31. Winter v. Natural Resources Defense Council, Inc., 555 U.S. 7, 24 (2008).

Appendix

1. Since the critique of the real business cycle theorists in the 1970s and 1980s—see, e.g., Finn E. Kydland and Edward C. Prescott, "Time to Build and Aggregate Fluctuations," *Econometrica* 50, no. 6 (1982): 1345–1370; Robert E. Lucas, "Expectations and the Neutrality of Money," *Journal of Economic Theory* 4 (1970): 103–124; Robert E. Lucas, "Econometric Policy Evaluation," *Carnegie-Rochester Conference Series on Public Policy* 1, no. 1 (1976): 19–46—the Keynesian IS-LM model has been augmented by

more sophisticated neo-Keynesian models in academic research. See, e.g., Michael Woodford, *Interest and Prices* (Princeton, NJ: Princeton University Press, 2003), 9–10 and chap. 3. Neo-Keynesian models derive similar (but not identical) conclusions to the IS-LM model, but they derive these conclusions from microeconomic behavioral assumptions rather than the more ad hoc assumptions of Hicks and Keynes. IS-LM is still featured in most macroeconomics textbooks and is the framework within which many macroeconomic policymakers make their decisions. See N. Gregory Mankiw, "The Macroeconomist as Scientist and Engineer," *Journal of Economic Perspectives* 20, no. 4 (2006): 1–26, http://scholar.harvard.edu/files/mankiw /files/macroeconomist_as_scientist.pdf. As Olivier Blanchard, a noted macroeconomist recently observed, "I strongly believe that ad hoc macro models, from various versions of the IS-LM to the Mundell-Fleming model, have an important role to play in relation to DSGE models." See Olivier Blanchard, "On the Future of Macroeconomic Models," *Oxford Review of Economic Policy* 34 (2018): 43–54.

2. The IS-LM model also implicitly models a third market—the market for bonds. Savings can be held as cash or bonds. Cash facilitates transactions, but bonds pay interest. The IS-LM model is thus a three-market general equilibrium model, where the three markets are (1) goods and services, (2) money, and (3) bonds. By Walras's law, however, a point that represents equilibrium in two of these markets, in this case the goods and money markets, also depicts equilibrium in the third (bonds) market. See Paul Krugman, "How Complicated Does the Model Have to Be?," *Oxford Review of Economic Policy* 16 (2000): 33–42.

3. This discussion follows Paul Krugman's lucid explanation of the Hicksian IS-LM model for readers unfamiliar with economics: Paul Krugman, "IS-LMentary," *New York Times,* October 9, 2011, https://krugman.blogs .nytimes.com/2011/10/09/is-lmentary/.

4. Krugman, "IS-LMentary."

5. Ibid.

6. Ibid.

7. See John R Hicks, "Mr. Keynes and the Classics: A Suggested Interpretation," *Econometrica* 5 (1937): 153 fig.1, 153 n.8, 158.

8. Lawrence J. Christiano, Martin Eichenbaum, and Charles L. Evans, "Monetary Policy Shocks: What Have We Learned and to What End?," in *Handbook of Macroeconomics, Volume 1,* ed. J. B. Taylor and M. Woodford (Amsterdam: Elsevier, 1999), 65–148. In a more recent review of the empirical literature, Ramey supports this finding but observes that true "shocks" to monetary policy have become very rare; Valerie Ramey, "Macroeconomic Shocks and Their Propagation," in *Handbook of Macro-*

economics, Volume 2, ed. J. B. Taylor and H. Uhlig (Amsterdam: Elsevier, 2016), 71–162.

9. By purchasing long-term bonds that they normally shun, unconventional monetary policy by central banks also directly lowers the nominal interest rates on long-dated assets. Like short-term bonds, long-term bonds must yield at least zero nominal interest, however, lest investors migrate to cash, limiting this effect. Moreover, this effect may not even succeed in bringing interest rates on long-term assets to zero. Because there are powerful factors that typically induce a positive relationship between asset term and nominal interest rates, zero nominal interest rates on short-term assets may require above zero yields on long-term assets. Robert J. Shiller and J. Huston McCulloch, "The Term Structure of Interest Rates," in *Handbook of Monetary Economics, Volume 1,* ed. B. M. Friedman and F.H. Hahn (Amsterdam: Elsevier, 1990), 627–722.

10. Paul Krugman, "It's Baaack: Japan's Slump and the Return of the Liquidity Trap," *Brookings Papers on Economic Activity* 29, no. 2 (1998): 137–206; Gauti B. Eggertsson and Michael Woodford, "The Zero Bound on Interest Rates and Optimal Monetary Policy," *Brookings Papers on Economic Activity* (2003): 139–233.

Acknowledgments

I am incredibly grateful to the innumerable people and institutions who contributed to the writing of this book. I wish I could thank you all by name, but the length of the acknowledgments would approach the size of the text.

I thank my colleagues at Yale Law School for a decade's worth of illuminating debates and conversations. I have no doubt that you will see your influence on many of these pages. In particular, I thank Ian Ayres, Roberta Romano, and Bruce Ackerman, all of whom read earlier versions of the book and made comments that substantially improved the manuscript. John Witt provided invaluable strategic guidance on the publication process. Nick Parrillo and later David Schleicher spent more time than they ever imagined listening to the half-baked versions of the ideas found here and helped refine them immensely. I also thank Harold Koh, Robert Post, and Heather Gerken for the institutional support I received from Yale Law School. It's a great place for writing a book.

Great thanks go to my editor at Harvard University Press, Thomas LeBien, for wise and thoughtful advice throughout the publication process. Simon Waxman was an invaluable line editor, improving the flow of every paragraph. Thanks also to Kathi Drummy, Debbie Masi, and Julie Palmer-Hoffman.

I thank Andy Mun, Eliza Pan, Anirudh Sivaram, William Vester, Catherine Chang, and Shlomo Klapper for invaluable research assistance. In many cases, their perceptive comments and suggestions caused me to rethink whole sections of my work.

Thanks to the Newton Free Library and to the head office of Fick & Marx LLP for providing excellent work spaces for a vagabond academic. Dan Marx and Bill Fick offered regular (and urgently needed) reality checks over many a miso soup.

I thank Princeton University for giving an unconventional candidate the opportunity for graduate study in economics. Anne Case was an incredibly supportive adviser, even when I decided to head to law school. Thank you. And thanks also to Ben Bernanke, Michael Woodford, and Oliver Hart, whose thoughtful discussions of macroeconomics and finance initiated the reactions that led to this book.

I thank Richard Posner for being an intellectually exhilarating (and ever kind) boss, mentor, and role model.

Thanks so much to my parents, Barbara and David Listokin, and my in-laws, Sharon (who passed away in 2016) and Fred Wexler, for their unflagging support during the writing of this book and beforehand. Thanks also to my wonderful siblings and siblings-in-law, Siona and Perry, Miri and David, and Eric and Rachel.

An extra special thanks to my kids, Ami and Shira. It is amazing to me, and a source of great joy, that you are so interested in what your dad does for work.

Finally, I dedicate this book to Steph, my life's partner. You are the rock of our family. It is no exaggeration to say that this book would not have been possible without you.

Index

www.ingramcontent.com/pod-product-compliance
Ingram Content Group UK Ltd.
Pitfield, Milton Keynes, MK11 3LW, UK
UKHW041833260225
455625UK00008B/93/J